THE WORSHIP OF GOD

*Some Theological, Pastoral,
and Practical Reflections*

by
RALPH P. MARTIN

WILLIAM B. EERDMANS PUBLISHING COMPANY
GRAND RAPIDS, MICHIGAN

Copyright © 1982 by Wm. B. Eerdmans Publishing Co.
255 Jefferson Ave. SE, Grand Rapids, MI 49503

Library of Congress Cataloging in Publication Data
Martin, Ralph P.
  The worship of God.

  1. Public worship. 2. Liturgics. I. Title.
BV10.2M33   264   82-7397
ISBN 0-8208-1934-6   AACR2

FOR
ALLISON ELIZABETH
AND
PHILIP MARTIN

*Who came into the world as joy-bringers
while this book was being written.*

Contents

Preface

Near the close of his study *The Concept of Worship* Ninian Smart writes: "God is reached down a certain corridor . . . and this is the corridor of worship." Smart's book is but one of recent verdicts on the central role worship plays in both our formulation and practice of the Christian faith. Not only the philosopher of religion but the biblical scholar and theologian as well endorse the judgment that worship holds a vital place in our understanding of what we call Christianity. This assessment needs to be weighed by the seminary student and working minister.

It is time to reap some of the gains of these recent studies, and I offer this small book, primarily directed to ministers and students in theological schools as well as to lay leaders in the churches, as a compact guide to some of the main themes of the public worship of God.

The scriptural basis for worship has been largely assumed, and I have tried not to overlap the material presented in *Worship in the Early Church* (1964; reprinted in 1975). The present book seeks to erect on the basis there laid a model of Christian worship that is, I hope, both theologically adequate and pastorally helpful. With a desire to help readers to think theologically about worship and to apply these exercises to their own church situations and opportunities in some practical ways the book is now sent forth.

RALPH P. MARTIN

Fuller Theological Seminary
Pasadena, California
Easter 1981

THE WORSHIP OF GOD

CHAPTER ONE

Let us Worship God

"Worship": How Meaningful is it?

"Christian worship is the most momentous, the most urgent, the most glorious action that can take place in human life."[1] These words of Karl Barth will strike a responsive chord in all who are concerned for the renewal of the church in our day. Yet the truth is that many—if not most—Christians find public worship less than the exhilarating experience Barth wrote about. The situation is a perplexing one. It suggests a deep-seated conviction that the worship of God is indeed a vital part of the church's life and witness. And equally it reflects a wistful yearning that contemporary worship could be vastly improved and given a more satisfying rationale.

On the one hand the importance and centrality of Christian worship is acknowledged through all sections of christendom, with repercussions ranging from the Liturgical Movement within Roman Catholicism to an insistent renewal of interest and concern among Reformed and Free churches. The idea of the "Parish Communion" and the influence of the charismatic movement inside the Episcopal church have led to some startling results among traditionally stolid and settled congregations. These innovations suggest a response to a scene where Christian leaders and laity alike have become vividly conscious of the poverty, deficiencies, and disfigurements of much that passes for public worship today.

The other side of the picture is that most of the attempts at liturgical renewal, with experimental forms of worship and increasing lay participation, have led to a painful impasse. "Renewal of worship" is indeed a noble slogan, but the

1. Karl Barth, quoted in J. J. von Allmen, *Worship: Its Theology and Practice* (London: Lutterworth, 1965), p. 13.

results that have accrued after two or three decades of serious study, suggestive adaptations, and revised liturgies have been meagre. The outburst of energy associated with the charismatic revival has not yet touched the majority of worshiping congregations.

One reason for this scantiness lies in a failure to construct a systematic theology of worship. Christian theology has been busy and fruitful over the centuries in its work of confessing the faith by which the church lives. But, strangely, there is little to record regarding a "theology of worship." Every person is left apparently to his or her own best ideas and emotions, resulting in a veritable kaleidoscope of patterns and forms of worship throughout christendom. In fact, there is far more variety and flexibility in regard to the meaning and practice of the corporate worship of God than in relation to what Christians believe about God, the world, or the person of Christ—even in these days of doctrinal latitudinarianism.

A second way in which recent efforts at liturgical renewal have been largely abortive touches on the ferment within churches traditionally committed to set forms of divine service. In a perceptive contribution to the literature in this field T. G. A. Baker, Dean of Worcester Cathedral, England, assesses the credits and debits in the account of liturgical reform. After reviewing some substantial gains, mainly dealing with the sweeping aside of "suffocating formalism and fussiness in worship" in the interest of joyous celebration and a humanizing of worship with increased lay participation and more contemporary language forms, he still wonders aloud whether such gains have been purchased at too great a price. In particular he lists on the debit side of the ledger the loss of the "sense of the numinous," leading to aesthetic, emotional, and spiritual impoverishment, and a failure to catch popular interest and imagination by making the new liturgy directly relevant to national needs. He remarks that liturgical revision is largely a preoccupation of the clergy and the specialists.[2]

A third, more corrosive element that has worked against a recovery of vital worship in our day is that of "seculariza-

2. T. G. A. Baker, *Questioning Worship* (London: SCM Press, 1977), pp. 10-19.

tion."[3] The term reflects a modern attitude to life that calls in question some common assumptions that underlie "worship," as that word is usually understood.

Evelyn Underhill describes "worship" in a couple of ways that will illustrate what is meant by the inroad of the secular spirit. She defines worship as "the response of the creature to the Eternal" or, alternatively, "an acknowledgment of God as transcendent."[4] It is precisely at the point of stressing the presence of God as "eternal" and "transcendent," that is, "above" the world and occupying a space known as "holy," that Christian worship finds it difficult to convey anything meaningful to society in the 1980s. J. G. Davies has put his finger on several component parts of worship as it is ordinarily understood and shown how they stand at odds with a secular person's attitude toward life.[5] Rudolf Otto's analysis of the "mysterious" element in religious experience led him to propose that worship is a "creaturely feeling in the presence of Deity."[6] God is the holy one; human beings feel their uncertainty and frailty when confronted by his almighty power and holy person. Yet this picture of a God "out there" or "up there" is one that has lost much credibility in recent times, and men and women do not usually live in "dread and fear" of God.

Besides, the secular world view refuses to accept the dichotomy of "secular" over against "sacred." Notions that suggest that worship is a "drawing aside" from the world or "entering" into a different world from the one we normally live in are hardly acceptable to our culture, which resists the distinctions between "this" world and a world "above" us or "beyond" us. Certainly pictures of heavenly worship, led by angels in chorus, are not immediately relevant to our times. Thus worship defined in a way that suggests a correlation between two worlds, ours and God's, has a hard time in making sense to those in our society for whom the "real" world is exactly the one they can see, touch, and use. Talk of "another"

3. See *Studia Liturgica* 7 (1970) for collected essays on this theme.
4. Evelyn Underhill, *Worship*, 3rd ed. (London: Nisbet, 1937), ch. 1.
5. J. G. Davies, *The Everyday God* (London: SCM Press, 1973), pp. 243-260.
6. R. Otto, *The Idea of the Holy* (London: Oxford Univ. Press, 1923).

world, above and beyond our world, sounds like meaningless gibberish or a string of nonsense syllables. The two persistent criteria by which reality is tested are: is it verifiable? is it usable? Applied to the exercise of worship in our traditional modes of singing, speaking, and "communing with the eternal," these criteria would put us on the spot. How can we verify a "holy thought"? Or compute the effectiveness of a choral anthem? These are questions J. G. Davies asks pertinently.

What we need, therefore, is a reminting of an old coin. To proceed with our discussion of worship requires a fresh look at the term and a recasting of its meaning in such a way as will express its essentially theological dimension and yet will relate its practice to the concerns, interests, and needs of men and women in our world. John Richard Neuhaus seeks to do just that when he writes of the purpose of the church, saying that it exists "to sight, signal, support, and celebrate the coming of the Kingdom."[7] He proceeds to show how the last verb in his manifesto exactly focuses on the ministry of worship. In worship the church raises the celebration of God's praises by which his rule over all human life is confessed, proclaimed, exerted . . . and enjoyed.

Defining the Term

We propose a definition, then, that may do justice to the issues involved. *Worship is the dramatic celebration of God in his supreme worth in such a manner that his "worthiness" becomes the norm and inspiration of human living.* Several factors merge in this summary statement.

First, our proposed statement places God at the center and emphasizes the theological weight of worship. God's "worthiness" ensures that this motive will not be obscured or compromised. In the 1975 Hartford Appeal the reminder was clearly made: "We worship God because God is to be worshipped." It follows that Christian worship at its highest and noblest expression and intention will be unique, both as an activity and as a desire to seek his honor and "worth." Neuhaus again helps us with his warning words:

7. J. R. Neuhaus, *Freedom for Ministry* (New York/San Francisco: Harper and Row, 1979), p. 105.

The activity called worship is not true worship if it can be done legitimately in any other context. . . . Worship, if done in response to anything other than the mystery of God in Christ, is idolatry.[8]

Secondly, understanding worship in the way we have suggested delivers us from the tyranny of subjectivism. The invitation that is in current usage, given implicitly if not made so blatantly as in the church bulletin board observed by Neuhaus ("Join Us For Worship. You Will Feel Better For It!") fails to recognize what worship is essentially all about. Admittedly most worshipers anticipate that their church services will lift their spirits and give them a rosier outlook on life. But that "experience," whether it is found or not, cannot be the aim of worship; it is at best a by-product, a spinoff from the original intent.

The chief aim of worship is God himself. An encounter with him may be painful and entail a call to sacrifice, commitment, self-denial. In spite of the devaluing of holiness—which suggests God's apartness from the world and his "infinite qualitative distinction" (in Kierkegaard's phrase) from man—it is precisely this quality that gives to Christian worship its special ethos and its raison d'être. Therefore, the call is not so much "Smile, God loves you," as "Repent," "Weep," "Tremble" for the precise reason given. God's love expressed in Christ's cross, suffering, and victory is no cheap idea or weak sentiment. It can only be celebrated with reverence and wonder; it will almost certainly entail a searching decision to share its agony and conflict. And the role of the minister has to be seen in this light. He or she is a celebrant, not a cheerleader intent on whipping up enthusiasm or offering the people a psychological boost. The minister is preeminently a servant of Christ and a steward of the divine mysteries (see 1 Cor. 4:1).

A third justification for looking at worship in the way we have adopted will lead us directly to consider the truest pattern that expresses the term's meaning. If the celebration of God's worthiness is meant to lift us into the light of his presence, that elevation will provide a place from which we see our lives in a fresh light. The vision of God, as Calvin

8. J. R. Neuhaus, *Freedom*, p. 122.

noted, leads to a heightened appreciation of who we are: "in thy light we see light."[9]

Worship is thus directed to God but it is offered by those whose spirits are enlivened to receive impressions from the God they address. One of the most exciting and important rediscoveries of our time has been the dialogue shape of Christian worship. The distinctive genius of corporate worship is the two-beat rhythm of revelation and response. God speaks; we answer. God acts; we accept and give. God gives; we receive. As a corollary to this picture, worship implies a human response in terms of giving to God. The theological code word for man's offering to God is *sacrifice*. The worshiper is not a passive, motionless recipient, but an active participant, called upon to "make an offering."

The Legacy of the Past

The contemporary revival of interest in our theme cannot be understood without some looking backward. Two periods in church history in particular claim our attention.

1. The legacy of the Puritan tradition has been a dominant one within the nonestablished churches over three centuries. S. F. Winward[10] among others has described the outstanding features of the Puritans' idea of worship in the 1600s and extending to the next century:

a) The sole criterion was the written Word, found almost exclusively in the New Testament. The Old Testament was treated as belonging to the Jewish people whose worship, centered in Tabernacle and Temple, had given way to a more spiritualized mode. Moreover, only those items of worship that were specifically mentioned in the New Testament could claim authority. Musical instruments, for example, which are not explicitly referred to in the New Testament church, were treated as distracting from "pure" worship. No room was given to innovation or to a sense of a developing tradition. Indeed, on the contrary, a stifling literalism effectively blocked

9. See Edward A. Dowey, Jr., *The Knowledge of God in Calvin's Theology* (New York: Columbia Univ. Press, 1952), pp. 28f., citing *Institutes* I. ii.2.

10. S. F. Winward, *The Reformation of our Worship* (London: Carey Kingsgate, 1964), pp. 22, 63, 87ff., 105.

any notion of creative spontaneity in the forms of worship to be employed.

b) The sermon was made the climax and culmination of the service. This led inevitably to a devaluing of other forms of worship, for example, the eucharistic. Even those parts of the service that were not strictly "preaching" or exposition were made the vehicle of instruction. Pulpit prayers were chiefly didactic in content and tone; and Scripture readings were interspersed with the preacher's homiletical comments on the text. Congregational participation was reduced to a minimum, especially to the ministry of hymns or psalms singing.

c) The freedom of the Spirit was seen in the cultivating of worship from the heart and the stress on personal religion. Written prayers were frowned on if not roundly condemned, since it appears that the Puritan objection was to the exclusive use of the Prayer Book, thus denying free prayer.[11] Sole reliance on prearranged orders of service was regarded as a quenching of the Holy Spirit who leads God's people in a face-to-face encounter with divine realities.

d) By a strange quirk, while the priesthood of all believers was cherished as a theological conviction and the concept of the church as a "gathered community" prevailed in theory, a Protestant clericalism developed, with the minister occupying a central and determinative role as leader and chief performer in the service. The preaching of one man in a raised pulpit took pride of place, and this arrangement reduced the worshipers to the level of an inert body of passive auditors.

2. The social forces of the nineteenth century only served to distort the picture and upset what might have been a redressing of the balance. Several factors from that era confirmed the worst features of the earlier centuries and deepened the need for reform of the church's worship.

New inventions and facilities in mass communication—the press, radio, telephone—coupled with the rise of universal education gave fresh impetus to the power of human words.

11. H. Davies, *The Worship of the English Puritans* (London: Dacre Press, 1948), p. 115; cf. pp. 256f.: "Gradually, objections to a particular liturgy, the Book of Common Prayer, became objections to any liturgy, as extemporary prayers ousted pre-composed forms."

At political meetings audiences were swayed and moved by the oratory of speakers as later they would be stirred and in-fluenced by the written word in pamphlet and social tract. The persuasive powers of human speech enhanced the authority of those leaders who could command a hearing. And the same was true of church leaders who excelled as plat-form orators and—so the phrase ran—"pulpiteers." The preacher's rostrum became the church's sounding board and the minister's throne. This led to a style of worship that was heavily intellectualized and notional. The worshiper was thus subtly dehumanized by being treated solely as a mind to be informed, his person the target of a barrage of words. It is a moot point whether precisely at this level the church's contact with a rising generation of proletarian and manual-working men and women in factory, shop, and mine was broken off simply because the preacher's language could move his con-gregation only superficially. When worship became exces-sively devoted to the ministry of the word, thus ignoring the human being's many-sided personality which includes appre-ciation of visual art in architecture, painting, sculpture, and drama, something was lost. And sermons that were severely expositional and didactic lost their appeal because "the pro-letarian . . . does not live and move in the realm of abstract ideas."[12]

Individualism took its toll as worship became narrowly per-sonalized. Each person in the church pew was made to feel his or her individual worth (in itself a worthwhile and necessary discovery), but at the expense of a social context and respon-sibility. The hymnbooks of the later nineteenth century tell the story of religious experience that is inward-looking and pulse-taking without the counterbalancing social sweep of Wesley and Watts.

Laissez-faire economic theory invaded the church with a surprising consequence. A free church tradition that cher-ished and thrived on its enjoyment of "freedom" overplayed the antithesis between liturgy and liberty. This kind of dichotomizing drove an unnecessary wedge between a fixed, written order of prayers and ceremonial acts on the one side, and a spontaneous, uninhibited exercise of freedom "as the

12. S. F. Winward, *Reformation*, p. 7.

Spirit moves" on the other. One would suppose that unrestricted freedom, tied to no set pattern, would lead naturally to a full participation of the entire assembly of believers (as in the scene depicted in 1 Cor. 14:26). But, as we saw, this did not happen. Protestant worship focused attention on the one man in the pulpit who did everything, especially in praying extempore and preaching by divine afflatus, with the result that his audience became little more than a company of inert and submissive hearers.[13] If this state of affairs was not bad enough, the malaise of worship was aggravated by the role of that single leader. He organized the entire service at whim, and with apparently little or no sensitivity to the past history of the church's liturgy he proceeded to operate with a new set of criteria:

a) What aroused the feelings of the congregation and enforced the message of the sermon was regarded as spiritually effective. All the parts found in the earlier division of the worship service were treated as preliminary to the sermon and subservient to it. The climactic "message" of the preacher's biblical exposition and its evangelistic thrust became the dominant feature; all else was but a preparation for it, with prayers and hymns serving to "soften up" and predispose the congregation in anticipation of the "orgasmic" effect of the proclamation.

b) In liberal Protestantism of the period, the evangelistic opportunity of the sermon was replaced by a chance to ventilate social issues of the day. Thus the Christian pulpit became little better than a sounding board for the discussion of current political, social, and economic concerns as these were understood by the reigning liberal theology. While liberal theology lost its force after the first World War, traces of its legacy lingered on into the twentieth century in the form of "civil religion." Patriotism and national honor became part of the fabric of the church's life, and this colored the worship.

c) The "garnered wisdom of the ages" was lost and the church's long liturgical heritage despised in the interests of

13. See Ivor Bailey, "The Challenge of Change. A Study of Relevance versus Authority in the Victorian Pulpit," *The Expository Times* 86 (Oct. 1974), pp. 18-22.

"free" worship. Free church worship services were characterized by shapelessness and novelty, with no discernible structure and progress as the service proceeded. That situation is largely still with us today—in spite of a growing awareness of dissatisfaction caused by a failure to offer a pattern of worship that, while not losing its warm-hearted spontaneity and directness, respects the coherent flow of the service and its development from one theme to another.

Agenda for Reform

The time is ripe for a fresh evaluation of what we intend to do when we participate in corporate worship. In the following paragraphs we will discuss what seems to me to be the main ways that patterns or styles of worship in the churches today could reflect and embody the vast amount of research, study, and conclusions that have marked the past few decades of scholarly interest and productiveness in this discipline. What follows will also set the stage for our discussion in subsequent chapters as we review the traditional parts or ingredients of the diet of public worship.

1. We have already noticed how worship is the human response to divine revelation, set in a dialogue pattern. The two-beat rhythm of God's approach to us that meets with and evokes a reacting offering of ourselves to him seems as basic to the Christian view of worship as it is to the essence of all biblical religion. The sequence of these movements is highly significant.[14]

The divine initiative is safeguarded by the emphasis (which is not to be obscured) on God's prior action. He starts the entire process by his freely willed choice of Israel, seen in the call of Abraham and continued in the election of the chosen people. We acknowledge this initiative by ascribing to him praise and by publishing his "mighty acts" in creation, calling, and redemption. The celebration of God's grace offers a fixed point in worship; indeed, it is the Archimidean point on

14. As illustrated in Paul W. Hoon's book, *The Integrity of Worship* (Nashville: Abingdon Press, 1971), p. 77: "Christian worship is God's revelation of himself in Jesus Christ and man's response; it is the dialogue between man and God through the Word."

which all else turns. All worship of God finds its origin in the objective "moment" when God acts and comes to our world in free love.

What we do in response to this "coming" concerns our role as involved sharers and participants. The receiving of God's gifts quickly merges into a giving to him of thankfulness, obedience, and trust. There are no fewer than eight different words in the New Testament that emphasize human activity in worship; of these the most common are "service" (diakonia), "liturgy" (leitourgia), and "worship" (latreia). All are terms of human activity and enterprise. All speak of our responsibility to "ascribe to the Lord the glory due his name; [to] bring an offering, and [to] come into his courts" (Ps. 96:8). "Worship the Lord in holy array" (v. 9) is the call that completes the picture.

2. If worship involves and is expressed by the activity we perform, it embraces the whole person. Protestant evangelicalism has given a rightful prominence to the "speaking/hearing" aspects. The word of God is spoken in Scripture readings and sermons; it is the duty and privilege of the worshiper gladly to hear and obey. But this concentrated insistence on "the word" gives, as we have seen, an undue weight to fellowship with God expressed in noetic and intellectualized ways. What is excluded is the appreciation of beauty and truth in visual forms, leading to a stimulation of the imagination and an illumination of the inward eye.

The posture of a seated company of worshipers, set in serried rows and ranks, is not the only possible—nor maybe the best—one for the use of our motor limbs in upraised hands and arms, the celebration of God in sacred dance, and the religious vehicle of dramatic art. These are all other ways in which worship can take on a richer meaning and a fuller flavor.[15]

3. Worship should seek comprehensively to incorporate both set forms and the freedom of the Spirit. This is a thesis admirably set out in Winward's book. What we may

15. See Anne Long, *Praise Him in the Dance* (London: Hodder and Stoughton, 1976).

offer is a brief recital of the reasons why there ought not to be any hiatus or conflict between the two ways of looking at worship today. Both styles have much to offer. Yet each way of worship stands in need of the complementary role of the other.

The adoption of set forms of worship ensures that there will be fidelity to the "shape of the gospel," provided that such forms are so put together that they express the major themes of creation, man's need, and human redemption in this world and beyond. Then, the heritage of the past is best preserved by a liturgy that draws on the church's history and experience down the ages. The danger of simply repeating fossilized and archaic patterns in traditional and often outworn language is clearly present; but recognizing the legacy of the past need not entail such a conservative attitude. Finally, a prearranged order of service places a firm control on the subjective tastes and fancies of the minister, and delivers the congregation from his more glaring foibles! It gives some flexibility for creative thinking and planning, but sets boundaries within which the truest worship, worthy of the historic gospel, is offered.

In complementary ways room must always be left for the present activity of the Spirit whose role is to lead the church into a deepening apprehension of God's truth and to make the gospel contemporary. It follows that there will be space for worship that is spontaneous and suited to the needs of the present hour. "Do not quench the Spirit" (1 Thess. 5:19) is Paul's word of caution in circumstances that suggest an attempt to canalize the Spirit's operation and to squelch some charismatic ministries, though we can only guess the precise setting of the admonition. Liturgies *can* have this dampening effect, though their right use need not lead to such a suffocating of the Spirit. Moreover, there is always a need to be alive to what the Spirit is saying to the churches in our times and to fashion our prayers, confessions, hymns, and proclamation to speak relevantly to our contemporaries without betraying the ancient message of God's truth.

4. We distinguish between the Christian's private and family devotional life and his or her sharing in the public

worship of God as an act of corporate fellowship. In the latter sense, worship is by definition a communal enterprise that is much more than the sum total of individual practices of prayer, meditation, and Scripture study. The extra dimension stems from the enrichment of the assembled congregation at worship. The church is more than a convenient meeting place for men and women whose individual interests and religious experience draw them together but who remain separate and detached from one another. The worship of the church means the pulsating of a "common life" *(koinōnia)*[16] that flows through the body of Christ and in which the individuals participate through their baptism by one Spirit into one body (see 1 Cor. 12:13). To conceptualize the church at worship as made up of isolated units, however personal, each worshiping in a self-contained compartment, however closely associated, is really to mistake what the New Testament means by the church. As E. Schweizer well illustrates,[17] the ideal set forth in the pages of the apostolic church is that of fellowship-in-worship. He deals critically with the latter-day notion of the Christian community as split between one speaker and a silent body of listeners; and equally his study rebukes the excessive individualism of what passes for worship in many modern churches. Recovery of the wholeness of the church's life as "life together" in Christ, in Bonhoeffer's phrase,[18] would go a long way to set our worship as a corporate exercise on a stable basis, and deliver modern congregations from "ministerial monopoly" with one person conducting a virtuoso performance on the one side, and overemphasis on the narrowly individualistic—such as disfigured the Corinthian assembly where *koinōnia* had tragically broken down—on the other.

16. On the various meanings of *koinōnia* in the New Testament I may refer to my book *The Family and the Fellowship: New Testament Images of the Church* (Grand Rapids: Wm. B. Eerdmans; Exeter: Paternoster Press, 1980), ch. 3: "Fellowship: The Anatomy of a Word." See also N. Turner, *Christian Words* (Edinburgh: T. and T. Clark, 1980), pp. 163-168.

17. E. Schweizer, "The Service of Worship" in his *Neotestamentica. German and English Essays 1951-1963* (Zurich: Zwingli Verlag, 1963), pp. 333-343.

18. D. Bonhoeffer, *Life Together* (New York: Harper and Row, 1954). See Neuhaus's use of the term in *Freedom*, pp. 101-104.

5. The classic description of the Christian *synaxis*, that is, gathering for worship, divides the service into two parts, corresponding to "word" and "sacrament." The "liturgy of the word" is succeeded by the "liturgy of the upper room." The former is arranged with the general public congregation in view, the latter restricted to the baptized faithful.

This model has stood the test of time and has done much to conserve the liturgical heritage of the centuries. If it lacks one obvious feature, it still operates within the framework of the notional and severely didactic. Admittedly the eucharistic climax of the service offers a visual contact with the realities behind the bread and the wine. Yet it still remains the case that worshipers are there to be instructed, taught, edified, and prepared to contemplate the heavenly mysteries of the communion table. What perhaps is needed to make the circle complete is a vision of worship as related to life and society. The ministry of intercession, whereby the prayers of God's people reach out to lift up the world to him, has always had an honored, if somewhat obscure, place in the history of the liturgy. We need to recover its importance, for it carries with it a reminder that while worship is directed primarily to God, it fits and equips God's church to be the agent by which his will is done on earth and through which the church's prayers for the world are largely answered.

6. Our final prescription must therefore be one of worship related to life, for worship serves an ancillary function of preparing the assembled company to accept its role as Christ's servants and stewards over the entire range of human existence. In the high moments of public praise and prayer and communion with God we discover our full personhood, since we see ourselves "under the aspect of God" whose name and presence we invoke and enjoy. Worship does indeed transcend the barriers of time and space, bringing us into touch with heaven's reality and fulfillment, as the author of Hebrews knew well (Heb. 12:22-24). It permits us to see within the veil, and actualizes in our temporal experience what truly belongs to the eternal state where God is "all in all" and his will done perfectly. So Barth's fulsome description of "the most momentous, the most urgent, the most glorious action" is exactly the case. But it carries the cor-

responding summons that out of this vision and awareness of heavenly joys and perfections we should see our present life and lot, cast in a less-than-perfect world and still laying its claim to service and work upon us, in such a way that we are eager to play our part in promoting God's interests and human well-being here and now as we move from worship in the sanctuary or chapel to mundane living. Paul can glide from his statement of "spiritual worship" (Rom. 12:1) into a series of the most practical, down-to-earth applications of what that "worship in everyday life," in Käsemann's phrase,[19] will entail (Rom. 12:9-21).

19. E. Käsemann, "Worship in Everyday Life: a note on Romans 12," in *New Testament Questions for Today* (Philadelphia: Fortress Press, 1969), pp. 188-195, and his *Commentary on Romans* (Grand Rapids: Wm. B. Eerdmans, 1980), pp. 326ff.

CHAPTER TWO

Praises with Understanding

The Call to Worship

We have already called attention to the so-called "crisis of worship" that was discussed at the Uppsala sessions of the World Council of Churches in 1968 and often remarked on since then. The crisis arose partly because the secular version of the gospel called into question the relevance of worship in its traditional forms, and partly because the concept of transcendence and the "numinous" has been challenged in recent times. To be sure, modern worship must reflect the idiom and life-style of the day we live in, and there is no virtue in a mindless repetition of archaic forms and language that carry no meaning to our contemporaries. Changing the address of God from "thou" into "you" is a case in point;[1] and it has yet to be shown that worship is less "dignified" or less evocative when this transposition is made. These, however, are marginal matters. Attempts to restructure worship and to recast its traditional modes in the interests of modernity have gained only slight acceptance among Christians generally.

The critique of transcendence is much more radical since a denying of God's "apartness" and uniqueness would strike a blow at a cherished and pervasive biblical image of God seen, for example, in Isaiah 57:15:

1. As in *The Alternative Service Book 1980* (London: Hodder and Stoughton, 1980), except in Rite B. See D. L. Frost, *The Language of Series 3* (Bramcote: Grove Books, 1978), pp. 7, 8. The lively contributions to *Crisis for Cranmer and King James* (Manchester: Carcanet: Special Issue of *PN Review* 13, 1980) show how the debate continues.

For thus says the high and lofty One
Who inhabits eternity, whose name is Holy:
"I dwell in the high and holy place."

To remove this picture of God's holy and majestic presence
would leave an empty void in man's understanding of the
divine nature that no updated version of immanence or idea
of God as the "ground of being" can fill. Such a denial is
unnecessary once we recall that God's "aloofness" is not at
the expense of his nearness. The prophet therefore completes
his sentence of Yahweh's oracle:

"and also [I dwell] with him who is
of a contrite and humble spirit,
to revive the spirit of the humble,
and to revive the heart of the contrite."

To be at all meaningful in any Judeo-Christian context,
worship must address God the creator who is at once above us
and yet graciously near, "the beyond who is in the midst."[2]
There are two corollaries of this premise that bear on the
theme of praise.

One is *the theocentric nature of worship*. Worship is an
exercise of the human spirit directed primarily to God. As we
saw, the worshiper embarks on an enterprise undertaken not
simply to satisfy his needs or to make him feel better or to
minister to his aesthetic taste or social well-being, but to express the worthiness of God himself. This observation is in
line with the derivation of the very word we use. Worship by
its etymology means "worth-ship." We can use the term

2. The most telling illustration remains in Kenneth Grahame's *The
Wind in the Willows* (cited by Howard Booth, "The Glory of the Lord,"
The Expository Times 92 [Dec. 1980], pp. 83ff.). J. G. Davies, *The Everyday God* (London: SCM Press, 1973), p. 245 comments on the climax of
the encounter as Mole and Rat recall their sense of "august presence":
    "Rat!" he found breath to whisper, shaking. "Are you afraid?"
    "Afraid?" murmured the Rat, his eyes shining with unutterable
love. "Afraid of Him? O, never, never! And yet—and yet—O, Mole, I
am afraid!"
    Then the two animals, crouching to the earth, bowed their heads
    and did worship.
"Kenneth Grahame has conveyed in a remarkable way that blend of awe
and delight, of fear and fascination, which is said to be induced by the
numinous and to demand worshipful obeisance" (p. 245).

loosely when we say of an individual, "He worships his money" or "she worships her home," meaning that such people attach inordinate value to these objects. At a different level, in the Marriage Service of the Book of Common Prayer, the prospective husband greets his future bride with the words, "With my body I thee worship."[3] This is a pledge of utter loyalty and devotion to the woman who is worthy of this, at least in his eyes. Now if we can elevate this idea to the realm of God-man relationships, we have a working definition ready made for us; and that includes, as we insisted already, the ascribing to God of supreme worth, for he is uniquely worthy to be honored and acclaimed in this way.

For confirmation of this proposal we need only glance at the Psalms, the hymnbook of the Second Temple: "Ascribe to the Lord the glory due his name" (Ps. 96:8). Because the Lord is great, he is "greatly to be praised" (Ps. 96:4). "Extol the Lord our God, and worship at his holy mountain" is the call of Psalm 99:9, with the reason given, "for the Lord our God is holy."

The "holiness of God" is then at the heart of the Christian idea of worship with its dual effect of inspiring in us a lively awareness of creaturely dependence and frailty because of our sinful selves (see Isa. 6:1-9 for this reaction, complemented by Peter's response recorded in Luke 5:8), and yet bidding us draw near since the divine character is "attractive," to use R. P. C. Hanson's interesting title.[4] The men and women of Scripture's story invariably feel initial discomfort and unease when they become aware of the divine presence: Abraham in his colloquy with Yahweh (Gen. 18:27); Moses at the place of fiery revelation (Exod. 3:5); Manoah when confronted by life's mystery (Judges 13:17, 18, 22); Job overwhelmed by an inexplicable theophany (Job 42:5, 6); Peter at the lakeside, as we saw; Saul of Tarsus arrested by the bright light and the voice out of the sky (Acts 9:4); and John as he sensed another's presence on Patmos (Rev. 1:17). Yet man's creatureliness in the encounters with deity leads on to a reassur-

3. In the 1980 version this has become "With my body I honour you," but option B earlier retained "worship": "To love, cherish, and worship/ Till death us do part."

4. R. P. C. Hanson, *The Attractiveness of God: Essays in Christian Doctrine* (Richmond: John Knox Press, 1973).

ance of divine pardon, God's intimate nearness, and his commissioning summons to service of whatever form. The sequel may vary, but what is uniform is the insistence that no mortal can remain unmoved or unchanged before him who is "of purer eyes than to behold evil and [cannot] look on wrong" (Hab. 1:13) but whose tender mercies never fail in their offer of forgiveness and renewal (Ps. 130:3, 4).

The cry "Thrice Holy" of Isaiah 6 is carried forward to the throne-room drama of John's vision (Rev. 4:8), and as the *Trisagion* it found a place in early liturgies. God's holy nature sets the pattern for Christian worship that is different from a cosy intimacy with God as our partner or "pal." "Mateyness" with the God of the Bible is the last relationship you would expect with one who is "a consuming fire" (Heb. 12:28, 29).

A second corollary stemming from our view of worship is *the claim laid upon the worshiper to offer what is his best* and so to demonstrate by his offering of praise, prayer, and giving the seriousness with which he regards this religious exercise and duty. True worship will entail a response that is thoughtful, costly, and worthy, appropriate to the high occasion and in line with the serious intent of a person's coming into the presence of the all-holy who is the all-gracious God. The Old Testament rituals and ceremonies heavily accent this need for the worshiper's preparation for the cult. David "will not offer burnt offerings to the Lord my God which cost me nothing" (2 Sam. 24:24). "You cannot serve the Lord" was Joshua's admonition (Josh. 24:19) to a people who in their easy-going, idolatrous ways had forgotten that Yahweh is "a holy God" who required a wholehearted and unshared dedication to his name. Put into modern terms these biblical verses stress the seriousness of our worship and the claim it lays upon us to have done with all that is slipshod and flippant—not to say frivolous—in our approach to God and our leading others into his presence. Such a careless or indifferent attitude is obviously out of place in the religion of the new covenant where Jesus' words preserved in the Johannine community reflect what is the essence of genuine worship: "God is spirit, and those who worship him must worship in spirit and truth" (John 4:24). The office of the Holy Spirit is directed precisely to this goal, as we see if Paul's words are taken at face value: "we worship by the Spirit of God" (Phil. 3:3, RSV margin). For the Spirit may be relied on to direct and inspire our praise in such a manner that is acceptable to God, if we are prepared to take the offering of praise with fitting attention to what we are doing and why we are doing it. Anything that is merely formal, casual, or routine can hardly be regarded as set "within the magnetic field of the Holy Spirit," as W. C. van Unnik graphically describes true worship;[5] nor will it prove satisfying to the participant.

Praise: Old Testament–Style

The people of Yahweh were summoned into existence to be a people of his own possession and to make his praise "glorious" (Ps. 66:2). Verbs most often used of the worshiping people's approach to God—"to bow down" and "to serve" —are matched by other action words that tell us how pious Israelites thought of their offering of praise to the covenant God. Three verbs are expressive:

1. "To make a noise" (Hebrew root is *hālal*) underscores the obvious point that praise involves the use of words audibly expressed. Silent prayer is not a Hebrew practice; the reading of Scripture, on the other hand, is an exercise that involves the vocal chords (see Acts 8:30; Philip can *hear* the Ethiopian as he reads the prophetic writing). Notice the way Eli thinks that Hannah is drunk because she prayed without forming the words to be heard (1 Sam. 1:12-14).

The Hebrew verb we have noted provides the "prime expression of all praise,"[6] namely, Hallelujah which means Praise Yah/the Lord (Ps. 135:3, and often at the beginning and end of psalms). The noun for "praise" from this root is *tehillāh,* which has a wide range of meanings but is used chiefly in relation to God whose mighty deeds are sung and acknowledged. In this way God's honor or fame is proclaimed in all the earth (Hab. 3:3).

5. W. C. van Unnik, *"Dominus Vobiscum:* The Background of a Liturgical Formula" in *New Testament Essays in Memory of T. W. Manson,* ed. A. J. B. Higgins (Manchester: University Press, 1959), p. 294.

6. *Interpreter's Dictionary of the Bible,* vol. 3 (Nashville: Abingdon, 1962), p. 857.

2. In a number of cases Yahweh's praise is celebrated by bodily movement and gesture. Singing with Miriam (Exod. 15:20) and dancing with David (2 Sam. 6:14) as examples—they go together in the scene depicted in 1 Samuel 18:6—are part and parcel of this exuberant expression of praise (the verb "to praise" is taken from the Hebrew *yādāh;* connected possibly with the hand, *yād,* it means "to give thanks"). The psalmist knows this type of locomotive activity to be one way in which God is exalted (Ps. 149:3), with hands as well as voices upraised (Ps. 28:2; 134:2) as a tribute of "thanksgiving," the basic meaning of *tôdāh.*

3. The verb *zāmar* (in the form *zimmēr,* which the Greek Bible translates as *psallō:* "to sing hymns") covers musical activity, including the playing of instruments and singing in honor of Yahweh. The best translation is "to make melody." Individuals offer this type of praise; but choirs too may join their voices, as in the antiphonal responses of Psalm 136 and even more dramatically in Psalm 24. A variety of musical instruments is mentioned in Psalm 150:3-5, ranging from the trumpet blast and clashing cymbal to the sweet melody of flute and harp. All unite to "praise the Lord" (v. 6).

God is praised in the Old Testament church for a number of reasons. Psalm 150, quoted above, is written in celebration of his "mighty deeds" (v. 2), a thought characteristic of much of the Old Testament with its emphasis on "holy history" as the story of the saving acts of Yahweh on his people's behalf. We may identify four main areas of life in which Israel rejoiced to praise her God:

1. Nothing rivals the celebration of God's power in setting his chosen people free from the tyranny of slavery in the time of Moses. As a German scholar might well express it in his native idiom, Yahweh was ever regarded as "the out-of-Egypt-bringing God." The redemption and the exodus became and remained the focal point of Israel's joy in God's saving grace and power, and at every Passover in Scripture and in the liturgy of the seder the story was retold and divine deliverance rehearsed. Chapters 12-15 of Exodus are con-

stantly appealed to in later books as the outstanding document in which this emancipation is told, culminating in the "song of Moses" which Miriam picks up:

> Sing to the Lord, for he has triumphed gloriously;
> the horse and his rider he has thrown into the sea.

2. What was done at the Sea of Reeds took on added significance once the drama was completed at the mountain of revelation, Sinai, with the giving of the law and the establishing of the covenant (Exod. 24, 34). So later psalmists exult in Yahweh as the God of the covenant (e.g., Ps. 106) who saved the nation from the foe "and delivered them from the power of the enemy" (v. 10). God's faithfulness to Israel persisted in spite of the people's fickleness and perversity (this is the theme of Hosea); and running through all her history is this confidence, even if sometimes distorted and misplaced, as Jeremiah was to expose, that Israel was bound to Yahweh by covenant ties and pledges. Hence the call to praise God for his covenant fidelity is often heard.

3. The renewal of the covenant became a central feature of Israel's cultic year. Some scholars have maintained (in agreement with S. Mowinckel who pioneered this type of research),[7] that her liturgy was shaped and molded by the annual New Year festival when the covenant was reaffirmed. But behind the New Year celebration of Yahweh's kingship lay the praise of God as Lord of the harvest and giver of all life. The chief locus here is Deuteronomy 26:1-11, where the presenting of a basket of harvest produce is the occasion for a classic "confession of faith"—Israel's version of the Apostles' Creed—which retells God's goodness in choosing, redeeming, and preserving the nation (26:5-9). All this is set in a framework of God's gift in the bountiful harvest field and orchard; and not surprisingly both themes are conducive to "worship before the Lord your God" (v. 10) with glad and grateful hearts.

4. Responding to pressures from pagan polytheisms and nature worship, Israel offered her conviction of God as

7. S. Mowinckel, *Zum israelitischen Neujahr und zur Deutung der Thronbesteigungspsalmen* (Oslo: Dybwad, 1952).

sole creator (Gen. 1) and Lord over all peoples. The futility of idols and idol-makers is exposed with merciless scorn by the exilic prophet (Isa. 40:19, 20; 44:9-20). Out of this matrix was born Israel's praise of God as the only, sovereign Lord, the king of creation. He made the world and all its inhabitants, both animal and human. His power controls the turbulent sea (Ps. 95:5), exerting an authority that showed Yahweh's mastery of the monster that is associated with the deep ocean (Ps. 89:9, 10; 93:3, 4; 106:8, 9; Isa. 51:9, 10).[8] The drama of Psalm 107:23-30 is a vivid, real-life portrayal of man's innate fear of the presence of demonic forces (symbolized in the raging sea) which Yahweh alone can control and subdue. Small wonder that Yahweh's people will want to acclaim him as Lord of creation and king over the world!

Praise: The New Testament Picture

Some special uses of the term "praise" will not directly concern us here. God is worshiped by the angels (Luke 2:13, 14 and often in the Apocalypse); and man is praised by God and by his fellows (Phil. 4:8; Rom. 13:3; 1 Pet. 2:14). Paul occasionally refers to his praise of the churches (1 Cor. 11:2) or to praise of his colleagues (2 Cor. 8:18). But the warning is not absent: that the praise of man should not obscure nor diminish God's praise. And that confusion is to be avoided since in the highest sense only God is praiseworthy (Rev. 9:10).

The chief emphasis naturally falls on the praise Christian believers offer to God. Indeed, the raison d'être of the church's life is to show forth the praises of God who has called the redeemed to himself (1 Pet. 2:10). The success of Paul's Gentile mission is applauded by the Gentiles who "praise God" (Rom. 15:9-11). And for the author of Hebrews there is nothing more fitting than that the old ceremonial offerings of the Tabernacle should give way to "the sacrifice of praise to God," expressed in vocal acknowledgment of God's name (Heb. 13:15).

The life of praise is the hallmark of Christian existence, since it demonstrates that the believing community has already anticipated the last day of God's final victory and is stretching out to share in its glories, even if the end is not yet attained. When the "consummation of the ages" is reached,

8. H. Ringgren, *Israelite Religion* (London: SPCK, 1966), pp. 107ff.

the psalmist's call will be answered (Ps. 115:13): "Praise our God, all you his servants"—an acclamation John the seer views as at least partially realized as the church on earth joins with the heavenly worship (Rev. 19:5). On the negative side, what describes and condemns the state of pagan society for Paul is that, although men and women have a dim picture of God, they do not honor him or give him thanks (Rom. 1:21). "Praise" therefore acts as a litmus test to decide whether or not men are on God's side. Either they give him praise or they withhold that acknowledgment and live only for themselves. So the phrase "Give praise to God" in John 9:24 (based on Josh. 7:19 and various Jewish texts) carries the meaning "Admit the truth."[9] It implies that when men make a truthful confession of who they are they cross over the threshold to a life of praise.

The themes of public praise are worth mentioning.

1. We have just referred to the role of the church as a mouthpiece of and witness to God's "excellencies" (Greek *aretai*) according to 1 Peter 2:10. The subject of the church's celebration seems to be drawn from Isaiah 43:21 in the Greek Bible, where God's excellent greatness evokes the people's "praise" (the plural "praises" is rendered by the same word as Peter's in Isa. 63:7). F. J. A. Hort[10] suggests that Paul's doxology in Romans 11:33-36 in the light of Romans 8:28-39 may have been in Peter's mind as he sums up in one graceful expression the "great deeds of God" *(magnalia Dei)* which center on all he has done for the church in the new age of salvation. "The author has in mind especially the redemption brought about by Christ's death and resurrection, and the divine wisdom, love, power, and mercy which lay behind it and in it" is E. G. Selwyn's comment.[11]

2. God's universal gifts bestowed on his creatures in creation and providence are the subject of such episodes as

9. C. K. Barrett, *The Gospel According to St. John*, 2nd ed. (Philadelphia: Westminster Press, 1978), p. 362.

10. F. J. A. Hort, *The First Epistle of St. Peter i.1-ii.17* (London: Macmillan, 1898), p. 129.

11. E. G. Selwyn, *The First Epistle of St. Peter* (London: Macmillan, 1947), p. 167.

Paul's exclamations at Lystra (Acts 14:15-17). Divine care for humankind is seen in fruitful harvest fields and beneficent protection, a second theme also picked up in Paul's Aeropagus address (Acts 17:26). Praise to God for his gifts of food, drink, and marriage (see 1 Tim. 4:3-5; Heb. 13:4) are invariably couched in the form of a protest against a false devaluing of these parts of human experience by Christian "spiritualizers" known as Gnostics. When their teaching became formulated in the second century, these two areas of human life—in attitudes toward food and sex—were precisely the ones where they maintained an ascetic and negative stance in a way already published by Paul's opponents at Colossae: "Do not handle, Do not taste, Do not touch" (i.e., engage in sexual relations) (Col. 2:21). The Pauline pastor has an effective answer to these denials of the goodness of God's gifts to his creatures. The prayer of thanksgiving offered for these gifts "consecrates" them by making them available for human use on the principle that "the earth is the Lord's" (Ps. 24:1, quoted in 1 Cor. 10:26) and its produce are rightly used as God's bounty to man. It is eminently fitting therefore that God should be thanked as the giver of "every good endowment and every perfect gift" (James 1:17).

3. At least one example is found in the pages of the New Testament of specific praise related to an individual's own needs and God's answer to his request. The case is a classic one, since the character involved, Abraham, becomes something of a test issue throughout the various books and theologies of the New Testament writers. With remarkable consistency the teaching of the Gospels, Paul, Peter, the author of Hebrews, and James the Just appeal to the example of Abraham as a model believer, an idealized "Christian" before the time, an archetypal specimen of the trusting individual.[12] Paul so regards him clearly in Romans 4 in a discussion climaxing with the remark that Abraham "grew strong in his faith as he gave glory to God" (v. 20). Abraham's

12. So James Denney characterizes Abraham in "The One Right Thing to Do," *The Way Everlasting* (London: Hodder and Stoughton, 1911), p. 258: "All the New Testament writers who wish to prove anything about the true religion say, 'Look at Abraham.'"

praise of God was called forth by a fulfillment of the divine promise. Making good God's promises provides an occasion for Paul to build a rudimentary liturgy as he summons the Corinthians to share in his confidence in the gospel that centers in God's promises fulfilled in the Messiah and gladly acknowledged in the church's response of "Amen" uttered in public worship (2 Cor. 1:20).[13]

4. Benedictions that "bless God" and salute his gracious gifts and doxologies that ascribe to him the praise which is his due are alike characteristic of the New Testament way of looking at life. Paul in particular punctuates his epistles with such outbursts, sometimes spontaneously (as in 2 Cor. 11:31), and occasionally when the theme requires it with a suitable ejaculation of praise (as in 2 Cor. 9:15). But also, because there is a pattern in apostolic writing derived from the Jewish liturgy, Paul can open his letter writing with a measured statement of praise to God, expressed in terms such as "Blessed be the God and Father of our Lord Jesus Christ" (2 Cor. 1:3; similarly in Eph. 1:3; 1 Pet. 1:3) or the more proselike epistolary form, "I thank [my] God" (Phil. 1:3) or "we always thank God" (Col. 1:3). These notes of praise are a direct legacy from Jewish worship, evidenced in the synagogue and among the community of the Dead Sea scrolls, and they illustrate how Paul in the main can take a conventional frame and place in it a tribute of praise which is unmistakably Christian in tone and content. He does this partly as a suitable way of securing his readers' goodwill and interest, and partly to summarize his teaching which the ensuing letter will elaborate. But what is just as clear is the liturgical temper of his writing so that he expects his letters to be read out in congregational gatherings (see Col. 4:16; 1 Thess. 5:27). He is already giving to the letters a kind of worship flavor and even a quasi-canonical (i.e., authoritative) tone as "holy scripture" by prefacing his more obvious didactic and argumentative pieces with an invocation of the praise of God.

13. "Here we come very close to a definition of worship, for the glorifying of God, the response of faith which issues in praise, thanksgiving, and supplication is exactly what we are doing in worship" (J. D. Crichton, "A Theology of Worship," in The Study of Liturgy, ed. C. Jones, G. Wainwright, E. Yarnold [London: SPCK, 1978], p. 9).

Conclusions

What sort of picture emerges from this outline of corporate praise that runs through the New Testament materials (and that we have looked at only cursorily)?

First of all, the character of God is a deciding factor in the evocation of praise. In our offering him the homage of our hearts we are really confessing him as a beneficent and gracious God. His hands are full of gifts and we receive them with a gratitude that overflows into praise.

Chiefest of those gifts is the matchless love of God seen, for all the New Testament authors, in the coming or sending of his son Jesus Christ who both revealed the Father's name and fulfilled the Father's will for the world's salvation. This is why the characteristic note of New Testament praise is exultation in God's saving act centered in Christ, "his inexpressible gift" (2 Cor. 9:15), and realized in the human experience of forgiveness and new life (Col. 1:12-14). The epitome of this saving deed is seen in the doxology of Ephesians 1:3-14, which, arranged in a trinitarian format, also traces the out-working and unfolding of God's eternal plan (1:3-5), historicized in Jesus Christ the son whom he loves (1:6-11), and made real in experience by the Holy Spirit who applies that "plan of salvation" to those who are its beneficiaries (1:12-14). After each section of this clearly constructed hymn the refrain is added: "to the praise of his glory" (vv. 6, 12, 14), as though to mark out the threefold character of the plan corresponding to the three activities of the triune God.

Second, we observe how the biblical teaching invites us to praise in the light of historical events that transpired independently of human engineering or forethought. Certainly men and women are enlisted to be God's agents in helping forward his plans in the world. When God willed to set his people free, he first found and called Moses through whom he worked—a roundabout manner of doing things that scandalized Jean Jacques Rousseau and many others since.[14] And men and women are invited to avail themselves of what God does "over their heads" as it were, or *extra nos,* outside of us,

14. John Baillie, *Our Knowledge of God* (Oxford: University Press, 1939), p. 185 quotes Rousseau's question, "Is it simple, is it natural, that God should have gone and found Moses in order to speak to Jean Jacques Rousseau?"

as the theological phrase runs. But it is God's decision to act and he always reserves the initiative. So praise is directed to God who "works wonders" (Ps. 77:14) sovereignly.

Praise therefore is not an exercise suspended on human feelings or governed by our emotional state. Even when the worshiper is low in spirit, he is bidden to raise up his head and contemplate the "mighty works of God" done "out there," whether or not he "feels" at that moment like entering upon a celebration of God. And it is that recall and contemplation of what God once did that can be as cordial to his drooping spirits, as the psalmist found when life's mysteries were too enigmatic and threatening for him (Ps. 77:9-12).

Third, the prominent verb associated with corporate praise is one (Greek *eucharistein)* that has given a word to our language, "eucharist," with the special nuance of thanksgiving at the Lord's table. Paul draws on this verb in 1 Corinthians 11:24 in the context of Jesus' actions in "giving thanks" to God before breaking the Passover loaf at the Last Supper. In 1 Corinthians 10:16 ("the cup of blessing which we bless") the Greek verb is *eulogein;* but this verb along with its partner *eucharistein* seems to be drawn directly from the Old Testament Jewish vocabulary (in the Hebrew *bērak/ berakah)* of "blessing God." The evangelists Mark and Matthew use the two verbs interchangeably: *eulogein* is the verb before the bread, *eucharistein* before the cup.[15]

The action of "blessing God" is given sharp focus in Judaism in the series of "graces before meals."[16] Jewish law required that no food be eaten before the blessing—of God, not the food, it should be noted—is offered. "It is forbidden to man to enjoy anything belonging to this world without a blessing; he who enjoys anything of this world without a blessing commits a violation" (Babylonian Talmud, *Ber.* 35a).[17] Blessings open with the statement "Blessed be thou,

15. On the equivalence of the two verbs, see J. P. Audet, *La Didachê*, Etudes bibliques (Paris: Gabalda, 1958), pp. 386-393.

16. On such Jewish "Prayers After Food" *(birkath hammazon),* see *Prayers of the Eucharist. Early and Reformed,* ed. R. C. D. Jasper and G. J. Cuming, 2nd ed. (Oxford: University Press, 1980), pp. 9f.

17. See G. Kittel and G. Friedrich, eds., *Theological Dictionary of the New Testament,* trans. G. W. Bromiley, vol. 2 (Grand Rapids: Wm. B. Eerdmans, 1964), p. 760 for this quotation (H. W. Beyer).

O Lord our God, king of the universe" as though to claim emphatically that the whole world is his and finds it proper place under his lordship. And the mealtime closes on the note of benediction as God is thanked again for his provision. The principle at stake here, say the rabbis, is one of "how much more." If we are to be grateful to God before we eat, how much more should we be grateful after we have received.

In Christian worship these ideas were given special significance. The Jewish-Christian prayers in a document known as the *Didache* or Teaching of the Twelve Apostles acknowledge God's provision in our daily food but quickly pass on to the theme of spiritual food and drink made available to the church in Jesus, God's servant. The sequence follows the pattern of John 6 where the debate between Jesus and his audience turns on this distinction.

So Christian praise of God is eucharistic through and through. We shall return to the special case of *the* eucharist or Lord's Supper service later. Here we note that true worship consciously sets God at the center of all life, celebrates his gifts in creation and providence, but reserves an unshared place for what he has done in the redemption of the world through our Lord Jesus Christ.

One practical result emerges from our study at this point. Our approach to God is above all else one of adoration. Thus, *true worship is that exercise of the human spirit that confronts us with the mystery and marvel of God in whose presence the most appropriate and salutary response is adoring love.* Adoration confesses that there is more in God than our finite minds and limited capacities can absorb; love rejoices that this God, "the beyond in our midst" wears the human face of Jesus Christ whose distinctive name for God was Father. A title that sums up the worshipful invocation is "Holy Father"; and God's holiness and fatherhood meet in Jesus who is the inspirer of all authentic praise.[18]

---

18. "The language of worship begins with the vocative. In worship one addresses the focus of worship . . . invested with qualities of personhood when [it] is addressed in worship" (N. Smart, *The Concept of Worship* [London: Macmillan, 1972], pp. 11, 14).

CHAPTER THREE

Praying Together

Introduction

The Bible is often seen as a library of assorted books; nevertheless, many pervasive themes run through each section. Obviously the writers reflect a consciousness of God that no book lacks—not even Esther, which does not explicitly refer to the divine name. At the same time the books of the Bible emerge out of a setting of human life in this world, with all the attendant challenges and problems and enrichments that such an experience, both societal and personal, brings with it. The activity that draws together a conviction of the living, loving God on the one hand, and the human condition of national, family, and personal existence in the world on the other is *prayer*. Praying to God the source, giver, and goal of all life is a common bond uniting most if not all the biblical characters.[1] The men and women who people Scripture's story page are invariably those who have left a record of turning to God in all manner and circumstance of their experience and seeking communion with God in prayer. This is so self-evident that it becomes an almost impossible task to detail the prayer habits of these men and women; their practices are as manifold and diverse as the characters themselves.

Corporate Praying

Our task has a more limited scope. We are not here concerned with private prayer or with individuals praying; rather, the focus of interest is the corporate aspects of prayer, as the assembled congregation joins together. When we try to apply scriptural precedents to our modern church life we are

---

1. The most useful source of documentation is the article "Prayer" in *The New International Dictionary of New Testament Theology*, ed. C. Brown, vol. 2 (Grand Rapids: Zondervan, 1976), pp. 855-886.

immediately put on our guard, and several points must be clarified at the outset. First, the language of this kind of praying is "we," not "I." Even if one individual vocalizes the prayer it is on the understanding that he or she is the mouthpiece of the community and not acting as a "private" individual whose praying happens to be in public. Many pulpit prayers, especially in the Free church tradition, fail precisely at this point. The minister or leader has yet to learn the distinction between a type of praying that, devotionally and directly, voices personal needs and desires and one that endeavors to express the community's aspirations and fears, which the individual is seeking to represent as their spokesperson.

Second, this consideration means that there is a lowest common denominator in public praying, making it as meaningful and relevant to all persons in the assembly as is humanly possible. The emphasis will fall on simplicity and straightforwardness in approaching God and in the use of the language, idioms, and concepts as these reflect spiritual experience. Prayers that presuppose an intimate knowledge of scriptural metaphor or theological doctrine will soar over the heads of most worshipers; just as serious is the leader's reflecting his or her own maturity in such a way that the congregation is left behind or, worse, made to feel that they cannot attain the degree of spirituality their leader has so obviously reached. Care needs to be taken to avoid the two extremes of an oversimplified kind of "nursery" praying which most will find embarrassing, and a convoluted or esoteric style of praying that leaves the people confused and threatened. Dignity need not be sacrificed at the expense of simplicity; and simplicity need not be reduced to the language of the kindergarten.

Third, our praying is always addressed *to God*—an obvious remark but often, alas, forgotten, as when the leader "uses" prayer to direct an admonition horizontally to the assembled group or to impart information. Then prayer is misused. It is cowardly and improper to administer a pastoral rebuke in the language of prayer, and it destroys the authentic spirit of worship to turn the prayer segment of the divine service into a rehearsal of the church announcements for the coming week or a bulletin of family activities, even if the family is the church family.

Corporate prayer is indeed part of church family life but as there is a place for specific mention of individuals and their needs in small groups, so there is a limit to what may effectively be done in congregational worship where the focus of vision is the entire church under the eye of God.

Some Biblical Precedents

Three considerations govern our study of the scriptural models.

1. The first Christians were Jews to begin with, and they brought over with them into the early congregations a liturgical legacy from the Temple and the synagogue. The attitude of the Jerusalem believers in Jesus as messianic head of a new community almost inevitably meant that theirs would be an ambivalent attitude to the Temple. Jesus had foretold its destruction and its replacement by a new spiritual shrine, his body. If the record in Acts is anything to go by, they venerated the sanctuary as a holy place and attended its hours of prayers (Acts 3). But before long they came to see the dangers inherent in that attachment as men like Stephen capitalized on the tradition that there was a new Temple since Messiah's death and resurrection and that God dwells in no earthly, man-made shrine but in human lives (Acts 7). The sacrificial system would equally fall under the rubric of an old order that had passed away with the coming of Israel's Messiah and his sacrifice, which in turn brought the Levitical offerings to their true fulfillment and supersession (the theme of the letter to the Hebrews).

It was somewhat different in the case of the Jewish synagogue. On every count the network of synagogues, especially in Galilee and the Dispersion, played a more significant role in the progress of early Christianity. As an institution, the local meeting place had the edge over the Temple since, for people outside of Jerusalem, it was near at hand, convenient to use, and open (though not restricted) to males, ten of whom could choose to form a quorum by banding together as a *minyan*. Thus a synagogue was born and could function without the presence of a priest or the cultus of sacrifice and offering. It is historically provable that Christian worship developed along lines set by the synagogue and owed much more in its genesis and evolution to the synagogue pattern than to the Temple. We should, therefore, look to the synagogue and its format of worship as the matrix out of which the first Christian church's liturgy emerged.

W. Schrage's very complete essay on the Jewish synagogue,[2] demonstrates its central importance to Jewish religious and social life in the period of the New Testament. In particular, the synagogue's worship, in line with its furnishings, was built upon a set pattern of praise, prayer, and instruction. Praise of God took prominence since the acknowledgment of God as creator and Savior is openly made in a way that sets the tone for the entire service. Another invariable feature of synagogue liturgy is Scripture lections, comment, and homily. But the framework into which the worship is fitted is prayer. After A.D. 70 with the destruction of the Second Temple it was said by the rabbis that prayer is even better than sacrifice.

We can observe how the chief ingredients of synagogue worship are enclosed in the prayers. The credal statement "Hear, O Israel, the Lord is one" is framed in benedictions in which God is honored. The reading of Torah is made with appropriate praises and prayers for illumination. The chief prayer, the *Kaddish,* praises God's name and expects his kingdom; and at the heart of the service is the *Tephillah* or *Amidah,* the standing prayers, which later developed into the set "Eighteen Benedictions."[3] They are far-ranging prayers, covering many facets of Jewish life, part praise, part supplication, part intercession, but all flavored by the praise of God in the language of the Old Testament, especially the Psalter. There are personal elements that seek forgiveness based on repentance. There is a yearning for redemption and healing. There is a harvest petition, seeking fruitful seasons. Wider interests extend to include the gathering of the exiles, scattered in the Dispersion, the prospect of judgment, and the reestablishing of Jerusalem as God's city under the Davidic king.

2. W. Schrage in G. Kittel and G. Friedrich, *Theological Dictionary of the New Testament*, trans. G. W. Bromiley, vol. 7 (Grand Rapids: Wm. B. Eerdmans, 1971), pp. 798-852.

3. The prayers are reproduced in C. Brown, ed., *New International Dictionary*, pp. 865ff. from R. A. Stewart, *A Rabbinic Theology* (Edinburgh: Oliver and Boyd, 1961), pp. 183-186.

While it cannot be shown that the *Shemoneh Esreh*, as this prayer came to be called, played any significant part in early Christian worship—the case of the "blessing (= cursing) of the heretics" that was later added to identify the presence of Jewish Christians is a special one—it is interesting that the liturgy underlying some chapters in 1 Clement (a document dated around A.D. 96) reflects several of the ideas of the Jewish model. Moreover, set prayers are already established by the time of the *Didache* (around A.D. 80), though the prophets are permitted to engage in free prayer as they will. New Testament prophets, notably at Corinth, led the congregation in prayer (1 Cor. 14).

2. Free, spontaneous praying is a feature of Christian gatherings recorded in the book of Acts. As the messianic pietists worshiped at the Temple, they also met in houses and later in other locations such as at the harbor of Miletus (Acts 20:36) or on the beach at Tyre (21:5). House congregations are mentioned (2:46; 4:42) as later Lydia's home at Philippi (16:15, 40) and Philip's house in Caesarea (21:8) became venues for Christian congregations.

Some special needs drove these men and women to prayer. They sought God's guidance (Acts 1:24) and the threat of trouble brought them together for personal encouragement (4:24-30) or to intercede for Peter in prison (12:5, 12). A particular instance of united praying is to be inferred from the scene at Antioch when the Spirit's call came and Barnabas and Saul were commissioned by the corporate decision of the Antiochenes at worship (13:1-3; 14:26).

3. Emerging as it did from the womb of Jewish messianism, the early church yet became innovative in the parts of prayer-speech that have left their deposit in the strata of New Testament literature. It is relatively easy to spot these "fossils" since they stand out as foreign-sounding words in the Greek New Testament.

a) Pride of place goes to *Abba* as the characteristic name for God in both the practice (Mark 14:32-39) and teaching of Jesus (Luke 11:1). The absolute uniqueness of this household word, used by a child for his earthly parent and best rendered "Dear father," is still being debated. What seems indisputable is that Jesus avoided the more formal appellation, "Our Father" *(Abinu)*, found in the synagogue prayer, and deliberately chose a nursery word to convey the thought of God's fatherly love, care, and provision for men and women as his children. Paul knew this Aramaic tradition and passed it on to his Gentile churches with suitable translation into their native Greek (see Gal. 4:6; Rom. 8:15). The context of these two passages suggests public worship which, led by the Spirit, was the occasion when believers confessed God as Father and received the assurance of their adoption into the divine family. Specific "moments" such as baptism or the recital of the prayer "Our Father" imparted as a privilege to new converts have been suggested as the setting of the cry "Abba, Dear Father" (see also 1 Pet. 1:17).

b) *Marana tha* is a precious fragment of prayer that may claim the distinction of being the oldest surviving specimen, with one other possible exception. Dividing the Greek word into its two components (in Aramaic originally) is not simple, but parallels from other places (Rev. 22:20; *Didache* 10:6, which uses the exact phrase) suggest that the translation should run, "Our Lord, come" (see later p. 148). It is a prayer of invocation, beseeching the risen Lord to come, either to the eucharistic meal or in his final appearing. Perhaps the first event was regarded as a foretaste of the final parousia.

c) The familiar tone of *Amen* (heard in 1 Cor. 14:16; 2 Cor. 1:20, and as a title in Rev. 3:14) should not dull our ears to the novelty of this term, which normally today finds a place at the close of our prayers to denote agreement or endorsement of what has just been said. The practice is ancient, and from the Corinthian passage mentioned (1 Cor. 14:16) we may picture the scene of prayers that could not be assented to because they were unintelligible to the "simple listener" (C. K. Barrett's translation)[4] who did not appreciate the language of the Spirit. "He does not understand what you are saying," and so the Amen is withheld, a situation Paul deplores. The reason is, as Schweizer[5] and Barrett make plain, that it is the responsibility of the church as a whole to

4. C. K. Barrett, *The First Epistle to the Corinthians* (London: A. & C. Black; New York: Harper & Row, 1968), p. 321.

5. E. Schweizer, *Church Order in the New Testament* (London: SCM Press, 1961), pp. 96f., 100, 190f. (sec. 7f, k, 23c).

hear, understand, test, and control all that goes on in the public offices of prayer and worship. This is a far-reaching consideration, and effectively checks all ideas of "ministerial monopoly" referred to earlier, and all types of idiosyncracies in worship that have no meaning for the congregation in general.

d) Two other foreign-sounding liturgical cries are recorded; both of them are firmly habituated in Christian worship. *Hosanna* (see Matt. 21:15) means "Save us now, we pray" and derives from Psalm 118:25. *Hallelujah*, "Praise to Jah" (Yahweh), is found in Revelation 19:3-8 as a shout of acclamation and triumph, anticipating Christ's final victory. It is not difficult to see how these two ejaculations, whatever their original context in the life of the Old Testament worship and the New Testament church, would quickly find a niche in the liturgies of the later church. Hosanna was used to greet the Lord who comes to his people as they gather in his name. Hallelujah (sometimes in the Latin form Alleluia) because of its onomatopoeic associations was taken over to convey the sense of exuberant praise as the mercies of God were contemplated and celebrated.

Common Prayers: A Model

Recalling our interest in the offering of public prayer as part of divine worship, let us ask if our preceding discussion offers help to the church in our day. Clearly, with the Jewish model before us, we should expect united praying to be orderly and sequential. While there is nothing resembling a set of rubrics or headings that has come down to us in church history, the theology of worship suggests a certain order.

First, prayer opens with the adoration of God in his character and revealed person. The note of objectivity is immediately sounded by our rehearsing in praise who he is and what he has done. Friedrich Heiler speaks of adoration in prayer as "the contemplative surrender to a supreme good";[6] and it is in that initial contemplation of God that a genuine spirit of fellowship with God who is praiseworthy is born.

Second, in the light of God's holiness and righteousness,

6. F. Heiler, *Prayer: A Study in the History and Psychology of Religion* (London: Oxford University Press, 1932), p. 360.

the worshipers confess and acknowledge their need of his pardon and grace. Such an act, since God is gracious and merciful, is met by the assurance of his forgiveness and the absolution of sins.

Third, the theme of thanksgiving takes up the next phase of the prayer sequence, since the now penitent and forgiven worshiper will want to express gratitude to God for all his gifts, chiefly the redemption and new life that is freely offered and thankfully embraced in Christ and the gospel. The common mercies of life in health, safety, and provision of our bodily and temporal needs will be part of this thematic thanksgiving.

Intercession, where the one who prays is concerned as mediator and intercessor before God principally for the needs of others, has much biblical precedent going back to Abraham (Gen. 18:22-23), Daniel (Dan. 9:3-19) and Ezra (Ez. 9:6-15). Paul uses the style of a wish-prayer in his letters as he joins in this ministry of supplication for his people. The more theologically grounded basis for our intercession is Christ's praying for his church (Rom. 8:34; Heb. 7:25; John 17). The language here is one of request or petition, with the basic idea of "wanting something," usually for other persons in need—the sick, the afflicted, the persecuted, the hungry and homeless, the aged, and our enemies. But coming to God with our own desires and requests is part of this kind of praying. Indeed, the verb "to ask" occurs frequently (some 70 times in the NT) in this context.

True prayer merges into the surrender of the worshiper to the God he invokes. A rabbinic prayer states the relation between prayer and God's design for our lives in a paradoxical way: "Lord, help me to do thy will as though it were my will, so that thou may'st do my will as though it were thine." The "end" or goal of prayer is to seek God's highest interests in our lives and to receive his grace to fulfill his will with all our powers. Prayer "succeeds" when it melts into commitment and obedience; it fails when it is treated as a recital of our needs and an attempt to force God to act.

The scheme suggested above indicates a progression in our common praying, set by the pattern of the Lord's Prayer and following the chief loci of Christian doctrine: creation, fall, redemption, illumination, and union with God in Christ. We begin with God in his glory and grace and close with the doing of his will in us and through us as we step out in daily living.

Public Praying: An Agenda

We are now ready to enter upon some practical application relating to the prayer ministry of the church in the light of our brief resumé of the biblical data. We can best consider the pros and cons of the two types of public praying found in the church.

1. *Set prayers* have several features that commend their use. They offer a common ground of language and thought on which all the congregation can stand as they focus unitedly on shared themes. The unity in the assembly is also a wider one as on any given day in the ecclesiastical calendar widely scattered congregations feel a sense of kinship by joining in common prayer. The heritage of the past is respected as "the accumulated wisdom and beauty of the Christian Church, the garnered excellence of the saints"[7] is capitalized. Such is made available for our use and enrichment today. Set prayers in unison preserve the dignity and orderliness of worship, and when the prayers are skillfully arranged in sequence they can immeasurably add to the "flow" of the service.[8]

On the debit side, however, there is no denying that repetition of standard prayers can make for formality and staleness. Even such gems as the Lord's Prayer require real effort of concentration and vitalized imagination if they are not to be prayed by rote and in an unthinking manner. Then, what set prayers gain in dignity and decorum they may lose in their being impersonal and unrelated to present needs. Such prayers can stifle the creative urge of the leader who, in

7. Percy Dearmer, cited in *Christian Worship: Studies in its History and Meaning,* ed. N. Micklem (Oxford: University Press, 1936), p. 234.

8. Calvin offers three reasons for the insistence on set prayers: first, that they provide help for the unskillfulness and simplicity of some; second, that the consent and harmony of the churches one with another may appear; and third, that the capricious giddiness and levity of such as effect innovations may be prevented (cited by John E. Skoglund, "Free Prayer," *Studia Liturgica* 10, 3/4 [1974], pp. 151-166 [p. 153]).

heavy-handed dependence on such written compositions, may well lose his or her sensitivity to the present and pressing needs of the men and women in the sanctuary.[9] Often the repeated use of a prayer book will set up a barrier between leader and people who get the impression, even if mistakenly, that he or she is simply "doing a job." Obviously this is a danger here, and under all conditions praying should be, as Paul said, both "with the mind" and "in the Spirit" (1 Cor. 14:15).

2. Turning to *free praying*, as it is called, without the use of written aids and following no set pattern, we may register the obvious fact that the leader is (ideally at any rate) relying on the Holy Spirit—an attitude Paul commends in Romans 8:26 though without exclusive reference to this kind of activity. Spontaneity, creativity, immediacy: these are all made possible when the minister enters himself into personal communion with God, and out of that dynamic experience utters prayers for the benefit of all. He or she can be alive to given situations[10] and is allowed room to express personal convictions, unhindered by the pages of a book and untrammelled by rubrics and conventions. Isaac Watts commended this type of praying, while he insisted that the minister should have prepared himself in heart and mind in advance. "Conceived prayer" is Watts's description.

On the other side of the reckoning, a congregation that knows only free prayer from the pulpit or desk is certainly at the mercy of what are termed "ministerial moods"; the people are exalted or debased according to the whim of the pastor whose own spirits may be either high or low according

9. The Amsterdam Baptists of the early seventeenth century made their objection plain:

Because true prayer must be of faith uttered with heart and lively voice, it is presumptuous ignorance to bring a book to speak for us unto God. . . . We may not stand reading a dead letter instead of pouring forth our petitions. . . . Therefore we must not read when we should pray (quoted by Skoglund, "Free Prayer," p. 155).

10. Watts, "Guide to Prayer," *Works*, vol. 4, p. 127:

Our circumstances are always altering in this frail and beautiful state. We have new sins to be confessed, new temptations and sorrows to be presented, and new wants to be supplied. . . . And all these can never be well provided for in any prescribed composition.

to his health, his feelings, or the weather. The same people may find themselves subject to a type of praying that is undisciplined, expansive, and plain rambling; even worse it may be what Oswald Chambers once bitingly labelled, ''mooning before the Lord.'' By a quirk those who oppose set prayers often find themselves falling into stereotyped expressions and cliches that are brought out with monotonous frequency and given a public airing. It is hard to distinguish the routine use of favorite expressions from a ritual that is printed and read. Moreover, with all the virtues and strengths of spontaneous prayers led by an inspired leader, there is still the searching question of Jeremy Taylor, ''How can a congregation say Amen to that which they have not considered?''

The upshot is that both kinds of public praying have strengths and weaknesses. They both need each other, and the happy solution would be a thoughtful combination and integration of Watts's ''conceived prayer'' with the occasional use of printed materials to give variety and a change of pace. The treasures of the past can be neglected only at our loss, yet we need fresh prayers for new occasions.

The same Isaac Watts in his *Guide to Prayer* counsels ministers to avoid these two extremes: (1) A confining ourselves entirely to precomposed forms of prayer, and (2) an entire dependence on sudden motions and suggestions of thought.

One other aspect remains. ''There was silence in heaven for about half an hour'' (Rev. 8:1). We all imagine that we are only praying when our voices are upraised, whereas the warning against ''much speaking'' from the cynicism of Ecclesiastes 5:2 to the excoriating words of Jesus (in Matt. 6:7) would dictate the opposite. There is need for silence to allow praying to take place. Admittedly the use of silence requires much discipline lest our wandering thoughts and awareness of distractions spoil the opportunity. But silent prayer is a needed protest against the strictly verbal concept of prayer. We forget that prayer is communion of the spirit with the divine Spirit and often at a level of experience too deep for words, as Paul knew well (Rom. 8:26, 27; 1 Cor. 2:10-16). Provided we are prepared to cultivate the ''silent spirit,'' and to enter corporately upon the time of prayer not to ''use

God'' but to "enjoy him'' (in Luther's distinction), the moments of silence will do something spoken prayer may fail to achieve. They will give a pause for God to speak to our inward ear and to approach us at a deeper level than the audible word can reach.

> The Lord is in his holy temple;
> Let all the earth keep silence before him.
> (Hab. 2:20)[11]

---

11. Of special interest for this chapter is P. F. Bradshaw, *Daily Prayer in the Early Church* (London, SPCK, 1981), which I was not able to use.

CHAPTER FOUR

Hymns and
Sacred Songs

The Role of Hymns

A memorable baptismal service took place in Milan 1600 years ago. It was the climax of a long spiritual pilgrimage on the part of Augustine of Hippo in North Africa, who was destined to become one of the great formative figures in Christian history. In retrospect he recalled the part of the service that left its abiding impression: the intense emotion engendered by the hymn singing of the assembled congregation. Christian testimony ever since has repeated this experience. "Singing is the most genuinely popular element in Christian worship," reports Geoffrey Wainwright, supplying the reason: "Familiar words and music, whether it be repeated response to biddings in a litany or the well-known phrases of a hymn, unite the whole assembly in active participation to a degree which is hardly true of any other component in the liturgy."[1]

Church history looks back on the significant part played by hymns, whether in the propagation of "orthodox" faith or (more strikingly) in the dissemination of theological opinions that the later church adjudged "heretical." An example is the *Thalia* or drinking song of Arius, the arch-foe of Athanasius. This was a popular medley of prose and verse[2] used to make Arius' understanding of the godhead known in the churches. From the orthodox side Hilary wrote a "book of

1. G. Wainwright, *Doxology. The Praise of God in Worship, Doctrine and Life* (London: Epworth Press; New York: Oxford Univ. Press, 1980), p. 200.

2. See J. N. D. Kelly, *Early Christian Creeds*, 2nd ed. (London: Longmans, 1950), p. 210.

hymns," to be followed by the immensely influential hymnody of Ambrose of Milan (A.D. 339-397) and Prudentius Clemens (A.D. 348-410) whose legacy has come down in at least two translated hymns appearing in our English hymnals.

Nor is it possible to overlook the role of hymns in the Lutheran reformation, which produced in Martin Luther not only a great leader and preacher but a gifted hymnist. Methodism, too, was "born in song" and spread its message partly through village and open air preaching but equally by means of the prolific hymn writing of Charles Wesley, to whom are attributed 6,500 hymns.

But what is it about a hymn that has given it such an important part to play in the church's worshiping life? This question is easier to ask than to answer. For one thing the definition of what constitutes a hymn is elusive. Most authorities appeal to Augustine whose summary statement has found wide acceptance: a hymn is "a song with praise to God."[3] Three features stand out: a hymn is praise; it is intended to be sung; and it is directed to God. To test the validity and adequacy of Augustine's definition we should go on to elaborate each of its three components. (1) "Praise" obviously will carry a wide range of meanings and include the introspective glance that leads naturally to a confession of sin and a seeking of forgiveness, coupled with aspirations to such "amendment of life" as will prompt the worshiper to a fresh dedication. (2) The variety of literary and musical forms will encourage us to expect a wide diversity in the way "music" and "words" have been wedded. Sometimes the verbal side has predominated, giving rise to a practice of rhythmical speaking or cantillation of the words, a device borrowed from Jewish reading of Scripture. At other times the melody has carried the hymn whose theological and devotional content as a written composition has been painfully lightweight. A "good" hymn manages to blend the verbal and melodic elements in happy proportion. (3) The most discussible part of Augustine's sentence is the inference that all hymns worthy of the name should be addressed formally to God. Clearly the syntax of a hymn may vary as between the traditional second person:

3. Augustine, *Commentary* on Psalm 148.

> We praise, we worship *Thee*, O God
> (based on *Te Deum laudamus*),

and the third person:

> A safe stronghold/Our God is still
> (from *Ein' feste Burg ist unser Gott*).

In both instances God is the center. In the majestic line of
Isaac Watts, sometimes claimed as the greatest single sentence in any hymn, this is so: "God is a name my soul
adores." And Watts in this splendid example is perpetuating
and enlarging the tradition that goes back to the period of the
Greek-speaking church whose "most remarkable characteristic of . . . hymnody is its objectiveness." Julian further
writes:

> Whether the theme be the mystery of the Triune Godhead or the Incar-
> nation, or the mighty periods of Christ's incarnate work in earth or
> heaven; or whether some life or narrative of Holy Writ, considered in its
> doctrinal or typical reference—the attitude of the poet is always one of
> self-forgetful, rapt, or ecstatic contemplation.[4]

The issue turns on whether or not it is permissible to include also under the rubric of "hymn" elements that balance
austere objectivity with a warm subjective expression of "the
human aspects of the divine encounter."[5] Such aspects would
include not only elements of confession and petition (which
are justified on other grounds, as we observed), but intercession, moral reflection, witness to the world, and above all the
Christian's own faith set in the style of personal affirmation
and testimony, as in "Now I have found the ground where-
in/Sure my soul's anchor may remain . . ." (this couplet
may well summarize the Wesleys' contribution).

Some recent hymnologists are putting in a bid to enlarge
our horizon and include a wider definition. One such revision
says that a hymn is a "metrical composition intended to be
sung by *everyone* in a religious service" or more simply,
"words sung by the people in worship."[6] Whether or not this

4. J. Julian, *A Dictionary of Hymnology* (London: John Murray, 1892),
p. 465.

5. N. P. Goldhawk, *On Hymns and Hymnbooks* (London: Epworth
Press, 1979), p. 38.

6. John L. Gardner, *The Hymn Society of Great Britain and Ireland
Bulletin* vol. 7, no. 5, p. 110, quoted by N. P. Goldhawk, *On Hymns*, pp.
13, 94 (the latter definition is Goldhawk's own preference).

is a helpful improvement will need to be considered later, and in any case some safeguards and criteria will need to be applied, as we shall see. All the experts seem agreed, however, on the point that hymns, both of the objective variety or the inward-looking kind, have a twofold function in the service of praise.

1. *The hymns play an impressive role* as an aid to worship by putting us in the right frame of mind and heart. To approach the divine mystery of God in a true worshipful spirit requires suitable preparation and adjustment, lest what we attempt is undertaken in a routine or formal way that lacks proper motivation and authentic intent. Music plays that role, as we hear it; and our singing can lift our spirits to new heights of contemplation and expectancy that makes genuine worship possible. "Since singing is so good a thing, I wish all men would learne to sing," wrote William Byrd (1543-1623), organist at the Chapel Royal in London and composer of much music for the Reformed English Church. He continued in the preface to one of his collections of songs: "The better the voice is, the meeter it is to honour and serve God therewith, and the voice of man is chiefly to be employed to that end."

There are snares to be watched for in the exercise of the musician's art and craft, as Augustine sensed. The music may be enjoyed as an end in itself instead of leading the worshiper into the divine presence. The Puritans voiced that objection and some of their successors have taken the hard line of banning all musical instruments from the service of worship. But in the Puritan movement the other side is clearly seen in one of their most illustrious representatives, John Milton. His poem *Il Penseroso* describes the writer's exultation of spirit as he appreciated all that "man-made" music could bring to the enrichment of worship:

> There let the pealing organ blow
> To the full-voiced quire below
> In service high, and anthems clear,
> As may, with sweetness, through mine ear,
> Dissolve me into ecstasies,
> And bring all Heaven before mine eyes.

2. The complementary aspect is *the expressive role of music-in-worship*. Praise is now seen as finding its rich medium in the vocal expression of a hymn sung to God. In a way not possible in ordinary speech, the hymn conveys and articulates all that believers would want to express in their response to God who in goodness and grace has first come to them. The part played by hymn singing caters to many expressions of the human response. It provides a way of attesting the faith we have and indeed of deepening and confirming that faith. The verdict of experience is that once we have given vigorous expression to a conviction—such as is possible in singing a hymn—the stronger is our grip on that conviction.

There is also a socializing function, for music is "a social art, an activity in which all can join,"[7] since it provides a common medium for the corporate expression of praise. J. O. Dobson makes a perceptive point when he remarks on the harmony of the music, heard in both instrumental and vocal melody, as symbolizing the fellowship of the church at worship:

> It is a significant thing that harmony developed in the music of Christian worship. For harmony is an expression of fellowship in a common intention, a common allegiance variously declared, yet without discord. . . . So it corresponds to a deep and essential need of the Christian spirit.[8]

One further comment needs to be added. For the churches in the Free church and Reformed tradition, hymns have always provided opportunity for the congregation's active participation. Bernard L. Manning's often-repeated dictum reminds us of the role of hymns in the churchly ethos that stands under the inspiration of the Wesleys and Watts. "Hymns are for us Dissenters what the liturgy is for the Anglican. They are the framework, the setting, the conventional, the traditional part of divine service as we use it . . . . We mark times and seasons, celebrate festivals, and expound doctrines by hymns."[9]

7. H. Davies, *Christian Worship. Its Making and Meaning* (Wallington: Religion Education Press, 1946), p. 74.

8. J. O. Dobson, *Worship* (London: SCM Press, 1941), p. 118.

9. B. L. Manning, *The Hymns of Wesley and Watts* (London: Epworth Press, 1942), pp. 133-135.

The importance of Manning's statement is seen when we set hymn-singing practices in many of our churches today over against the way worship was practiced in medieval christendom. Then the chief actors were the priests and the choir; the people were content to take a passive part. While it would be untrue to say that lay people had no part, it still remained that such persons, like those in an audience, were not vocal.[10] The Reformation and its aftermath gave the laity an active share in the liturgy, and hymns as well as the full eucharist were restored to the congregations.

Even within the churches of the Reformation faith the place given to hymns can be demoted—as happens when hymn singing is "used" to fill up a space while the offering is received or made part of a choral procession. The upshot of Manning's observation would be to restore the hymn to a place in its own right where hymn singing is not an accompaniment of something else that is going on in the service contemporaneously but an act of the divine worship demanding and receiving the concentrated attention of all concerned.

A moment's reflection will confirm what we have sought to emphasize so far. If worship gains full meaning only as it represents our wholehearted response to God's action in Christ, then our hymns cannot be less than our devoted focusing of all our powers on the themes they poetically and musically bring before us. The preface to *Congregational Praise* sums up finely the purpose of our celebration of worship in hymns:

> A hymn is intended for singing, and for singing together. Its subject must therefore be worth singing about, and it should express the common faith of Christendom. Nothing is so worthy of our singing as the glory and majesty of God, His creative power and redeeming grace. The greatest hymns are never far from the sublime scenery of our redemption.

Precedents of our Hymns

Christian hymnody owes a debt to both the Greek and Roman religious tradition of the world into which it was born and the Jewish community of faith that formed its matrix and cradle.

10. E. Routley, *Hymns for Church and School* (London: Novello, 1964), p. iv.

The Greco-Roman practice of singing hymns to gods and goddesses goes back a long way, but it reaches its peak at a time when the finest and most sensitive spirits in late classical civilization were becoming conscious of their need of ''salvation.'' The immediate occasion was an onset of pessimism and despair, caused partly by Greek science that offered a naturalistic explanation of the universe, and partly by eastern astrology that placed a vast distance between human beings and the gods whom Homer had described in some personal detail. A valiant attempt to relate the traditional deities to human life was made as an answer to belief in impersonal ''fate'' or ''chance.'' We can see a fine specimen of this religious aspiration in Cleanthes' *Hymn to Zeus:*

> Thou, O Zeus, art praised above all gods: many are thy names
> and thine is all power for ever.
> The beginning of the world was from thee: and with law thou
> rulest over all things.
> Unto thee may all flesh speak: for we are thy offspring.
> Therefore will I raise a hymn unto thee: and will ever sing of
> thy power.

Written by Cleanthes (*c.* 331-232 B.C.), this poem represents a fine statement of stoic belief in the rule of ''law'' that governs the universe, and a readiness to apply the idea of Zeus as father of the gods to humankind (see Acts 17:28 for a similar connection made in Paul's Athenian sermon). But the stoic lacked a firm conviction regarding God as personal and the hymn does not really break out of the imprisoning circle of ''fate'' by which human lives are controlled. So the noblest sentiments expressed here served only to show the need for some confidence in a personal God whose ways are known and can be trusted.

The story of the long history of the Jewish people and their religious practices offers a more promising anticipation of what came to full flower in Christian hymnology. At creation, all the heavens rejoiced in celebration of the creator God (we read in Job 38:7); and this fixed belief of later Judaism found narrative expression in the first chapter of Genesis. The first recorded mention of singing on the part of men and women comes at the passage of the Sea of Reeds (Exod. 15:1, 21) when the antiphonal refrain praised Yahweh's deliverance:

Sing to Yahweh, because he has won a glorious victory;
He has thrown the horses and their riders into the sea.

At Solomon's Temple services there were choirs and
musical contributions, according to the Chronicler's account
(2 Chron. 5:11-14). Several antiphonal or responsively sung
psalms in the Davidic psalter may belong to this period (Ps.
24, 118, 136), even if that accumulation of psalms is better
called "the hymn-book of the second Jewish Temple,"
erected after the exile (cf. Ezra 3:11; Neh. 12:24, 36). The so-
called "Royal Psalms" in praise of the Hebrew monarchy may
well have been linked with enthronement ceremonies, royal
anniversaries, preparations for battle, and so on (Pss. 45, 72,
110).

The wide gamut of human experience in its heights and
depths is covered by the Hebrew "Book of Psalms."[11] How
far some of these expressions of piety and doubt simply represent individual laments and thanksgivings or embody the corporate confessions and confidences of the community of Israel
is not easy to say. A lot of examples are situation-less,
although it is traditional to find links between what the writer
confesses and events in the life of David the king or Moses the
lawgiver (e.g., Pss. 51, 90). The expressions of sure confidence in God are timeless (Pss. 23, 46), as are the numerous
thanksgiving psalms that look back to Yahweh's gracious in-
tervention in time of sickness, trouble, exile, and fear (for example, Pss. 16, 67). The "songs of pilgrimage" are naturally
associated with journeys to the Temple at festival times (Pss.
84, 122), while other types of psalm liturgy are pure praise of
God whose creative (Pss. 104, 147, 148) and redeeming
power (Ps. 103) are known in the nation's life. The Israelite
singers were not slow to borrow from their neighbors, as we
can see from Psalm 104 which has ideas similar to Pharaoh
Akhenaton's remarkable "Hymn to the Sun," composed in
the fourteenth century B.C.

Yet the factor that stamps the Psalms as distinctive in the
canon of religious literature and so provided Isaac Watts with
inspiration to employ the language and idiom of the Hebrew
psalter—with necessary transpositions "to make David speak

11. See the recent study, *Singing to the Lord. The Psalms as Hymns,* by
Michael Ball (London: Bible Reading Fellowship, 1979).

like an English Christian,'' as he said[12]—is the firm anchor-
age of divine revelation in historical events and specifically in
those acts that showed Yahweh's power to liberate and to
save his people.

The use of hymnic praise at the festivals, notable at Passover and the "Ingathering" (later known as Tabernacles or
Booths), may seem to endorse Israel's religion as essentially
agricultural and related to fertility rites. But it is clear that
whatever such festivals were originally, their place in Judaism
was regarded as celebrating, both in retrospect and with a forward looking, God's redemption under Moses and his pledge
to save his people from all their oppressors. A specific illustration of the tie between the past and the future is seen in the
hymns of the people at Qumran whose praise of God's goodness and expectation of a coming new age finds a memorable
tribute in the Dead Sea scrolls. The hymnist (in the *Hymn
Scroll*, 12) raises a voice of praise:

> I [thank Thee, O Lord],
> for Thou hast enlightened me through Thy truth.
> In Thy marvellous mysteries,
> and in Thy loving kindness to a man [of vanity
> and] in the greatness of Thy mercy to a perverse heart
> Thou hast granted me knowledge.[13]

The *Hymn Scroll* is throughout a fine expression of personal faith and desire to glorify God for his revelation to the
community. But even these tributes lack the note that is characteristic of the New Testament hymns.

Our conclusion stands that, in spite of many noble sentiments of religious and devotional longing for God and a life
that is worthy of high ideals, such hymns as we have surviving
from the ancient world of Greco-Roman and Jewish culture
express poignantly a sense of unfulfilled desire. Hymnic spec-

12. Sometimes Watts took exceptional liberties in revising the Hebrew
psalter in the interest of contemporary relevance. Thus Psalm 100 ("Make a
joyful noise unto the Lord all the lands") becomes
> Sing to the Lord with joyful voice;
> Let every land his name adore;
> The British Isles shall send the noise
> Across the ocean to the shore.
13. G. Vermes, *The Dead Sea Scrolls in English* (Harmondsworth:
Penguin Books, 1968 ed.), p. 175.

imens are an eloquent witness to that *praeparatio evangelica* that made the world ready for the coming of the new age in Jesus Christ who is both Israel's hope and the world's Savior. He is therefore properly regarded as both the true worshiper and the person in whom Christian worship finds its focal point. It is not unexpected that the writers of the New Testament church will join together the picture of Jesus as the ultimate celebrant of the divine praises, and tributes of hymnic worship that center on him, his person and his saving deed. In Hebrews 2:12 the language of the Jewish pietist (in Ps. 22:22) is boldly applied to Jesus:

> He says to God,
>   "I will tell my brothers what you have done;
>   I will praise you [literally, I will offer hymns to you]
>   in their meeting [or the church]"

And one of the keenest interests in some recent New Testament study has been the detection, classification, and appreciation of specimens of "hymns to Christ" already seen in the literature of the apostolic communities.

The New Testament Data

The best evidence we have that the early church, even in New Testament times, was a singing church is seen in Colossians 3:16, which is roughly parallel with Ephesians 5:19. There "psalms, hymns and sacred [or spiritual] songs" are mentioned. Not much success has followed some recent endeavors to go back to earlier ways of distinguishing these compositions; but even so, it still is possible that distinct types of liturgical praise are to be understood.

1. "Psalms" could refer to the Hebrew psalter since we have the witness of Acts (e.g., 4:24f.) that the first Christians found in selected passages material that was useful not only for apologetic purposes or for theological reasons, but also to nourish and sustain their common life in fellowship and prayer. "Is anyone among you in trouble? He should pray. Is anyone happy? He should sing praises (or psalms)" is the exhortation given to some early Jewish Christian community (James 5:13). This passage, which uses a verb to play the harp or to sing without instruments, "shows that from the

earliest days the Church possessed a rich treasury of praise,''
as one commentator notes, citing *The Odes of Solomon* as
well as some New Testament passages, but strangely over-
looking the fund of hymnic jubilation in the psalter.[14] The
inclusion of the Old Testament psalms in this category is suggested further by Jesus' own example of appealing to the
psalms in his teaching (Mark 12:1-12), using the *Hallel* section as a preparation for Passover (Mark 14:26 from Pss.
116-118), and encouraging the disciples in the postresurrection appearances (according to Luke 24:44) to find
messianic fulfillments in the same Davidic psalter.

2. "Hymns" *per se* would be such tributes of worship
directed to God whether in a Jewish setting (as in Rev., e.g.,
4:8, 11; 15:3, 4 where God is praised as creator) or in an incipiently Christian context. In the latter category the prime
examples are the canticles preserved by Luke in his birth
stories (Luke chs. 1, 2). There are four such specimens in
which Old Testament models (such as the song of Hannah in
1 Sam. 2, which is transposed to express the advent of messianic hope with God's fulfilling his promise to the Jewish
fathers, Luke 1:46-55) and Old Testament yearnings are the
launching pad for the community's celebration of the new
age shortly to dawn in the coming of Messiah.

The *Gloria* of Luke 2:14 is characteristic. God is hailed as
the provider of "peace" on earth since his saving favor is
known to the people he has chosen. It has been with sure instinct that the church down the centuries has incorporated
these Lukan hymns, especially the *Magnificat* (Luke 1:46-55)
and the *Nunc Dimittis* (Luke 2:29-32) into its weekly liturgy.

It remains true, however, that other New Testament
hymns share a different matrix. The "hymns" preserved in
the Pauline churches took a christological turn and were exclusively devoted to a recital of the "events of salvation"
wrought out in the mission and achievement of Jesus. The
New Testament teaching on the person of Christ is virtually
contained in those passages most likely to be classified as early
hymns of the church: John 1:1-18; Philippians 2:6-11; Colossians 1:15-20; 1 Timothy 3:16. The common feature that

14. James Adamson, *The Epistle of James* (Grand Rapids: Wm. B.
Eerdmans, 1976), p. 197.

unites these sublime texts, even if they derive from a variety of church situations, is their interest in the preincarnate Lord who came to reveal the Father and to restore a lost creation. The link-term connecting revelation and cosmic renewal is *redemption*. At the cost of his life given over to the will of God in sacrifice and self-offering, Jesus died the sinner's death and released those forces into human experience that make possible a true basis for forgiveness of sins and new life. But the message, though authenticated in human experience as a reconciliation to God, has wider ramifications. It proclaims a new world set right with its creator, the overthrow of evil powers, and a fresh start to human history that will eventually lead to a universe restored to its pristine glory and harmony. The sweep of these hymns is as vast as that world in whose ultimate destiny no refractory or alien elements are permitted to continue. The New Testament hymns tremble on the verge of a cosmic Jubilee when God will be "all in all" (1 Cor. 15:28) as all things are brought under the sole headship of the reigning Christ (Eph. 1:10).

3. "Sacred songs"—where the adjective may mean either "spiritual" over against "secular" or worldly or, as is more likely, "songs inspired by the Spirit"—apparently formed a separate group. They were the result of immediate inspiration, as in the scene in 1 Corinthians 14:26 where improvised compositions, whether or not involving ecstatic experience or glossolalic speech—Paul includes both in verse 15 of that chapter—are brought to the assembly and used in worship. They may well have been no more than single-line statements, such as Paul has to refer to in 1 Corinthians 12:3. They could possibly have been confessional chants used notably at baptism; and of this type the best attested example is Ephesians 5:14 (cf. 2 Tim. 2:11-13). Everything about this verse in Ephesians suggests its independent setting in a service of initiation, not least its idioms of light and life to betoken a dawning Christian experience, its style as poetic and rhythmical, and its place in the flow of the chapter. Above all, it gains in significance in offering us a fragment of evidence that the first Christians thought of "hymns" as a means of mutual encouragement and challenge aimed horizontally at a group of fellow believers.

Hymns in Historical Perspective

As we embark on a brief overview of the lines of development taken by the church's hymns, let us keep in mind some conclusions we have reached, though they may be stark in their simplicity. First, early Christian praise was hewn out of the quarry of what those far-distant believers claimed as holy Scripture. In particular, the language and forms of the Old Testament gave Christian hymnody its working tools and its materials. We can see this in the use made of the Psalms and such Old Testament passages that lie in the background of Ephesians 5:14 (see Isa. 60:1-3).[15] The great "Hymn of Christ" in Philippians 2:6-11 is resonant with several Old Testament motifs (Adam, the servant of God, and the universal dominion of Yahweh, proclaimed in Isa. 45:23 and Jewish synagogue prayers), just as Colossians 1:15-20 is built on the ideas of "wisdom" in Proverbs 8 and some intertestamental texts.

Secondly, the arrival and enjoyment of a new age, discovered in Christ who is exalted as enthroned Lord of all powers, human and demonic, loosed Christian tongues to celebrate in an unparalleled way all that God had done in and through Christ. That Christian hymns should be largely christocentric is not to be wondered at, even if the precise turn of phrase "a hymn to Christ as to God" awaits the subapostolic age in Pliny's description, at secondhand to be sure, of what the believers in Bithynia did at their Sunday morning gatherings. Yet with all their christocentricity the hymns remain staunchly within the Hebraeo-Christian orbit of monotheism and true "theo"-logy. It is the glory of God the Father that the Christ-hymn (Phil. 2:11) eulogizes. With equal insistence this God is uniquely made known in the condescension and sacrifice of his son who, now exalted, came to his glory only along a *via dolorosa* of obedience unto death. The descent/ascent movement should prepare us for the use of dramatic poetry imaginatively set to work to portray the greatest of all God's acts. "That the Maker should become man and should even go to death for the love of man—that astonishing thing evoked *rapturous praise* from believers."[16]

15. As G. G. Findlay suggests in *The Epistle to the Ephesians*, The Expositor's Bible (London: Hodder and Stoughton, 1892), p. 335.

16. G. Wainwright, *Doxology*, p. 206 (his italics).

Whether professedly Christian hymns in the subsequent church have always echoed that "rapturous praise" or been faithful to the scriptural heritage of the church's faith are perhaps questions to be borne in mind as we rehearse the way our hymns have evolved.

There are roughly four periods or landmarks in the history of hymns:[17]

1. *The early and medieval period.* Outside the New Testament the earliest hymn with an extant full text is one used at a candlelight or lamplighting ceremony (about A.D. 200 or earlier) and called appropriately from its first line (translated by John Keble from the Greek), "Hail, gladdening Light." Other Greek hymns have been collected and translated by J. M. Neale. Examples are "The day of resurrection" and "The day is past and over."

In the Latin period the most famous is *Te Deum laudamus,* traditionally ascribed to Ambrose but most probably written by Nicetas, bishop of Remesiana in the late fourth century. Ambrose used hymns in an anti-Arian crusade, as we saw, and (more significantly) placed hymns firmly in the order of public worship services.

Medieval hymnody is largely the story of Latin hymns with contributions by monastics such as Bernard of Clairvaux (1090-1153) to whom tradition ascribes "Jesus, the very thought of thee," Abelard (1079-1142), and Francis of Assisi (c. 1181-1226). From the thirteenth century came the influential "Day of wrath" *(Dies Irae),* the great hymn associated with preparation for the reading of the Gospel at the mass. This is an example of sequences, that is, metrical verses similar to the hymns used in the "offices" of worship. The popularity of such sequences tended to lower their quality, and at the Council of Trent they were discontinued. *Dies Irae,* however, did survive and remained in the Roman Missal of A.D. 1570. A later sequence gained recognition as *Stabat Mater* ("At the cross her station keeping / Stood the mournful mother weeping"). Thomas Aquinas' great eucharistic

17. There are many surveys of Christian hymns. I refer to one such, John S. Andrews, "Hymns," in *The International Dictionary of the Christian Church,* ed. J. D. Douglas (Grand Rapids: Zondervan, 1974), pp. 494-496.

hymn, rendered as "O Bread to pilgrims given," deserves a mention.

Much of the remaining hymnody from the medieval time stands in the Catholic tradition, which expresses the worship of God as creator and our communion with him in a "mystical" sense. The legacy was picked up by the Oxford Tractarians and in writers such as Faber, Keble, and Newman, whose hymns are now part of an ecumenical treasury. "Lead, kindly Light" and "Praise to the holiest" are good examples, but some lines such as "And that a higher gift than grace" and "There is welcome for the sinner/And more graces for the good" (F. W. Faber) raise some serious theological questions.

2. The Puritan movement largely stayed within boundaries set by the importance given to the metrical psalms. The Church of Scotland has looked to this source as the chief vehicle of praise, thanks to Calvin's admonitions. The "Old Hundredth" (Psalm 100) lives on as a separate "hymn" in most modern hymnals. Earlier collections of the Psalms of David held the field until 1696 when a new version by Tate and Brady supplanted them. The *Scottish Psalter*, in use among Scottish Presbyterians, goes back to A.D. 1650.

The year 1623 saw the appearance of George Wither's *Hymnes and Songs of the Church,* which is claimed as "the first attempt at a comprehensive English hymnbook," with notable contributions from George Herbert, John Milton, and John Bunyan. Among Dissenters, chiefly Baptists, early hymnbooks appeared in 1671 and 1673.

Isaac Watts (1674-1748) set a new pattern, notably by christianizing the Psalms and writing in a way that liberated his contemporaries from the rigors of the metrical psalms. His innovations, however, partly in criticism of the Psalms for containing aspirations and sentiments he judged to be sub-Christian, were treated as radical by many of his fellow Congregationalists. Watts's quiet humor and concern for children's hymns gave him a fresh outlook on the value of hymns in Christian worship and living. With an added touch of genius and a fervent belief in "experimental religion," Watts carved a niche that well qualifies him for the honor of being the church's finest hymn writer. But he had distinguished company around and following him in Philip Doddridge and James Montgomery. ''Hark, the glad sound'' and ''Hail to the Lord's anointed'' from these two men come close behind Watts's finest and justly famed pieces.

3. In Charles Wesley (1707-1788) the Methodist movement found its ''sweet singer'' and the most effective exponent of its message. *The Collection of Psalms and Hymns* compiled by his brother John in 1737 contained not unnaturally a large proportion of Charles' output, estimated to be in the region of six and a half thousand, but also including John's own translations (mainly of Moravian compositions). From the Moravians John had received under God the assurance of personal faith in Christ and the impetus to follow his destiny. The later *Methodist Hymn Book* (1933) stands as a repository of the founder's teaching, emphasizing the prominent characteristics of the Evangelical Revival of the eighteenth century, namely, universal grace freely offered to all, the centrality of faith in Christ, and personal assurance of the Spirit's sanctifying power.

In this same period and reflecting some of the Revival's major contributions to Christian life and thought were A. M. Toplady (''Rock of Ages'') and John Newton, who with William Cowper produced the memorable selection of *Olney Hymns* in 1779.

Another prolific hymn writer in the Presbyterian tradition was Horatius Bonar who is credited with 600 or so hymns, while the nineteenth century produced its further crop of hymn writers in persons such as Charlotte Elliott (''Just as I am''), E. H. Plumptre (''Thy hand, O God, has guided'') and S. J. Stone (''The Church's one foundation''). These names suggest Christian poets as diverse as their titles indicate, but united by a desire to express biblical truth with robust style and in plain rhythm; and their words were blessed with matching tunes to carry the message home to heart and mind.

4. The twentieth century has seen various attempts to express the historic faith in new dress. A recent essay devoted to ''The Hymn Today—The Challenge of the Words''[18]

18. Brian Wren, *Hymn Society Bulletin* (Jan. 1977), p. 138, cited by N. P. Goldhawk, *On Hymns*, p. 52.

writes of modern hymn-writing under the captions of (a) the
desire to give faith a "respray," and (b) the bid to bring the
world to the church. The first attempt is to examine the age-
old faith in a new light. Sometimes this involves rewriting the
traditional or biblical message in a contemporary fashion as in
Sydney Carter's two pieces, "Lord of the dance" and "Every
star shall sing a carol," or Richard Jones's "God of concrete,
God of steel." The second way of expressing the church's
faith reflects, more controversially, a suggested "openness to
the twentieth century," as Wren calls it. The ruling concern
is to compose lines that spring out of experience in the "real"
world in which we live. So human activity is a common
feature of hymns that are strong on social responsibility,
stewardship of the world's resources and the environment,
race relations, world peace and international problems, but
including too the ecumenical yen for the church's visible
unity. F. Pratt Green, one of the most sensitive and gifted of
modern hymnists, highlights the need for hymns to reflect
Christian compassion about human plight and a concern to
call congregations to do something positive about it. He
rebukes our forgetfulness of the church's mission in the world
and our innate desire to seek the consolation of religion at the
expense of its demand and costly challenge:

> May our prayer, Lord, make us
> Ten times more aware
> That the world we banish
> Is our Christian care.

Three particular areas have produced innovative hymn-
writing: "pop" music with its lyrics and refrains, folk hymns,
and the Scripture recitations set to song in the charismatic
movement. Much of what passes for modern Christian praise,
however, carries all the marks of the ephemeral and frothy,
and seems destined to pass on to oblivion as new emphases
take its place.

The Enduring Quality of our Hymns

Openness to the Spirit who is ever our contemporary, and
alertness to the needs of the day in which our lot is set should
not dull our appreciation of the hymnic heritage we have received. So our concluding section may suggest certain criteria
for what makes a "good" hymn. Norman P. Goldhawk

devotes a full chapter to this issue[19] and leads off in a way that would relate to "good" hymns as well as "good" tunes. The good hymn, he says, is the one I like, for the personal reason that its words, theme, metre, and music instinctively and temperamentally appeal to me. More seriously he offers no fewer than ten standards by which we may measure an effective hymn: its faith-building character; its doctrinal soundness; its faithfulness to Scripture, expressing what is true in experience and doing so with an opening line or couplet that fastens itself on the mind; the criterion of clarity coupled with a "singability" and a unity of theme. Finally, the candidate will have a timelessness unrelated to passing fads or fashions in theology and churchly concerns, and it will raise our thoughts to God.

Putting much of the above in a different way, let me set down four criteria as tests of hymns that are worthy of a place in public worship. First, the hymn will articulate the praise of God the Father in whom his creation lives. This feature is shown and illustrated in the consensus choice of Watts's "Our God, our help in ages past" as the most popular hymn in English. Second, it will celebrate God's activity in history, both as a past deed and climaxing in Christ incarnate, crucified, risen, and ascended, and as a continuing reality in every age including our own. Third, it will register its sensitivity to personal experience of God's saving and renewing grace in Christ and in the Spirit, leading to an encouragement to God's people to rise to their full stature in Christ. Finally, the language should be readily understandable and express some aspect of Christian truth that may be applied at the social level where human life is spent in relationships, both personal and worldwide, brought under the aegis of the contemporary Christ.

From the start the Christian church has been a hymn-loving church. It sang in the cradle, as we see from Luke 2:10-14, and new songs will herald the final triumph of God according to the Apocalypse. In that interim we are invited to worship God in song as worthily as we know how.

19. N. P. Goldhawk, *On Hymns*, pp. 93-105.

CHAPTER FIVE

Bring an Offering

A Question of Definition

"Offering" is a term that carries many ranges of meaning in Christian worship. It may, of course, refer to the act of offering or to the thing offered to God. Liturgical scholars distinguish no fewer than four different senses:[1] (1) the self-giving of Jesus seen in the symbolism of the Last Supper and in its concrete act on the cross for the salvation of the world; (2) the celebration of the eucharist or Lord's Supper as a "memorial" of this self-offering; (3) the application to the material elements of bread and wine with which this "memorial" is made, following his command to "Do this in remembrance of me"; and (4) its application to the "consecration" of the worshipers who offer themselves "in Christ," in whom they participate as they celebrate the thanksgiving meal and become united with him in his perfect oblation to the Father.

Certain aspects of this classification have been the center of much and bitter controversy. In particular, the Reformers strenuously objected to describing the eucharist as an oblation, insisting that the only "perfect oblation" was offered by the Lord in his death on the cross. They were less averse to the idea of the people's oblation since it chimed in with the Protestant teaching on worship as the offering of "spiritual sacrifices, acceptable to God" (Rom. 12:2). In more recent times what has become prominent is a particular focus on the bread and wine as man's offering to God of the fruits of his labor and as a token response of all material creation to its creator. In the above discussion little has been said about

1. W. Jardine Grisbrooke, "Oblation," in *The Westminster Dictionary of Worship*, ed. J. G. Davies (British title, *A Dictionary of Liturgy and Worship*) (Philadelphia: Westminster Press; London: SCM Press, 1972), p. 281.

monetary offerings, since these do not properly fall within the exact and historical definition of the term. But with a newer interest in treating the eucharistic elements as a *pars pro toto,* representing the entire realm of human activity and productivity in God's world, the door is open to include ideas that are normally linked with man's stewardship of nature and God's gifts to him.

Historical Highlights

The early history of the church yields some interesting examples of different ways of looking at the offering. We shall return to the New Testament later. Here the starting point is the church of subapostolic times, which already was aware of the uniting of Christ's offering and his people's gifts. The "sacrifice of praise" for Clement of Rome (in A.D. 96) is worthy of Jesus Christ, "the high priest of our offerings" (36:1) who "ordered sacrifices and services to be performed" (40:2). The bishop, under the figure of the Old Testament high priest, fulfills his ministry with the particular duties of that office, just as the lower order of the clergy and the lay people are instructed to perform their "liturgies" according to their rank. "Each . . . must make thanksgiving according to his own order keeping a good conscience and not transgressing the appointed rule of his own liturgy" (40:5-41:1). The men appointed to episcopal office are installed "to offer the gifts" (44:4). Clearly Clement has a picture of a closely ordered structure of church life where each leader and lay member has a specific role to play in offering the gifts.

In Justin's *First Apology,* which describes worship in mid-second-century Rome, we meet the first clearly described structure of a divine service.[2] It is preceded by another source, however. The church manual known as the *Didache* belongs to an uncertain date but is clearly earlier than A.D. 150. Its prayers of thanksgiving (in chapter 10) praise God as the giver of "food and drink" that men may enjoy with thankfulness to God. The contrast is then drawn with "spiritual food and drink and eternal life through Jesus, your child." The placing

2. H. B. Porter, *The Day of Light* (London: SCM Press, 1960), p. 49 calls Justin's account "the oldest systematic description of Sunday worship."

of this prayer at a time "after you have finished your meal"
suggests that this part of the *Didache* relates to table fellowship of an agape variety. The prayers are patterned on Jewish
prayers of "grace before and after meals," and do not refer to
a solemn eucharist. A different scene is in view at *Didache*
chapter 14, where the writer is evidently rehearsing a service
of public worship on the Lord's day; its purpose is "to break
bread and give thanks." After confession of sins and the
making of an offering, linked with the "pure sacrifice" of
Malachi 1:11, there are injunctions for the appointment of
bishops and deacons, which suggests, says J. H. Srawley,[3] that
these officials were specially connected with the administration of both eucharistic elements (as in Ignatius, *Smyrnaeans*
ch. 8) and the people's gifts.

Justin's account is very similar to the above, especially in
chapter 67, which describes the Sunday gathering. The role of
"the brethren" who assist in the service is one of offering to
the "president" (Greek *ho proestōs*) the elements of bread
and a cup of wine and water. After a prayer of thanksgiving
the elements are distributed by these men, now called
deacons, who also take the bread, wine, and water to absent
members. The deacons (presumably) receive the money gifts
of the congregation and hand these over to the president:
"Those who prosper, and who so wish, contribute, each one
as much as he chooses to." What is collected is deposited
with the leader who is charged with responsibility for the
orphans and widows, the needy and the sick, those in prison
and "strangers who are sojourners among [us]." In short, out
of this fund, he is the protector of all those in need. And it is
an integral part of Sunday worship to receive such an offering.

Irenaeus, bishop in southern Gaul (*c.* A.D. 180), makes
some significant contributions to the early history of the
offering. In debate with the Gnostics who devalued the material creation as the product of an evil god, Irenaeus wants to
reassert the biblical teaching that all God's gifts are good. He
puts a sharp point on this insistence when he applies to the
eucharist phrases such as "the oblation of the church," "the

3. J. H. Srawley, *The Early History of the Liturgy*, 2nd ed. (Cambridge:
University Press, 1947), p. 21.

new oblation of the new covenant," and "the pure sacrifice" (from Mal. 1:11; incidentally, the use of this text is a justification of the Old Testament which the Gnostics also despised as inferior). He goes on to talk of the eucharist and its oblation as "the first fruits of the creatures." So when the prayer of thanksgiving is said at the table it leads to a "sanctifying [of] the creature." Notice the polemical thrust of such a conclusion. How can the bread, over which prayers of thanks are given, be the Lord's body and the cup his blood, if bread and wine are the product of an evil genius, the God of creation, as the Gnostics maintained? Here is a timely protest against an overspiritualized notion of both God and worship, which lays a foundation for a doctrine of God's goodness seen in his creation and our gratitude to be expressed in material offerings.

The next witness called in our short overview is Hippolytus, whose *Apostolic Tradition* is customarily dated A.D. 215-217 and is most likely located at Rome. This church order may be claimed as representing the local tradition of the Greek-speaking church of Rome, but with its subsequent influence in Egypt and Syria it obviously contains liturgical beliefs and practices of a wide region. It offers two orders of eucharistic service. In one of them, the deacons are expressly said to offer the oblation, thus elaborating Justin's description. The second relates to a baptismal eucharist and is interesting in that it adds to the gifts of bread and wine. Presbyters and deacons administer three cups to the people, one of water, another of milk and honey, a third of wine. The "milk and honey" are baby food, appropriate to the newly baptized, and mark their entry into the promised land of God's new Israel. Three additional features in Hippolytus' order are worth a mention. First, the new convert is told to bring some offering for the eucharist to follow his baptism. This fact confirms what was hinted at in Clement, namely, the share that deacons and lay persons had in the offertory rite. Second, Hippolytus makes explicit what was only suggested in Justin's account: a prayer for the action of the Holy Spirit in the oblation. Debate centers on whether the text of Hippolytus is sound at this point; and if so, is it a petition *(epiclesis)* directed to the descent of the Spirit on "the oblation of the holy church" including the gifts, or is it, as Srawley and others have contended, a prayer for the communicants?[4] Third, the rubric that insists that the bishop is "to lay hands upon the oblation with all the presbyters and to say the thanksgiving" suggests a practice of concelebration, that is, presbyters are closely associated with the bishop in the eucharistic offering.

The following centuries witnessed a distinct shift in the direction of confining the oblation to clerical action, thereby lessening the part played by the laity. In the East and especially with the Byzantine liturgy the focus was on the bishop's action as the climax of the "processional rite." The so-called "great entrance" concentrated all attention on the procession of ministers who brought the gifts of bread and wine to the altar. Augustine's pastoral counsel that the congregation was to see its life consecrated on the altar was passed over. Instead of the laity coming up to the altar to hand over their offerings, the pope and his clerical assistants (in the later Roman rite) went down to receive those gifts; and inevitably the importance of lay participation was diminished—a feature that has persisted from the adoption of a uniform liturgy in both East and West by the year A.D. 800 through the Roman missal of A.D. 1474 to the revision in Pope Paul VI's time.

Recent reforms in the Roman Catholic church have restored lay activity in the offertory. The gifts are now brought up to the altar. Bread, wine, and water are offered with prayers of blessing and consecration, to which the church as a whole responds. The "secret prayer" offered silently or in a low voice over the gifts has become articulate or sung in the new *Ordo Missae* (1969). This reform has served a pragmatic function in making the people's offering a more visible and realistic part of worship and opening a fresh vista on "offering" as closely connected with Christ's self-giving in sacrifice, which we celebrate as both salvation-bringing and exemplary, so preparing us to use our material possessions to help our neighbors in their need.

4. See G. J. Cuming's note in *Hippolytus: A Text for Students* (Bramcote: Grove Books, 1976), p. 11.

Offering: The Biblical Picture

The idea of the presentation of gifts to the deity or to a number of gods and goddesses is as ancient as religion itself.

1. In the classical tradition Homer speaks of sacrifices of burnt animals offered to the pantheon, and the ritual surrounding such sacrifices is attested from Pindar onwards. The standard term is "offering" (Greek *prosphora*), which meant originally bringing or presenting, and was used of a wide variety of objects—money, revenue as tribute, food in cereal form, and of course slaughtered animals in whole or in part. From the time of Sophocles, in connection with making an offering as a gift or expiation to the gods, the expression "offering" came to imply the submission of the worshiper to the deity in cultic acts.

2. The Old Testament documents offer considerable variation on this theme, and there is no one clearly articulated theory of offering in the worship of Yahweh. The levitical sacrifices, in particular, present several emphases, sometimes dealing with atonement for sins (as a "covering"), sometimes as an act of reparation, sometimes in symbolic fashion to convey the idea of complete dedication to God in sacrifices that "ascend" (i.e., in the fire of sacrifice), and often and persistently to express thanksgiving in the offering of a gift. The "peace offering" is occasionally thought to establish a mystical union with Yahweh (cf. Judges 6:18-21; 13:16; Ps. 50:12f.), but it is more likely that as the offering was eaten "in Yahweh's presence," the predominant thought is fellowship with him, not a feeding on him. Above all, offerings served to ratify the covenant with Yahweh—a fundamental notion in Israelite cultus. It suggests an attitude to God based on gratitude for his past mercies and gracious acts, and calls for an answering loyalty on the part of the nation. The link-term is the Hebrew word *hesed* (English, "mercy," "loving-kindness," or "loyalty"), which binds in covenantal union Yahweh, whose character is "gracious," and Israel, which is summoned to be a faithful people. *Hesed* represents two sides of a single coin. Much more than other theories of

sacrifice, which proposed the sacrifice to be food for the gods, or to release a life force through death, or to effect a physical unity with the deity, or to invoke his aid, this background in covenantal religion seems to be characteristic of Old Testament religious acts in the cultus. And from the perspective of the prophets of the eighth and seventh centuries, the genius of their understanding of Israel's faith as both in continuity with the Mosaic past and yet with high ethical seriousness and social responsibility shines out in their use of sacrificial idioms; but their teaching has an added dimension. We may refer to Isaiah 1:10-20; Micah 6:6-8; Hosea 6:6; Amos 5:21-27, and Jeremiah 6:20; 7:1-15. The prophets' standpoint is epitomized in 1 Samuel 15:22, with its stress on the inwardness of the religious observance, its call to obedience and sincerity, and its expression of a devotion to Yahweh that no mere routine ceremony can compensate for or, where it is missing, condone.[5]

3. The New Testament, in shorter compass, is as wide ranging as the Old in its many understandings of offering as the heartbeat of divine worship. Jesus takes up the same ambivalent stance to the Temple, its cultus and sacrifices, as his compatriots had done in the writing prophets of preexilic Judaism. There is both a veneration of the cultus as centered on his Father's house and an observance of the feasts and holy seasons, notably Passover, and a critical attitude to religious practice that is simply outward and perfunctory. The scribal laws of defilement and sabbath regulation are exposed to a withering rebuke in Matthew's Gospel (9:12f.; 12:7) in the light of Hosea 6:6, which is cited there. The Temple is cleansed, as all four Gospels report; although each has a different emphasis, all agree on the note of Jesus' coming to claim the Temple as its rightful Lord and purifying it as a true house of *prayer*. The sacrificial side of Temple worship is passed over. The messianic sign in fulfillment of Malachi's oracle (3:1ff.) suggests that a new day of religious obedience and service is about to dawn in a Temple not made with hands, in which fellowship with God will be set on a fresh basis, namely, the new covenant of immediate access to God

5. See H. H. Rowley, *Worship in Israel* (Richmond: John Knox Press, 1966), pp. 110-143.

and universal appeal (replacing priestly mediation), as Jeremiah had forecast (Jer. 31:31-34). There is thus in the early Christian traditions of Jesus' earthly life a double strain: he valued the Temple as a focal point of national unity and cohesion, yet he remained indifferent to its chief business of sacrifice, and greeted its prophesied disappearance from the scene (in A.D. 70 when the Roman armies leveled its buildings) with an equanimity born of hope that a new order would replace its cult.

The paradoxical nature of the above picture is reflected too in the ways the first theologians—Paul, Peter, the writer of Hebrews, the seer of the Revelation, and John—came to interpret Jesus' mission and achievement in retrospect. Jesus' "atonement saying" in Mark 10:45 to the effect that his life is to be surrendered as "a ransom for many" is conveyed in sacrificial terms, though with overtones of Isaiah's portrait of the servant of Yahweh (in chapter 53). All the writers we mentioned employ sacrificial categories to expound the meaning of Messiah's death, often in dependence on a previous Jewish-Christian outlook: Romans 3:25, 26; 1 Corinthians 5:7f.; 1 Peter 1:2, 18, 19; Hebrews 1:3; 2:17; 9:11-14, 26; 10:9, 20; 13:20, 21; Revelation 5:6-10; John 1:29; 19:31-37; 1 John 1:7; 2:1, 2; 4:10.

But all of these contributors to "New Testament theology," so diverse in their respective background and ethos, are united equally in offering a "spiritualized" application of both their statements of what Christ's death effected and its moral challenge to those who gratefully receive its benefits. Paul can go on: "let us keep the festival, not with the old leaven . . . but with the unleavened bread of sincerity and truth." Peter summons the people of the new Israel to accept as God's chosen ones (1 Pet. 2:9-10) a life that is holy with untarnished moral behavior (1 Pet. 1:14-16). Hebrews has severe warnings against ethical laxity and slovenly discipline of life and is careful to show how Messiah's sacrifice leads to a cleansed conscience and moral sensitivity no ritual could produce (Heb. 9:14; 10:14). The Apocalypse, full of Old Testament echoes, still calls its readers to a distinctive way of living and even suffering, by which God is honored and their persecutors put to shame. The Johannine community is set on its guard against false teachers who dealt cavalierly with sins, and its apostolic figure is the great exponent of love and liberty that never degenerate into license.

The upshot of this survey is to see how "offering" can take on a double meaning. Markus Barth illustrates this from Ephesians 5:2: "Your life must be controlled by love, just as Christ loved us and gave his life for us as a sweet-smelling offering and sacrifice that pleases God." He comments that the author has designated Jesus Christ's death as an atoning sacrifice offered by the pouring out of blood (i.e., sacrificial idioms drawn from the Old Testament). But the author is equally indebted to the prophetic (that is, ethical) strand of Old Testament religion as to the priestly. "Sacrifice" is both nonmetaphoral as well as symbolic, since the allusion to "love" shows how he has combined a double function. "The cross [of Jesus] is a once and for all valid saving event that cannot be duplicated or imitated, *and* it is an example which is to be followed."[6]

We are now ready to see how this fusion of historical event in the oblation of Christ on the cross and the call to "offer sacrifice" in his name is worked out in the early church's teaching and practice of "the offering."

A Test Case of New Testament Stewardship

The center of gravity of New Testament teaching regarding the offering is seen in one particular historical instance—the so-called "collection for the saints." To be sure, several parts of the teaching of Jesus allude to offerings made to the Temple treasury (see Matt. 5:23, 24; 23:16-22; Mark 12:41-44) and almsgiving directed to the poor and needy (Matt. 6:1-4). The latter duty was highly regarded in Judaism, and indeed one of the pillars of religion in Jesus' day was, in addition to the Torah and the Temple service, "deeds of mercy." This phrase is literally "the distribution of kindnesses"; it speaks of acts of human compassion, generosity, and concern for the widows, orphans, and needy by which faithful Jews showed their fellow feeling and practical sympathy for the disadvantaged in their society. The effect of Jesus' teaching was to pro-

6. M. Barth, *Ephesians*, The Anchor Bible, vol. 2 (New York: Doubleday, 1974), pp. 558f.

mote a sincere motive in such ministries of help, to warn
against ostentation in giving, and to stress the need for religious faith to express itself in a down-to-earth, practical way.
Several of his parables make these points in unforgettable
scenes (e.g., Luke 18:9-14 [the tax collector and Pharisee],
16:19-31 [the rich man and Lazarus], 10:25-37 [the kind
Samaritan]). There is even a paradoxical element in Jesus'
recorded teachings. He utters severe warnings against the
spirit of greed and possessiveness (Luke 12:13-20), closing the
door of the kingdom on those who trust in their wealth (Mark
10:17-31); but at the same time he uses the singleminded
shrewdness of the real estate manager as an object lesson for
his disciples (Luke 16:1-13), knowing that Caesar's benefits
of law and order and "peace" *(pax romana)* had to be paid
for in Caesar's coin (Mark 12:13-17).

It is Paul, however, who gives us the most explicit and systematic teaching on the place of the offering in Christian
stewardship. And Paul's teaching itself is linked with the circumstance surrounding the need to assist "the saints" in the
Jerusalem church. To that subject we must devote some
attention.

The Collection for Jewish Christians

The best starting point is in Paul's own words. As part of the
agreement made at Jerusalem, according to Galatians 2:10,
Paul accepted responsibility for "the poor." That he took the
task seriously is clear from the repeated references in later letters to a ministry involving the raising of a fund for the "poor
in Jerusalem" (1 Cor. 16:1-4; 2 Cor. 8, 9; Rom. 15:27-29) as
well as his intention, declared in the story of Acts, to visit the
holy city for the purpose of handing over the money so sub-
scribed (Acts 20:16, 22; 24:17; strangely, this aspect of his
visit is not prominent in Luke's detail).

The reason for the Jerusalem church's poverty can only be
guessed. It may be the church had grown in size, and with
increasing numbers of widows to care for the relief fund was
overburdened (cf. Acts 6:1-7). We know that elderly Jewish
families migrated to the holy city to spend their last days and
eventually to be buried there in expectation of the resurrection of the dead. Some scholars suggest that Galilean Chris-

tians undertook a similar pilgrimage to Jerusalem to await the advent of the Messiah whose appearing there was anticipated. A popular view is that the experiment of a "communism of love" (to use Troeltsch's term) involving the pooling of resources and the liquidation of assets (as in Acts 4:32-37; 5:1-11), had brought impoverishment.[7] C. H. Dodd offers this reason for the failure of the Jewish Christian experiment: "They carried it out in the economically disastrous way of realizing capital and distributing it as income."[8] On the external front, we may appeal to bad harvests reported in Judea in the mid-forties of the first century (see Acts 11:27-30) and the persecuting of the church by Jewish authorities which may well have added to its economic and social woes.

For whatever reason—and it may well have been a combination of circumstances—the Jerusalem congregations were in real economic distress. So Paul's offer of "remembering" (that is, actively aiding) them looks at first sight to be a simple, if noble, act of charity and compassion. Paul expected his Gentile churches in Macedonia and southern Greece to rally to the support of fellow Christians in their extreme need and to help them in a most practical manner. This seems clear enough from Romans 15:26 and Paul's line of reasoning in 2 Corinthians 8:13f. and 9:12.

Karl Holl's essay in 1928 put a fresh face on this discussion.[9] He maintained that "the poor" and "the saints" were both designations not of people who were in need but of the church in Jerusalem as such. They claimed to be a "holy" people whose "poverty" was akin to the "poor in spirit" of Matthew 5:3. Their self-designated status gave them a "right" to expect financial help from the Gentile churches since they were the mother church of christendom. There was precedent for the "right of taxation" in the way Jewish synagogues of the Dispersion were under legal obliga-

7. B. Holmberg, *Paul and Power. The Structure of Authority in the Primitive Church as Reflected in the Pauline Epistles* (Lund: CWK Gleerup, 1978), pp. 35-43.

8. C. H. Dodd, *The Epistle of Paul to the Romans,* Moffatt NT Commentary (London: Hodder and Stoughton, 1932), p. 230.

9. K. Holl, "Der Kirchenbegriff des Paulus in seinem Verhältnis zu dem der Urgemeinde," *Gesammelte Aufsätze zur Kirchengeschichte,* vol. 2 (Tübingen: J. C. B. Mohr, 1928), pp. 44-67.

tion to send a Temple tax to the holy city. Holl went on to argue that Paul accepted this claim, a concession betrayed in the language he chose to use in words such as "abundance" (2 Cor. 8:20), "service" (2 Cor. 9:12), and "collection" (1 Cor. 16:1f.).

The case presented by Holl and others seems exaggerated, but it is generally admitted that the collection for the saints was more than a simple expression of charity. As we look at the texts in 2 Corinthians and Romans it appears that Paul viewed this exercise as a powerful way of demonstrating the unity of the two wings of the church, both Jewish and Gentile. His appeal as "apostle to the non-Jews" was calculated to awaken in his converts a sense of gratitude for all the benefits they had received through Israel's hope in the messianic faith. Conversely, Paul fervently believed that such a sign of Gentile generosity would be interpreted as a way to cement relations—often strained—between the two cultural groups and win over the Jewish Christians to a full acceptance of the validity of the Pauline mission. There is an undertone of missionary strategy here as Paul adds in the thought that the way Gentile Christians act as proof of their new life in Israel's Messiah will goad the Jews into envy and encourage them to seek salvation (Rom. 11:14).

There is a special dimension of this hope. It begins with the attested fact that Paul was willing to visit Jerusalem with the collection in hand, being careful to surround himself with a large number of Gentile Christians. This was partly to protect the money (we assume); but more especially, it was to safeguard his reputation lest it should be damaged by innuendo that he was not to be trusted with sums of money. It is clear, too, that Paul was ready for this journey even though he feared that he would not be welcomed by the Jewish Christian leadership and would be exposed to danger at Jerusalem (Rom. 15:31). One side of the matter is that Paul was acting in a representative manner in offering "alms for Israel" as part of the notion that God-fearing Gentiles were encouraged to help the poor of Israel in order to express a desire to share in their faith in one God. There is evidence that some believed that such charitable gestures might make up for a lack of being circumcised, and serve to admit uncircumcised yet pious Gentiles into the covenant of Israel. If this is so, Paul's action was a powerful plea to have his Gentile churches accepted as a true part of the Israel of God. The use of idioms that Holl called attention to may thus be explained, even if there are other terms such as "brotherly love," "fellowship," "fair shares for all" that speak more of a human concern to stretch out a helping hand. The slightly flavored sacred-legal language may well be accounted for as Paul's way of overcoming resistance to the collection—especially at Corinth, where there seemed to have been a reluctance to accept responsibility, as we shall see.

One remaining item falls under consideration in this connection. Johannes Munck[10] and others have acutely noted how the presenting of the collection fits in with the winding up of the apostle's labors in the east (Rom. 15:23), and suggest that Paul regarded his mission service among these Gentile churches as successfully completed. The Jerusalem hierarchy gathered around James the Just may well have viewed this conclusion with dismay, suspicion, and fear; hence Paul's sensitivity that the gesture of the collection may be misinterpreted as though he were acting autonomously and independently of Jerusalem's claim to be God's elect people (see the hints of an animus to Paul in Acts 21:21, 28). In any event, this is how it worked out, and Paul's intention to unify the two factions of apostolic Christianity was broken on the hard rocks of increased suspicion and a reluctance of Jewish Christians to come to his defense when he was accused of fomenting trouble in the Temple area. So as an attempt to "prod the unbelieving Jews to profess faith in Christ, Paul's project was a crashing failure," as Keith F. Nickle sums up.[11] In a similar way Paul's valiant enterprise in seeking to draw Jewish Christians and their Gentile brethren together collapsed under the weight of mounting hostility, which may have resulted from pressure from Jewish nationalists, the Zealots who aimed to close ranks against the pagans and who could well have accused the Jewish Christians of national disloyalty in consorting with so-called "converted Gentiles."

Paul's laudable aim suffered yet one more blow. His

10. J. Munck, *Paul and the Salvation of Mankind* (Atlanta: John Knox Press, 1959, 1977), pp. 176, 193.

11. K. F. Nickle, *The Collection. A Study in Paul's Strategy* (London: SCM Press, 1966), p. 155.

pilgrimage to Jerusalem, bearing gifts from the nations, reflects the prophetic picture of the last days (Isa. 2; Micah 4), as the rabbis believed. Then, it was hoped, the obedience of the Gentiles would lead to the renewal of Israel and the onset of the new age of eschatological joy and blessedness. Paul's own work as an apostle would be validated by this climactic result, as he headed the large retinue of Gentile delegates to the holy city (Acts 20:4). His thinking seems to oscillate between the expectation of Israel's conversion (Rom. 11:26) and his continuing desire to evangelize in Rome and Spain (Rom. 15:24), but clearly the two are interrelated. Thus Paul views the offering of the collection as both a "salvation-historical" validation of his own ministry against his detractors and a means of "eschatological provocation" leading to national Israel's jealousy and turning to God. Alas, here again Paul's best hopes were doomed and crushed on the anvil of Israel's continued "hardness" and "blindness" and his own increasing disfavor among his compatriots.

A Study of 2 Corinthians, chapters 8, 9

The ground is now ready for us to look at some principles that are exposed in the chapters where Paul centers his thoughts on the collection for the saints. A lead-in verse is the call (in 2 Cor. 8:7) to "overflow in this grace [Greek *charis*] also." The Corinthians were rejoicing in several manifestations of the charismatic gifts of the Spirit: they were men and women of faith, speech, knowledge, and love that Paul had inspired in them. Now, he concludes, be sure to complement all these *charismata* with the "grace" of a generous spirit, and become leaders in the realm of cheerful giving. It is this gift of liberality he wishes to promote in a congregation full of spiritual gifts (1 Cor. 1:5-7; 14:12). The same admonition is there under the surface in 2 Corinthians 9:13 ("the generosity of your contribution" expressed to the Jerusalem saints in need); and both texts indicate that some inertia or even hostility to Paul's pledge to help has to be overcome. How would the Corinthian congregation rally to this call?

1. *Giving springs from a willing disposition* (8:12). The key word (Greek *prothumia)* means a "ready eagerness" to take action, and touches the mainspring of motivation,

since all Christian giving is worthwhile only if the motive is right. Paul can appeal to his own motive in arranging for Titus to visit Corinth, while Titus' own willing eagerness (Greek *spoudē*) to do so is commended (8:16, 17). In addition to Titus, the churches had appointed certain other unnamed brethren to travel; and their visits will show how God is glorified, Paul says (8:19), and will also demonstrate "our readiness," that is, his full consent and approval. That Paul's counsel did not fall on deaf ears is seen in the following chapter (9:2) where he builds on this precise quality of "eager purpose" to complete the collection, and uses it as a stimulus to the churches in Macedonia. He praises, in this context, "the zeal" of the Corinthians, perhaps making a pastoral plea that they should not disappoint him nor go back on their first promises, which underlie the writing of 1 Corinthians 16:1-4.

That earlier statement clearly presupposes the voluntary character of the giving. "On the first day of every week"— possibly their payday, but more probably the day of Christian worship—"let each of you put aside something, saving up what he has been prospered with." Both a readiness to respond to the appeal and the "free-will" nature of giving are for Paul a sign of God's grace within the person's life. He clinches the insistence that this must be so in a double way.

First, although the Macedonians have already answered the call by giving "according to their ability, indeed beyond their ability" (8:3), they have given *of their own free choice,* where the italicized words translate a single adjective meaning "of one's own accord" *(authairetos).* The ruling idea is "in good heart," acting without pressure or undue external constraint, though not quite "spontaneously" since Paul's request had triggered the giving in the first instance. But the response was free-willed in the sense that these people even begged Paul to have a share in the privilege of giving to the fund. That for Paul is the clear index of God's grace (8:1) at work in human lives—by disposing the inclination to give to others in a selfless regard for their privations and a ready desire to do something tangible to uplift them. Not surprisingly, therefore, Paul can remark on their example that they had first made a commitment to the Lord (8:5), and so they wished to put that response to the practical test of a ministry of giving to their fellow believers. We cannot fail to notice the subtlety of Paul's appeal on this basis: "grace" *(charis)* is God's gracious activity in predisposing the Macedonians to contribute, and then the same word becomes "the collection" (in 8:6) as the outward expression of the inward affirming of God's will as "good for them."

Second, Paul returns to the theme in chapter 9, although with a shift of emphasis.

> Let each person give as he decides in his mind, not regretfully nor under compulsion; it is the cheerful giver whom God loves. (v. 7)

The key term, to be sure, is the same as in the above discussion, with a concentration on free decision. The "happy giver" is one whom Yahweh loves, Paul had read in the Old Testament (Prov. 22:8; Greek: "God blesses a cheerful and bountiful man"; the Hebrew text [22:9] is still more expressive: "He who has a bountiful eye shall be blessed" by Yahweh). Here is the portrait of a giver who is motivated neither by stern, cold duty, nor external pressure. These negatives—"not out of sorrow" to see his money leave him, "nor out of compulsion" because such giving is expected of him or betrays a grudging spirit—are wonderfully picturesque. They allow true giving to shine in its own light by contrast, and convey the promise that such a disposition of freely motivated giving brings its own reward because no other reward is expected, not even from God (against C. K. Barrett who thinks v. 8 implies the promise of a divine recompense).[12] The spirit of Paul's counsel is summed up in 9:5:

> I want it to be forthcoming as a generous gift, not as money wrung out of you. (Moffatt)

2. *Giving strikes the note of generosity.* Paul has just coupled giving with a "joyful" acceptance of responsibility, so removing that obligation far from the world of legal or dutiful right and infusing it with a sense of gladness. He knows that such "generosity" (his word in 9:11) brings its own satisfaction and that God is thereby thanked for his bounty. Thanksgiving to him will dominate the remainder of

12. C. K. Barrett, *The Second Epistle to the Corinthians,* Harper's NT Commentaries (New York: Harper and Row, 1973), p. 236.

his discussion until the grand climax is reached in the ejaculation: "Thanks be to God for his gift beyond measure!" at the close of the chapter. Again Paul is playing with words. He began with God's grace *(charis)* in human experience; he completes his treatment in a doxological tribute of thanks *(charis)* to that God of all grace.

The intervening section, which uses the same Greek term no fewer than ten times (including 8:1 and 9:15), will focus on twin aspects of "generosity": the divine self-giving (8:9) and the human response and gratitude in action (9:11, 12). Both passages merit separate treatment.

a) Paul's standards are set by the highest appeal. In a powerfully expressed couplet arranged in a semicredal form, he brings the incarnation of the Lord Jesus into view as a tribute to his generosity *(charis):*

> You know the grace of our Lord Jesus Christ
> that for you he became poor, though he was rich
> that you by his poverty might become rich. (8:9)

Christ's wealth is a reference to his preincarnate life (cf. Phil. 2:6; Col. 1:15f.) when he enjoyed fellowship in the divine splendor, as John 1:1 expresses the mystery of his eternal being. Christ's poverty, voluntarily assumed—and *that* is the point of Paul's appeal—entailed his becoming man in the incarnation (cf. Phil. 2:7f.), with an obedience that led to his self-giving on the cross. Surprisingly, Paul does not take the thought to its logical extreme but stops short at the condescension of his becoming human in a dramatic kenosis or self-abnegation, suggesting he may be citing a confession. The richness of what he had is then meant to be shared with his people. Material poverty and wealth are not in question.[13] He became "poor" in the sense of his lowly submission to a life of obedience and piety, identifying with the "poor of the land" in Israel, the *anawim*. His exaltation means that his people are raised not to material prosperity but to the intimacy of communion with the Father to which he returned at his ascension.

What he did was the supreme act of love (so Paul's test in v. 8). By its nature love acts freely, as the testimony of the in-

13. Against J. D. G. Dunn, *Christology in the Making* (Philadelphia: Westminster Press, 1980), p. 122.

carnation shows. That kenosis of God's son displayed the divine generosity as no other human act could do. Now, Paul continues, prove your love in a generous response to my appeal. "This is what you ought to do" (v. 10); it is a fitting way to show your love and gratitude not in intention merely (they had made up their minds last year, v. 10) but in a freely accepted decision to contribute.

b) The "generosity" (Greek *haplotēs*, found with this sense in Rom. 12:8; 2 Cor. 8:2 as well as 9:11, 13) Paul commends is an answering response to God's goodness and grace in his giving. It is primarily addressed to God as a token of thankfulness. But it looks in the horizontal direction on the social plane as well. It supplies the need of the Jerusalem poor, and it gains "approval," says the apostle. No one is sure whose approval is intended, however. K. F. Nickle has suggested that the Jewish church in Jerusalem is in view.[14] They would respond positively to the Macedonians' and Corinthians' unreserved "lack of duplicity" (which is another meaning of *haplotēs)* in supplying relief for the poor, which was evidence of their—the Corinthians'—obedient confession of faith in Christ. The closing part of verse 13 endorses the interpretation that sees the "mother church" as the one who, Paul hopes, will react favorably to his people's open-handedness.

So Christian generosity serves many interests: it honors God the giver par excellence; it relieves human misery; it binds Christians together in a genuine unity of fellowship *(koinōnia* in v. 13) and dispels any suggestion of an uncaring indifference or supposed superiority; and it gives to our confession of faith and desire to spread the good news a down-to-earth reality that saves it from ethereal detachment from "real" life in this world.

3. *Giving entails the possibility of sacrifice.* Paul has opened the discussion with this prospect (8:1-3), but logically it comes at the conclusion of our analysis of his teaching.

The "joy" of giving is not lightly secured nor easily celebrated. Paul is sufficiently in touch with his Macedonian churches to know that the one feature of their early history was "affliction" (Greek *thlipsis,* a term of special meaning

14. K. F. Nickle, *Collection*, p. 105.

among the churches of northern Greece as we see from Phil.
1:29f.; 1 Thess. 1:6; 2:14; 3:2f.; 2 Thess. 1:4-10). The terminology embraces *both* economic privation caused by heavy
taxation under the empire (as Livy reports) and earthquakes
in certain Macedonian provinces in Claudius' reign *and*
pressure occasioned by persecution and disaffection within
their social groups. The upshot was "much testing by affliction" (8:2); yet paradoxically this trial released the gates of
"abundance of their joy" as their "extreme poverty overflowed in the wealth of their generosity." Indeed the hallmark of Macedonian Christianity is revealed as the sacrificial
side of their faith, as we learn from Philippians 4:14-20.

This Philippian passage is especially noteworthy not only
for its reminder of the Macedonians' generosity in supporting
Paul's ministry, but also by reason of the language Paul
uses —or rather, because of the terms he does *not* use. Not
once does he mention money in Philippians 4 nor does he explicitly say "thank you" to his friends; and there is a deafen-
ing silence also in regard to the precise term for "money" in
2 Corinthians chapters 8 and 9. As far as the Philippians section is concerned he turns rather to make a heavy concentration of liturgical idioms drawn from the Old Testament cult.
This is to impart to the congregation's giving the character of
a worshipful response to the gospel ministry they were supporting. So "gifts," "sweet-smelling offering," and "sacrifice" are all cultic keywords designed to tell the Philippians
that in assisting him they were more importantly offering
worship to God.

Their sense of ready willingness to give "beyond their
means" has already been noted; it stood for a trait Paul
reports without endorsement. Indeed, while he doubtless felt
gratified at this unmeasured response, he knows that what
counts in the end is giving proportionate to what a person
has, not according to what he does not possess (8:12). The
reason is clear: "not that there may be relief for others and affliction for you, but on the basis of equality," with fair shares
all around.

Still, the Macedonian example is illustrious, and Paul
wants to use it to stir the lethargic Corinthians to action and
endeavor. His call is for "equality" (8:14) on the basis that
where there is deficiency Christians who are blessed with "a

surplus'' should be the first to step forward. The law of the harvest field applies here (9:6-10). A niggardly sowing yields only a poor harvest, whereas a farmer who is prepared to ''lose'' his seed corn will, in favorable circumstances, receive back good measure. ''To give,'' says one ancient commentator, ''is not to lose, but to sow seed'';[15] and seed is sown in order to multiply (John 12:24). Paul enforces his point—that the measure of our satisfaction and inner reward in giving is decided by the depth of our involvement—by a frequent use of the Greek root *periss-*, variously rendered ''abundance'' (8:2), ''overflowed'' (8:2, 7), ''surplus'' (8:14), ''superfluous'' (9:1), ''multiply'' (9:8, 9), ''overflow'' (9:12). The lesson is an obvious one: costly involvement in God's work, like the farmer's singleminded attention to his fields even when he is called upon to take risks, does not go without recognition and will not fail to yield its true enrichments, which of course are not necessarily material. ''You will be enriched in everything for every kind of generosity'' (9:11) looks more to the eternal reward of God's final approval and the inner satisfaction that we have done our best, even at cost, to please him and meet such human needs as are within our power to assist and alleviate.

Conclusion

Christian worship involves us in the task of ''cooperating with God''; otherwise prayers die on our lips and praise is a cul-de-sac, leading nowhere. The authentic liturgy, endorsed by Scripture and history and reason, is that which looks both upward to God and outward on the world. In our ''offering,'' whether of our selves or our service (Rom. 12:1, 2), we bring together the mysteries of our faith and the stewardship of our resources; and with a faithful participation in the one, unique oblation of Christ, once crucified, now enthroned, we offer to God ''our sacrifice of praise of thanksgiving . . . and we offer and present unto Thee, O Lord, ourselves, our souls and bodies, to be a reasonable, holy, and living sacrifice unto Thee . . . [beseeching] Thee to accept this our bounden duty and service.''[16]

15. Quoted in R. H. Strachan, *The Second Epistle to the Corinthians*, Moffatt NT Commentary (London: Hodder and Stoughton, 1935), p. 142.
16. Cranmer's post-Communion prayer.

CHAPTER SIX

Confessing
the Faith

The Need for a Creed

This part of Christian worship is perhaps the most open to attack from those who are either uncomfortable with or positively hostile to credal expressions of religion. It is interesting to note how the various ecclesiastical creeds have suffered down the centuries. The so-called Athanasian Creed with its rigorous opening ("Whosoever will be saved . . .") and unremitting claims ("And the Catholic Faith is this") has never been popular in Anglican liturgical history. The Prayer Book of 1928 gave a permissive sanction to this formula, yet suggested some omissions from the printed text, especially the "damnatory" clause ("which Faith except every one do keep whole and undefiled: without doubt he shall perish everlastingly"). The Nicene Creed came under fire during the struggle with Deism in the eighteenth century. In our generation it has been the fate of the Apostles' Creed to be placed under a searching light because of its heavy trinitarian and christological language; and this latest phase of opposition reflects a general dissatisfaction with all credal religion in an age of tolerance and unrestricted theological exploration.

So "creeds" are under fire. Yet they have a long and varied history in the evolution of Christian worship; and it may still be claimed that there is a place in the worship of the people of God for a recitation of some statement that enshrines our common belief. But what is a creed?

Its name, taken from the opening of the Apostles' and Nicene Creeds in their Latin original (*credo*, I believe), implies a confession of personal faith in God. But more than that is involved. The faith confessed is that of the church. So a creed is "a short, comprehensive formula of the Christian faith, expressed in language of the first person and dignified enough for frequent use in public worship.''[1] Klaas Runia's opening definition has several parts to it. (1) The formula is short, not expansive; yet it is comprehensive enough to cover the main points regarded as essential. (2) The creed has a close connection with public worship. It is, we may say, dogma set to liturgy, producing a statement that is just as appropriately sung as said. Indeed it has been remarked that creeds *should* be sung rather than signed (when the proper name for such documents is "confessions" or "articles of religion" that originated as "position papers" over against certain doctrines or practices held to be erroneous). (3) The creeds, on the contrary, are not objective statements to be used in controversy nor is their primary function that of a teaching instrument. They are liturgical expressions, couched in the language of the first person, "I believe" . . . "We praise thee, O God" (the *Te Deum,* which is as much a creed as a hymn; the borderline between the two is very thin). (4) A further aspect of what constitutes a creed is brought out at the frontispiece to J. N. D. Kelly's magisterial work. He offers this definition: "a fixed formula summarizing the essential articles of [the Christian] religion and enjoying the sanction of ecclesiastical authority.''[2] The last clause emphasizes that the creed as it is used in public worship is not merely an expression of individual belief but carries with it a consensus, with all the weight of authority implied in that. The great "ecumenical" creeds are so termed because they are accepted as bearing some authority—or at least having some appropriateness—for use in public worship by almost all the churches of christendom, though, as we shall see, only one creed is universally approved: the Nicene Creed. Both the Apostles' and the Athanasian Creeds are treated with some suspicion by the eastern Orthodox because of their "western" flavor. Yet it remains true that with western Christianity, however fragmented it may have become, the profession of three great credal statements is one bright hope of unity amid multiple denominational disagreements and divisions. We may con-

---

1. K. Runia, *I Believe in God* (London: Tyndale Press, 1963), p. 11.
2. J. N. D. Kelly, *Early Christian Creeds,* 2nd ed. (London: Longmans, 1960), p. 1.

trast this state of affairs with the variety and confusion of "confessions of faith" within Protestant Christianity, all of which betray a tendency to divide the one body of Christ.

We are already nearing the threshold of our concern to defend the place of the creeds in worship. The acceptance and use of agreed teaching in those areas regarded as central to the Christian faith provides *a focal point of unity*. Transcending the divisions that have plagued the ongoing history and witness of the church in the world, the creeds point to a common heritage in which all Christians share. Whatever the precise historical and theological pressures and kinds of political opportunism that created the creeds—and these are considerable factors, as a reading of history up to the Council of Chalcedon in A.D. 451 will show—it remains that Christians today have inherited these "instruments" as their shared possession. We have an obligation to respect and honor our past, and not to squander nor treat lightly the legacy we have received. After all, we are not the first generation of believers on earth, nor is it proper to act as though we imagined ourselves to be the most theologically expert and informed. To jettison the creeds on the score that we have outgrown the truths they enshrine, or to deal cavalierly with the deposit of the gospel our forebears handed on to us is a mark of irresponsibility and a sign of poor stewardship. This defense, of course, does not commit us to an unthinking acceptance of the past heritage as though the last word had been uttered or important theological issues were foreclosed. To be a debtor to our Christian past is not to be its slave. But it does imply a keen sense of gratitude to those who have preceded us in the way of Christ, and a determination to retain the basic tenets of what makes our faith Christian, however much we may want to express it in an idiom or style suitable to the day in which we live. Here is the first line of defense of a "credal faith," and a justification for the use of its symbolic expression in worship.

Second, the provision of a place in a service of worship for one's beliefs to be acknowledged and proclaimed offers a moment when such beliefs can be crystallized and confirmed. It is a fact of experience that once we give utterance to a truth we have embraced it takes on a new significance. It becomes more "part of us" the instant we articulate it in a public way. There is thus in the reciting of the creed *both* an open declaration of what we as individuals believe within our membership of Christ's fellowship worldwide *and* a consolidating of that faith in our experience. The creed speaks to a deep human need to declare oneself, to take sides, and to do so in the company of others who are sharers with us of that faith and witnesses to our commitment as we verbally express it. Beliefs that are only secretly cherished or obscurely expressed are bound to be less than fully satisfying, even if they save us from intemperate and rashly made statements. If we are honest with ourselves, we admit that more often we hold back because of fear or embarrassment or a refusal to face life's searching challenge: What is the faith we live by? In our creeds we are invited to "come clean" and declare our interest. The situation for most of us will be quite unlike that of the great Harvard scholar H. A. Wolfson who gave "A Morning Chapel Talk" at the university. He presented the manuscript of what he had said to a friend who read it with a quizzical look, even though Wolfson claimed that he as its author liked it. "What do you think it is that I like best about this piece?" He continued, "You see, nobody will ever know whether I believe anything or not."[3]

Third, we will want to view the question of creeds in the modern church in a context of biblical revelation and authority. Granted that a full-scale creed in the sense in which J. N. D. Kelly defined it is not found in the New Testament, and that the so-called Apostles' Creed does not go back to apostolic times, it still remains true that the church's creed-making activity has already begun within the time frame of canonical Scripture. There are clear indications that what appear as credal fragments, set in the context of the church's missionary preaching, cultic worship, and defense against paganism, are already detectable in the New Testament. Nor may we overlook the data in the Old Testament and rabbinic Judaism, however much disputed, which give precedents to the apostolic writers to offer statements of various forms of a

3. Gershom G. Scholem in his review of Leo W. Schwarz, *Wolfson of Harvard. Portrait of a Scholar* (Philadelphia: The Jewish Publication Society of America, 1978) in the *Times Literary Supplement*, Nov. 23, 1979, p. 16.

"credo" that were treated as authoritative and binding, even
if other groups might not accept them.

The last-named qualification is important. Present-day
study of the New Testament documents has placed some
serious question marks against a too facile acceptance of the
unity once thought to characterize the New Testament "gospel." To be sure, highlighting the New Testament diversity
can be misleading if doing so suggests that the various centers
of believers were in competition or at hopeless odds among
themselves as to what they believed and proclaimed. The
multiformity is much more in areas of procedures and practices germane to worship—and we shall devote a subsequent
chapter to this theme, and suggest a line of development that
runs through the phases of early Christianity—rather than in
what the first Christians believed as the substance of their
kerygmatic message. The confessions of Christ crucified and
risen that build on firm convictions regarding the historical
incarnation and look for victory of God's kingdom in a future
expectation are the shared possessions of the different groups
in Pauline, Jerusalem, Petrine, and Asia Minor Christianity.
The unity here is what belongs to the heart of the faith as the
incipient "creeds" express it. Talk of a "different gospel" (in
Gal. 1:8, 9 and 2 Cor. 11:4) and controversies touching the
role of the law, the value of circumcision, and the observance
of churchly discipline are already brought to the touchstone
of what Paul regards as a logical extension of the original
kerygma of the person and place of Jesus Christ in salvation
history. The first christological disputes at Corinth and
Colossae are addressed in the light of the apostolic "traditions" (1 Cor. 15:3ff.; Col. 2:6, 7), just as the Johannine
leaders answer a prevalent docetism with its denial of a true
incarnation and the historical death of Jesus by recourse to
what was handed on "from the beginning." These appeals
presuppose a body of teaching, however rudimentary, that
was acknowledged as marking out Christians as distinctive
from their neighbors who adhered to other religions of Greco-
Roman society; the same "pattern of doctrine" (Rom. 6:17)
acted as a benchmark to distinguish what was "apostolic" in
the sense of adequately expressing the full significance of
Christ as divine son and the world's redeemer against those
who, while professedly Christian, doubted or denied his

being-in-God and his acting for God, or restricted the scope of salvation.

Walter Bauer in an influential book[4] maintained the thesis that later movements in gnosticism and Montanism were adjudged "heretical" partly because of their geographical origins and partly because the imperialistic character of the church at Rome managed to exert pressure by appealing—successfully, as it turned out—to its own creed, the "rule of faith"; and so this event ensured the dominance and continuance in the West of that Latin type of Christianity represented in the Apostles' and later creeds. This theory has met with some critical reception, notably by A. A. T. Ehrhardt[5] who accused Bauer of a failure to give a full picture of what made Roman Christianity distinctive, and of overstressing the geographical peculiarities as these were believed to have influenced the formation of Christian doctrines. But there is even less to be said for an opposing theory that the church's belief suddenly sprang into view at Rome at the turn of the first century and developed only slowly across the next centuries.[6] The way Catholic Christians were able to meet what Ehrhardt calls "the mysticism of the Gnosis as well as the asceticism of the Cataphrygians" or Montanists—the former offering a type of mystical rationalism, the latter a recast version of Christianity as sentimental enthusiasm—indicates that already the "catholics" were able to maintain a remarkably united front. Their appeal was to the "rule of faith" or "the traditions" or what Ignatius calls the "Gospel" *(Philadelphians* 5) or the "inviolable archives" (ibid. 8) which are Christ's cross, death, and resurrection. In a word, it is Jesus Christ known by faith as true man, true God, that constituted the essence of the faith. He is "no sham" (Ignatius, *Smyrnaeans* 1, 2) but "God revealing himself as a man, to

4. W. Bauer, *Orthodoxy and Heresy in Earliest Christianity* (Philadelphia: Fortress Press, 1971).

5. A. A. T. Ehrhardt, "Christianity before the Apostles' Creed" in his *The Framework of the New Testament Stories* (Manchester: University Press, 1964), pp. 151-199. See also Appendix 2 in Bauer, *Orthodoxy,* (pp. 303-306).

6. F. F. Bruce, *Peter, Stephen, James, and John: Studies in Non-Pauline Christianity* (British title: *Men and Movements in the Primitive Church*) (Grand Rapids: Wm. B. Eerdmans; Exeter: Paternoster Press, 1980), p. 75.

bring newness of eternal life" *(Ephesians* 19). In these noteworthy, semicredal statements Ignatius seems to be summarizing what the New Testament picture of Jesus Christ offers.
Already we meet in the pages of that worshiping community's records—Gospels, Acts, Epistles, and Apocalypse—a
"creed"-making and "creed"-confessing body of men and
women whose literary deposits, as sacred Scripture, we today
want to claim as normative and regulative for Christian
liturgy and the church's authentic worship of God.

The Biblical Data: The Old Testament

As we said earlier, "creed" takes on a special nuance when
we discuss what we discover from a form-critical study of the
canonical books and try to bring to light credal fragments and
confessions. "A credo [in this context] is a summary statement of belief encompassing the irreducible minimum sus-
taining a common faith," writes J. I. Durham.[7] The history
of Old Testament theology has yielded several notable examples where Israel's credo is thought to be a nodal point
around which the recital of God's mighty acts in her national
history played a role in the dramatic worship at the sanctuaries of Israel.

G. von Rad looked to Deuteronomy 26:5b-9 as the earliest
example of a brief historical credo, though previous suggestions had taken such patterns of "didactic exposition" of
events from the call of Abraham to the entry into Canaan
back to David's reign, or to even earlier cultic gatherings.
Von Rad's study, however, gave more weight to the content
of the credo. He isolated four themes: the patriarchs, the
oppression in Egypt, the march to and entry into Canaan, the
promised land and home of Israel. The language is stylis-
tically different from surrounding narrative prose, and suggests a setting in public recitation and tribal worship,
centered on Kadesh and related to the celebration of the feast
of Weeks at Gilgal (Josh. 24:2-13). For von Rad the events of
Sinai belonged to a different setting, and had their narration

7. J. I. Durham, "Credo, Ancient Israelite," in *The Interpreter's Dictionary of the Bible. Supplementary Vol.*, ed. K. Crim (Nashville: Abingdon Press, 1976), pp. 197-199. He cites the bibliographies of G. von
Rad and M. Noth.

as historical details in the sanctuary at Shechem and on the cultic occasion of the festival of Booths. Not until much later in Israel's history did the Kadesh-tradition merge with the exodus-Sinai complex of events.

The theory sketched above has been refined by Martin Noth who enlarged the number of credal themes to five by including the Sinai encounter as part of the existing credo, and denied the link with the sanctuary at Gilgal. It has equally been rejected by others who have questioned whether such a credo existed as a literary genre or held such a place in Israel's cultus or may be traced back to ancient sources. The debate rages, with perhaps only one agreed conclusion emerging: "That there was 'credo' in ancient Israel now seems assured."[8] The cultic connection is disputed, the precise form of the credo is largely unknown, and the *ad hoc* nature of the confessional material gives scholars pause in trying to date it exactly. What does seem to be shown clearly is that short phrases or single words (e.g., "Yahweh is king" or even just the divine name itself) and longer summaries (given in Josh. 24, Pss. 78 and 105) were Israel's way of conserving and transmitting the memory of her historical traditions; and it is as likely as not that in the sanctuaries and later in the Temple the form of words was preserved and rehearsed in celebration of what Yahweh had done for Israel and what his presence in history—past and continuing—meant. Of all the credal fragments, Deuteronomy 6:20-24 (the *shema)* came to hold an honored and distinctive place, and provided the synagogue with its daily *confessio fidei* as it did the heroic martyrs of later Judaism:

> Hear, O Israel, Yahweh [is] our God,
> Yahweh is one.

The New Testament Creeds

We have already recognized, with many modern writers, the presence of several embryonic creeds within the literature of the New Testament. The criteria used for detecting and isolating such "forms" are well known, since E. Stauffer

8. J. I. Durham, "Credo," p. 198.

listed them in some detail.[9] The most easily recognizable traits are: the use of verbs such as "believe," "confess," "proclaim" followed by appropriate clauses giving the substance of what is believed, professed, or proclaimed; the elevated and sonorous language employed, often with rare words or terms usually heavily theological in tone; the coupling of verbs "to receive"/"to hand over," indicating the presence of a tradition that was already in existence before the writer made reference to it; and a breakdown in grammatical and syntactical rules that betrays the insertion of quoted material.

The patient investigation of scholars over the past few decades has yielded a fruitful harvest. The outer shell of such allusions to "the apostles' doctrine" (Acts 2:42); the "traditions" (2 Thess. 2:15); "the deposit" (1 Tim. 6:20; 2 Tim. 1:12-14); "the sound words" (1 Tim. 6:3); the "confession" (Heb. 3:1); the "faith" (Phil. 1:27; Eph. 4:5; Jude 3); and the "gospel" (Rom. 2:16; 16:25; 1 Cor. 15:3ff.) has now been suggestively filled with a content suitable to the context and milieu of the passages concerned. The handing-on of apostolic teachings is identified in such places as 1 Corinthians 11:23ff.; 15:1-5; Philippians 4:9; and Colossians 2:6 with conclusions drawn that such specimens of Christian instruction are a combination of matters liturgical, kerygmatic, and ethical. Above all, the person and saving work of Christ was the theme of the good news that the first Christians saw as their joyous privilege and serious responsibility to "pass on"—whether by proclamation or by instruction—to other people, who in turn would ensure its promulgation.

The areas of life where these credal formulas played significant part were evidently the following:

1. At the obvious level it was through *the missionary preaching* of the church that men and women were summoned to faith and the call was heard, "Believe in the Lord Jesus Christ" (Acts 16:31). The Colossians heard the gospel from Epaphras' lips in these terms, according to Colossians 2:6. This emphasis on "Jesus as Lord" belongs to the outreach of the mission to Gentile regions where Paul and

9. E. Stauffer, *New Testament Theology* (London: SCM Press, 1955), pp. 338, 339.

others, such as his predecessors in the school of Stephen (Acts 11:19-21), evangelized pagans, using a language that was sufficiently understood in a society where there were "many lords" (1 Cor. 8:5, 6). It is natural, therefore, for Paul to use Jesus' lordship as a thumbnail summary of his kerygma (Rom. 10:9, 10). Where the audience was Jewish, the idiom used is more in terms of the messiahship of Jesus (as in what has been claimed as the earliest Christian confession, "Jesus is the Christ";[10] at least this is true logically if not chronologically). The Jewish confession in the *shema* of God's oneness is a presupposition in both spheres of evangelism (1 Cor. 8:4; 1 Tim. 2:5; James 2:19). A Jewish-Christian credo that emphasizes Jesus' true messianic credentials as "son of David" has been suspected to underlie Romans 1:3, 4, which extends the formula in Paul's hands to include a hellenistic dimension of Jesus' exalted status as "son of God." Here we see the process of credal adaptation at work which, as in the case of early hymns, extends the range of what is "received" to include fresh insights suitable to a new chapter in the missionary enterprise.[11]

2. *Cultic worship*—the adjective is needed to say that we are speaking of the church's public worship, not private devotional settings—provided scope for the devising and preserving of credal forms. The statement "Jesus is Lord" may well have appeared in a baptismal service as the initiate's response to the gospel and the validation of the ceremony shortly to follow. The creed "I believe that Jesus Christ is God's son," in the context of both an interrogation and a candidate's affirmation, is traced to the dialogue between Philip and the courtier according to the textual tradition of certain western authorities in Acts 8:37. Whatever the historical value of this incident, it certainly prepared the ground for a much more elaborate series of baptismal "questions-and-answers" in the later liturgies.

It is the same with the development of the eucharistic rite.

10. V. H. Neufeld, *The Earliest Christian Confessions* (Leiden: E. J. Brill, 1963).

11. H. Schlier, "Zu Röm 1, 3f," in *Neues Testament und Geschichte: Historisches Geschehen und Deutung in NT,* ed. H. Baltensweiler and B. Reicke (Zurich/Tübingen: J. C. B. Mohr, 1972), pp. 207-218.

Plausible suggestions have been made to trace certain hymnic and/or credal confessions to the Lord's Supper in the New Testament church (e.g., Rom. 3:24-26; Phil. 2:6-11; Col. 1:15-20). While it is probably more convincing to see baptismal ideas in the latter two passages, given some language such as "light," "image," "sonship," and Christ as Lord that can be matched with baptismal imagery (seen in Jesus' baptism, Mark 1:11 and Eph. 5:14), the eucharistic flavor of the other passage in Romans 3 together with sections such as Ephesians 1:3-14 paved the way for confessional prayers of thanksgiving for creation and redemption to find a natural place in the later celebration of the holy supper.

Nor should we overlook such cases as the first attested prayer, *marana tha* ("Our Lord, come"), as a credal cry, since it became embedded in the liturgy (as in *Didache* 10:6) in a context that looks to the presence of the risen Lord at the table and at the end-time. Gospel formulas of exorcism that confess Jesus as God's son found a place in the preparatory rites of exorcism conducted as a prelude to Easter baptisms in *The Apostolic Tradition* of Hippolytus: "And he [the bishop] shall lay his hand on them and exorcize all alien spirits, that they *may flee* out of them and never return into them." The verb reads like a quotation from the direct speech of what the bishop said, itself modeled on Mark 9:25 (cf. Acts 16:18, 19:13).[12]

3. Theories that associate the origin of our creeds with *catechetical instruction* derive from the pioneering work of A. Seeberg.[13] He sought to trace a prehistory of church creeds in a hypothetical "early Christian catechism" based on the Jewish pattern of instruction and discipline needed when Gentiles came over into the fold of Judaism from their heathen ways. C. H. Dodd[14] refined and improved upon this

12. G. J. Cuming, *Hippolytus: A Text for Students* (Bramcote: Grove Books, 1976), p. 17. See the discussion on the power of the Name to expel demons in R. P. Martin, *Carmen Christi: Phillipians ii. 5-11 in Recent Interpretation and in the Setting of Early Christian Worship* (Cambridge: University Press, 1967), p. 261.

13. A. Seeberg, *Der Katechismus der Urchristenheit*, ed. F. Hahn (Munich: Chr. Kaiser Verlag, 1966 ed.).

14. C. H. Dodd, *The Apostolic Preaching and its Developments* (London: Hodder and Stoughton, 1936).

idea, which has, however, been criticized severely in more recent times.[15] Dodd argued that a regular method of teaching *(didachē)* was applied to new converts to the Christian faith as they embarked on their new life in Christ. Perhaps some traces of this catechetical training may be seen in places such as Colossians 2:6, 7 and 1 John 2:12-14. But what we know for sure about a "creed"-observing catechumenate is very limited.

4. Not much positive conclusion stands also at the end of O. Cullmann's ingenious association of the rise of creeds with the *church's confrontation with Roman magistrates* (see ch. 10, p. 176 later). As it developed there is a side to creed formulation that suggests a way in which creeds became used as symbols of protest and summaries of the faith to be used apologetically when Christians were arraigned before pagan tribunals. To take this situation back to Paul's time is perilous (1 Cor. 12:3 seen in this way looks decidedly anachronistic: what evidence is there of a Corinthian believer called to Gallio's bench and faced with a choice that years later put Polycarp of Smyrna on the spot?). The setting of the Apocalypse seems more promising, and a recent idea that the credal "King of kings, Lord of lords" as well as the appellation of Jesus as "God" sprang out of a protest directed to the imperial claim to be "lord and god" has more cogency to it.

The continuing life, experience, and opportunities of the New Testament church, inheriting as it did the Jewish familiarity with statements of faith to mark the Jewish people out as exceptional in a world of idolatry meant that it would become a "creed"-building church. Creeds, however, took on different shapes. From the earliest limpid statements, "God is one," "Jesus is Christ," "Jesus is Lord" (Aramaic *marē*), the successful Gentile mission broadened the scope of missionary theology and subsequent worship forms. "Jesus is Lord" (Greek *kyrios*) became the most common vehicle of expression, reaching back to the faith's Old Testament roots (Yahweh had been rendered *kyrios* in the Greek Bible), and

15. See J. I. H. McDonald, *Kerygma and Didache. The Articulation and Structure of the Earliest Christian Message* (Cambridge: University Press, 1980), Introduction.

forward to an understanding of Jesus of Nazareth as Lord of
the world and ruler over every sphere of sentient life, angelic,
human, demonic (Col. 1:15-20; Phil. 2:6-11; 1 Tim. 3:16;
1 Pet. 3:22; Rev. 5:1-14; 19:16).

With all this heavy christological weight in the extant
"credal" formulas the cardinal belief in God the Father as
one God, as holy, righteous creator and judge, was not lost,
even if his name is there in the background, rather than in
prominent display. This can be accounted for phenomeno-
logically, if not theologically, for the church of New Testament times was caught up largely in the first flush of enthusiastic exultation in the enthroned Jesus Christ who had put a
new face on who God is and introduced the day of messianic
salvation and cosmic renewal. The "turning point of the
ages" in Christ's advent to earth and glory meant inevitably
that Jesus Christ would be the shorthand expression for that
new age, and that Christian faith in its first formulation
would be almost exclusively christocentric.

But we must be cautious and fair to the evidence. The
cultus that focused on Christ living in the midst of his people
was not a Jesus-cult. There was no compromise to basic Old
Testament monotheism, however much the new order of the
Spirit has antiquated the "dispensation of the old covenant"
(2 Cor. 3:6-7). If Jesus Christ is Lord, it is to the glory of God
the Father (Phil. 2:11).

Finally, it would be truer to say that New Testament creeds
are incipiently trinitarian. God is one, and Jesus Christ is Lord
and even God (though not so patently hailed as in Ignatius
and Justin); yet the Spirit is also divine and at least function-
ally clothed with attributes and characteristics that place him
on God's side as his agent and gracious presence in human
experience. There are the "raw materials" of the dogma of
the Trinity in sections such as Matthew 28:19; 2 Corinthians
13:14; and Ephesians 2:18, texts which will be before us later.
And it is a sure Christian instinct that these liturgical texts bid
us to reflect on the mystery of the three-in-one as we confess
and enact the adoration of the triune God.

> To the Father through the Son and in the Holy Spirit, is the underlying
> pattern of the history of salvation. So is it too of the liturgy.[16]

16. J. D. Crichton, "A Theology of Worship," in *The Study of
Liturgy*, ed. C. Jones, G. Wainwright, E. Yarnold (London: SPCK, 1978),
p. 19.

Creeds in the Church

The role of creeds has been one of gradual change. We can tabulate several ways in which the creeds have served purposes appropriate to the needs of the church at various times.

1. As we noted in a previous section, the most likely lifesetting of the New Testament creeds was that of baptism. This may be called *the initiatory* or *declaratory use* of symbolic forms. The "confession" of Romans 10:9 most probably belongs here. And perhaps too the situations envisaged by 1 Peter 3:21; 1 Timothy 6:12; Hebrews 4:14; and Ephesians 1:13; 5:26 relate to words spoken at the new convert's profession of faith made at baptism. The dialogue pattern of Acts 8:36-38, where Philip's question is met by the eunuch's response (in the western text), sets the stage for later development. In place of a single one question—one answer format more complex interrogations are found in Justin where passages in *Apology* 46, 61 seem to reflect a threefold interrogation. J. N. D. Kelly reconstructs these as:

> Do you believe in the Father and Lord God of the universe?
> Do you believe in Jesus Christ our saviour who was crucified under Pontius Pilate?
> Do you believe in the Holy Spirit, who spoke by the prophets?[17]

We may note the trinitarian structure of these interrogations; and presumably the ensuing baptism was administered in the triune name, after the manner of Matthew 28:19.

The same trinitarian form is seen in Irenaeus who at the beginning of his tractate *Epideixis* stresses the importance of faith in this manner:

> First of all, it bids us bear in mind that we have received baptism for the remission of sins in the name of God the Father, and in the name of Jesus Christ the son of God, who was incarnate and died and rose again, and in the Holy Spirit of God.[18]

A later reference to "the baptism of our regeneration [which] proceeds through three points"[19] or articles confirms that a series of baptismal questions was apparently part and parcel of the initiatory rite.

The suggestion is clinched by the data of Hippolytus'

17. J. N. D. Kelly, *Early Christian Creeds*, p. 73.
18. Irenaeus, *Epideixis* ch. 3, cited in Kelly, *Early Christian Creeds*, p. 77.
19. Irenaeus, *Epideixis*, ch. 7.

Apostolic Tradition, which are noteworthy as expressing
credal theology current in the church at Rome around the
year A.D. 200 and as containing an expanded version of the
trinitarian formula. Equally impressive is the threefold act of
baptism, following on each separate interrogation:

> Do you believe in one God the Father Almighty?
> [Or this may have been an affirmation sponsored by the deacon who
> assisted the baptizand]
>
> I believe in this way [baptism follows]
>
> Do you believe in Christ Jesus, the son of God, who was born from the
> holy Spirit from the virgin Mary, and was crucified under Pontius Pilate,
> and died, and rose again on the third day alive from the dead, and
> ascended into heaven, and sits at the right hand of the Father, and will
> come to judge the living and the dead?
>
> I believe [baptism repeated]
>
> Do you believe in the holy Spirit and the holy church and the resurrec-
> tion of the flesh?
>
> I believe [baptism a third time]

The same basic layout of a trinitarian statement is found in
the best known of all creeds, surnamed *The Apostles' Creed.*
The pious notion that this noble declaration originated with
the twelve apostles is found in the Latin author Rufinus who
wrote an exposition of its wording in *c.* A.D. 404, and in
pseudo-Augustine who developed the idea that each part of
the creed was contributed by a separate member of the
apostolic band: twelve apostles each in turn offering the
twelve clauses. We should observe the motive behind this
legend, which is to attach apostolic authority to the creed. In
fact, this particular creed has a long history behind it and its
wording seems to reflect the creed known at Rome in the second century.

The Old Roman creed that developed into the full-blown
Apostles' Creed by the late sixth or early seventh century and
became, probably through the influence of Charlemagne,
the official creed of the entire western church that he sought
to unify, functioned as a baptismal profession. Its pattern was

dictated, says Kelly,[20] by the Lord's threefold baptismal command, and its content was limited to those fundamental truths about God the Father, Christ Jesus his son, and the Holy Spirit which the church had either inherited from its Jewish past or received on the authority of New Testament Scripture.

But the Apostles' Creed is clearly marked out as a polemical document; it insists against a Gnostic devaluation of the world that God is "the Father almighty, maker of heaven and earth." Even if the last phrase is a later expansion, clearly the attribute of "almighty" (Greek *pantokratōr)* speaks of God's work in creation; and Irenaeus uses this name in his debate with the Gnostics who imagined a series of divine beings or emanations stretching between heaven and earth and only loosely under God's control. More clearly still, Jesus' divine sonship is cherished, but not at the expense of his humanity ("born . . . from the virgin Mary") and real death on the cross ("who under Pontius Pilate was crucified and buried"; the later text adds "suffered"). While it is not sufficient to explain the insertion of these clauses solely on the ground of their antidocetic (i.e., humanity-asserting) thrust, it still is true that second-century writers such as Ignatius and Irenaeus strenuously insist on the reality of the Lord's suffering and death in opposition to the docetists, for whom his passion was simply an illusion or an act of make-believe, impossible to associate with the divine who by definition cannot suffer. Dr. Kelly cautions against exaggerating this emphasis on the creed's polemics, but its major statements are still there as a bastion against the error of losing contact with empirical history and concrete reality. The declaratory expressions continue throughout the document to stress precisely those items in the Christian faith that caused offence in antiquity (resurrection, both Christ's and the believer's; judgment; the remission of sins). They served to give shape to a presentation of the early kerygma in terms of what was distinctive in an atmosphere where these emphases were most called for. Thus important matters such as the teaching of Jesus, the atonement, and the eucharist have been passed over—indeed, for

20. J. N. D. Kelly, *Early Christian Creeds,* p. 165.

various other reasons, such as in the case of the eucharist, the need to preserve the "rule of secrecy" *(disciplina arcani)* by which the church's sacred meal was not openly divulged to the public but restricted to the committed faithful.

The merging together of an initiatory setting (the creed as "confessed" in baptism) and a declaratory purpose (the creed as "handed over"—*redditio symboli,* as it is called—to new believers) seems to account for the way the Apostles' Creed evolved and became valued. It served as a "symbol" of the church's indebtedness to the past, specifically the apostolic era, and its awareness of present needs in the shape of false motives to be exposed and answered, as well as disputed elements in its faith to be highlighted and defended.

2. The use of creeds as *tests of orthodoxy* supplying a *recapitulatory role* establishes a clear landmark in the growth of credal theology. To be sure, in this area the polemical note is much to the fore, with the turning point coming at the council of Nicaea in A.D. 325. There "the custom became established . . . for ecclesiastics meeting in solemn conclave to frame formularies giving utterance to their agreement on matters of faith."[21] Such products were intended to have the weight of a more-than-local authority and to serve as tests of orthodoxy of Christians everywhere. The newer role of the creed is neatly summed up in C. H. Turner's dictum: "the old creeds were creeds for catechumens, the new creed was a creed for bishops"[22] as exponents of sound doctrine.

Not surprisingly, therefore, the creed grew considerably in complexity and in length. Heresies dealing with the person of Christ, which began with the debate between the followers of Arius, a leader in Alexandria, and his bishop Alexander, quickly assumed large-scale proportions, leading to the Council of Nicaea. There the password of orthodoxy, the term *homoousios* ("of the same substance"), was added to the existing local creeds to rule out Arius' notions of Jesus as merely a created being. As the discussion raged, producing several intermediate positions between Arius and Athanasius, the champion of Alexandrian orthodoxy, the second general

21. J. N. D. Kelly, *Early Christian Creeds,* p. 205.
22. C. H. Turner, *History and Use of Creeds and Anathemas in the Early Centuries of the Church* (London, 1910), p. 24.

council called at Constantinople in A.D. 381 reaffirmed the Nicene Creed and slightly augmented it. This is the form now used in the eastern church, and since that part of the church has never accepted the Apostles' Creed, the Nicene Creed has the distinction of being the sole exemplar of an ecumenical creed. Its heart is seen in the clause:

> We believe . . . in one Lord Jesus Christ, the only-begotten Son of God, begotten from the Father before all ages, light from light, true God from true God, begotten, not made, of one substance *[homoousios]* with the Father . . . .

As a weapon in defense of eastern orthodoxy touching the person of the Lord, the Nicene-Constantinopolitan Creed obviously was important, and it was introduced into the eucharistic service of the Byzantine churches in the early sixth century. Strangely, it became a weapon of a different sort. Originally fashioned to repel the Arians, the creed took on a role as a propaganda instrument for monophysitism, a tendency that exalted the divinity of Christ into the extremes of Apollinarius' position. He stressed the deity of Christ in such a fashion that the Lord's human nature was obscured and reduced almost to a vanishing point.

We may complete the story by remarking that the church "came back" to a centralist position by adopting—at the Council of Chalcedon (A.D. 451)—the so-termed Athanasian Creed, which emphasized the equality of the persons within the Godhead and sharpened the focus of Christ's person by its (Chalcedonian) formula of "one person, two natures" as a counterblast against the excesses that either minimized or maximized either the divine or the human in our Lord. Yet the inclusion of a "double procession" teaching, attributing the coming of the Spirit "from the son" (the *filioque* clause) meant that a less-than-universal acceptance throughout christendom was inevitable; and in the western church this "Athanasian" creed only gradually became acceptable for occasional use in public worship.

In the tangle of these convoluted debates and discussions that preoccupied bishops, theologians, and even lay folk during the first five centuries,[23] it is easy to see how creeds acted

23. See J. S. Whale, *Christian Doctrine* (Cambridge: University Press, 1941), p. 111, who quotes Gregory of Nyssa's scathing caricature of the amateur theologians in Constantinople in the fourth century.

both as repositories of dogma and as catalysts for continuing change in the formulation of Christian beliefs. What is less obvious is the role the creeds continued to play as part of the ongoing worship of the people of God.

3. The *doxological place* of the creeds reminds us that a creed, in its proper liturgical setting, is akin to a hymn. One argument for the original Latin version of the Old Roman Creed was that the Latin text has rhythmic qualities that are not present in the Greek text. The case for the original rhythmical composition of the creed is doubtful, but at least one ancient author, Faustus of Riez, has a phrase in which he describes it as a *carmen* or hymn—that is to give it its appropriate title. We are summoned to "offer" the creed to God—"to render it to the Lord," as Augustine counsels—as part of our worship. As a fitting tribute of praise, set in the liturgy, the creed gained a place in the daily and weekly office, though the exact position in the service varied. The Spanish position in the Mozarabic *missale* is before the communion, and the priest's reminder, "Let us say with our lips what we believe in our hearts," is an act of preparation. In the Roman order of worship the creed comes after the gospel (or later, after the homily) and so expresses the congregation's reception of the Christian message. Thus a person's baptismal faith is "repeated" and witness is borne. A daily reciting of the creed became for Augustine a part of his practice of submitting the entire day to God;[24] thence it entered the monastic daily liturgy in the West and eventually the Episcopalian *Book of Common Prayer* and other Protestant service books.

Problems with Creeds

An honest appraisal of the use and significance of "symbols" in the long haul of Christian history raises some questions of a critical nature. We have sought to accentuate the positive. Now we must turn to consider inherent dangers in the way creeds—and particularly later "confessions"—have been used. Here the distinction is important, since historically

24. See the references given in G. Wainwright, *Doxology. The Praise of God in Worship, Doctrine and Life* (London: Epworth Press; New York: Oxford University Press, 1980), pp. 187, 188.

creeds have been used as much to confess unity as to create it, whereas "confessions of faith" or "articles of religion" have emerged to define a given denomination's or sect's position over against its rivals or its opponents. The accent changes in such documents: it stresses the distinctives; the statement of faith is devised as a teaching vehicle; and it is frequently cast in an overtly polemical tone. This fact of history leads us to think about the three ways the creeds have posed problems and have become a disruptive, not to say destructive, force in the life of Christians.

First, it is a sad commentary on the perversity of human nature that we can give expression to lofty truths and yet remain uncommitted to what those truths really say in terms of their effect upon our lives. A "dead" orthodoxy is an unlovely thing, yet there are too many examples of what happens when the creed is recited with the lips or understood in the mind but not offered as an expression of living faith. Personal commitment—which is what the creeds were designed to articulate—can easily hide behind a merely correct form of words. The result inevitably is spiritual disaster.

Second, creeds have grown in size and scope, and in that process have taken on a combative role as they are employed as instruments of division and strife. The more refined they have become, the more insidious has been their use, not only for defining a church's stance on controversial matters but as a weapon to beat the head of the opposition.

Third, the outcome has been a tragic imbalance in Christian doctrine, as creeds have attempted to say too much and so to add to the minimal "requirements" for both personal salvation and the preservation of the evangelical truth by which the church lives. We all have to reckon with the existence of *adiaphora,* that is, matters of belief and practice on which there is disagreement in the church but which belong to the periphery of the gospel as most Christians maintain. We can illustrate this by reference to items such as the doctrine of the ministry, episcopal and otherwise; the theology and practice of baptism; the schemes of eschatology that attempt to set the future course of world events into a framework; and the validity and purpose of the "gifts of the Spirit" (Greek *charismata).* To build a creed around such matters is to invite immediate disputation over whether these

concerns are at the center or the circumference of the faith.
And the larger the creed is made to embrace these questions,
the more divisive the consequences.

Two warning lights flash at this point. One is that a creed,
however august and authoritative its pedigree, tends to
replace the role of Scripture as a *norma normans*, that is, as a
controlling authority. The way the Apostles' Creed escapes
such an indictment is correctly noted by Calvin:

> The whole history of our faith is summed up in it succinctly and in
> definite order, and . . . it contains nothing that is not vouched for by
> genuine testimonies of Scripture.[25]

The other unhappy result of an overemphasis on the fine
details and minutiae of credal statements is that Christ is
shunted out to the periphery. Calvin again spotted this
danger, and in defense of the Apostles' Creed maintained
that "Christ alone in all the clauses of the Creed" was its
safeguard and guarantee. His warning remains timely for our
day:

> . . . even if [some men not content with Christ] concern themselves
> chiefly with him, they nevertheless stray from the right way in turning
> some part of their thinking in another direction.[26]

The thrust of Calvin's rebuke is to keep the church on the
central track, which is Christ himself, and in effect to contend
that Christ in his person and all his offices remains the core of
Christianity. The earliest Christian symbol—the acrostic of
the word "fish" (Greek *ichthus*), meaning "Jesus Christ [is]
the son of God, the Savior"—after two thousand years of
Christian infighting and struggling to express the saving
truth, remains the best, because most adequate, expression of
what we confess in the worship and praise of God.

25. Calvin, *Institutes II*.xvi.18.
26. *Institutes II*.xvi.19.

CHAPTER SEVEN

The Role
of the Sermon

In the Beginning was the Sermon
This provocative dictum of the form critics reminds us that there is nothing in early Christianity more basic to its life than oral proclamation of what is called God's word. As far back as we can trace "Christian origins" in the church's life there never was a time when the sermon was lacking. Those who today are swift to cry that "the day of the sermon is over" may well ponder that fact of history. The first church came on the scene following the example of its Lord: it appeared "preaching the gospel" (see Mark 1:14, 15).

A sharp point is put on this contention by D. W. Cleverley Ford who stresses the novelty of preaching in the biblical story. Not that the people of Israel was without her preachers; clearly there was an honored succession of prophets who wore the preacher's mantle. But "preaching entered late into the life of ancient Israel, but it was there from the start in the life of the new Israel, the Church."[1]

The first chapter of church history is written on the day of Pentecost, when the Spirit came in a new way and the church, already in embryo, came forth. Not unexpectedly, since the church owes its existence to Christ her risen Lord, the church's birthday was celebrated with a sermon, as Peter got to his feet and explained the significance of that day in terms of the dawn of a new age. So it may be said with some confidence:

> No Church existed without, or apart from preaching; the Church came to birth *with preaching* and preaching came to birth *with the Church*.[2]

1. D. W. Cleverley Ford, *The Ministry of the Word* (Grand Rapids: Wm. B. Eerdmans, 1979), p. 53.
2. Cleverley Ford, *Ministry,* p. 53 (his italics).

Preaching as a medium of communication and a conveyance of divine truth to men is, of course, much older than Christianity. Seers and holy persons were highly regarded in the world of antiquity. Oracles were given at shrines such as Delphi and Epidaurus, while soothsayers and fortune-tellers claimed to have access to divine mysteries which they would reveal for a price. One graphic example comes in the scene at Philippi (Acts 16:16-22) where a girl ventriloquist possessed the "spirit of Python" and gave oracles: "she earned a lot of money for her owners by telling fortunes." Simon also lived handsomely from the practice of oracle-mongering in Samaria (Acts 8:9-13), and acquired a reputation as "that power of God known as 'The Great Power'." Itinerant teachers and prophets known collectively as "holy" or "divine" men flourished in Greco-Roman society.

At a different level, the prophets of Israel came with oracles that enshrined "the word of Yahweh." They too had their competitors in the person of those branded as "false prophets" by the writing prophets such as Micah and Jeremiah. It is not a simple matter to discern the criteria used to separate "true" from "false" prophets in Israel. Both groups claimed to convey "the word of Yahweh," as we see from the story in 1 Kings 22. Yet the test of credibility was not as straightforward as "Does his oracle speak of events that come to pass?" as Deuteronomy chapter 13 indicates. The deeper issue was evidently one of the prophet's character and personal integrity, which decided the question whether or not his claim to divine inspiration and authority was accepted. In later Judaism the test became one of fidelity to Torah, God's holy law, as the religion of the intertestamental period became increasingly one of a sacred book and its interpretation, believed to be an unerring guide to daily living.

Out of this situation the synagogue was born. Worship in the synagogue has always given pride of place to instruction based on Scripture readings and their expositions. Lections from Torah and the Prophets form the staple diet of Jewish liturgy. Aramaic paraphrases known as the Targums were intended to make these lessons understandable to the people who were more at home with spoken Aramaic than with biblical Hebrew. The rabbi's sermon was a homily designed specifically to elucidate and enforce the Scripture texts which preceded it in the order of worship.[3] But the homily still held a lower rank than the actual readings of Scripture, and it was given only if a person competent to give the exposition was present. This explains the scene in the synagogue at Pisidian Antioch (Acts 13:15), where Paul is invited to give a "word of exhortation" to the assembled congregation.

The speeches reported in the book of Acts present problems of several kinds. There is above all the matter whether they are authentic and verbatim records of what was said on those occasions or Luke's own inventive creations, based (it may be) on traditions he had received. The truth lies somewhere in the middle between these extremes, and allowing for Luke's own style and phrasing to show through the texture of his writing, we may still believe that he is giving us a faithful account of what early Christian preaching was like. The best way to look at these speeches[4] is to see in them *exempla* of what Luke regarded as models of Christian proclamation directed to different audiences but with each type of preaching being relevant for the church of his own day.[5] Thus there are speeches devoted to proclaiming a message suitable for a Jewish audience set in Jerusalem (Acts chs. 2, 7), a congregation in the world of the Jewish Dispersion (Acts 13), a motley crowd in pagan Lystra (Acts 14), a group of intellectuals in Athens (Acts 17), as well as a distinctively Christian gathering at Miletus (Acts 20). Not surprisingly, the motifs and lines of appeal in each case vary according to the type of audience present. But there are certain "constants," and these may well have formed a skeleton or frame of the "proclaimed message" (the *kerygma,* as Paul calls it in 1 Cor. 1:21).

3. G. W. Buchanan, "Worship, Feasts and Ceremonies in the Early Jewish-Christian Church," *NTS* 26 (1980), pp. 279-297 (p. 291: rabbinic homilies were interpretations of scripture designed to meet the current needs of the community, based on 2 Chron. 17:9).

4. In agreement with I. H. Marshall, *Acts*, Tyndale NT Commentary (Grand Rapids: Wm. B. Eerdmans, 1980), p. 33.

5. C. K. Barrett evaluates the motif of Luke's reporting like this: "If only Christians at the end of the century would preach like Peter and Paul, and live like Joseph Barnabas, all would be well!" ("*Theologia Crucis*—in Acts?" in *Theologia Crucis—Signum Crucis,* Festschrift für Erich Dinkler, ed. C. Andresen and G. Klein [Tübingen: J. C. B. Mohr, 1979], pp. 73-84 [p. 78]).

The Kerygma

Since the publication in 1936 of C. H. Dodd's seminal study *The Apostolic Preaching and its Developments*,[6] the debate over the precise configuration and content of early Christian preaching has been carried on over several generations with little by way of settled consensus emerging. Among the matters on which there is some measure of agreement is that the first preachers did (1) appeal to certain facts of recent history in which the life of Jesus of Nazareth was pivotal. Or, more precisely, the "event" of Christ as summing up a complex of happenings that involved Jesus' coming to earth, his death on the cross, and his exaltation to reign as Lord stood at the center of the proclamation. Moreover (2), the appeal was not made to "bare" facts but to happenings that were already clothed with a theological interpretation, asserting that in these "events" God himself was acting and was personally present. He "was in Christ reconciling the world to himself"—Paul's way of stating a piece of traditional teaching (2 Cor. 5:19). (3) And the invoking of such events was not intended just to inform the hearers but to move them to action. The kerygma was presented as a gracious offer, or sometimes as an imperious summons, but always designed to elicit a response, whether of acceptance or refusal. Paul can set the matter in clear light by comparing the two roads, either to salvation or to destruction (1 Cor. 1:18), or contrasting the double effect of his apostolic service as a "savor of life" or a "stench of death" (2 Cor. 2:15, 16). There is always an implicit "call to decision."

The apostle Paul is the great exponent of the "kerygma" that he believed God had entrusted to him, though, as he admitted, he was not part of the first generation of preachers (Rom. 16:1-16). He had "received" by tradition what he saw as his privilege and duty to hand on (1 Cor. 15:1-11). Nonetheless, it is Paul who gives the clearest expression to the theological rationale of preaching. Not simply is it that he heard God's call and answered it (Gal. 1:15, 16); nor that he discovered the secret of his life's work in preaching (1 Cor. 9:16). Rather, he came to see that in the proclamation of this message God was himself present: "God makes his appeal

6. London: Hodder and Stoughton.

through us'' (2 Cor. 5:20). The daring claim to be acting and speaking for God would be audacious enough; Paul's wording goes beyond that as he reverses the roles and insists that when he speaks the kerygma God himself is the chief actor and it is his voice that men and women hear and his authority that is brought to bear upon people's lives, claiming their allegiance. James Daane illustrates the striking audacity of Paul's high regard of preaching from Jesus' own teaching:[7] ''Whoever listens to you listens to me; whoever rejects you rejects me; and whoever rejects me rejects the one who sent me'' (Luke 10:16).

Recent studies on ''Paul the preacher'' have focused on the principal supports that buttressed his office as an apostle of the kerygma. In particular three matters stand out:

1. Paul's call and the exercise of his ministry are alike predicated on the *resurrection of Jesus*. The risen Lord summoned him to new life before the city gates of Damascus, according to the stories in Acts, and Paul renews the link between the reality of the exalted Christ and his vocation in 1 Corinthians 9:1: ''Am I not an apostle? Haven't I seen Jesus our Lord?'' The two rhetorical questions are meant to be taken together. As the presence and power of the resurrected Christ were a vivid reality to this man—see how he sums up his aspiration in Philippians 3:10—so he set the risen Lord at the center of his message to both his Jewish compatriots and his Gentile audiences (1 Thess. 1:9, 10; 1 Cor. 15:11, 12-19; Rom. 8:34). The reason for the centrality of the resurrection is not that thereby a man came back to life after death, but that in that act God was at work inaugurating a new eon of world history.

2. Paul's proclamation relied heavily on *the Spirit* who indeed is hardly distinguished at the level of experience from the exalted Christ (2 Cor. 3:17, 18). But the Spirit gave a dynamic to Paul's words that produced a powerful effect on the hearers, as is clear from the extended treatment in 1 Corinthians 2:3-14. The resources of a skilled orator and

7. J. Daane, *Preaching with Confidence* (Grand Rapids: Wm. B. Eerdmans, 1980).

debater were not sufficient, nor was an appeal to "human wisdom" legitimate for Paul, the herald of the cross. He deliberately renounced such devices and placed his confidence in "the power of God's Spirit" (1 Cor. 2:4), with the result that the faith of his listeners came to repose not on a human base but on "God's power." Paul even claimed that his actual words were "taught by the Spirit" (v. 13), and were appreciated by those who also possessed the Spirit. The second part of his affirmation is interesting, since it implies that he did not have a unique gift but only in special measure the gift of the Spirit common to all God's people. Paul expected his followers to be on the same "wavelength" as himself. And this factor or dimension gave to Christians an ability to discern the truth for themselves (v. 15; cf. 1 Thess. 5:21; 1 Cor. 12:10).

    3. The chief burden of Paul's preaching may be described as *reconciliation*.[8] In fact, this is exactly the term he used to denote his work; he is charged to fulfill a "ministry of reconciliation" (2 Cor. 5:18). The basic meaning of such a ministry is given in a modern rendering of the verse: "God . . . has changed us from enemies into his friends and gave us the task of making others his friends also." The task has a theme, explicitly stated as one "which tells how he makes them [humankind] his friends" (v. 19). The detail of how this transformation came about is elaborated in some neighboring verses, namely, God's action took place in Christ who was innocent of any wrong, and perfect. Yet in a mysterious "transaction" (in the words of a second-century writer, "O sweet exchange!"), the sinless Christ assumed the penal consequences of evil so that those who are united to him may share in God's righteousness and be restored to his favor. This way of expressing Paul's teaching owes much to A. M. Hunter. The latter comments on the adjective "penal": "Christ's suffering was 'penal' in the sense that he had to realize to the full the divine reaction against sin in the human race in which he was incorporated, and to which he had be-

---

8. See R. P. Martin, *Reconciliation: A Study of Paul's Theology* (Atlanta: John Knox Press; London: Marshall, Morgan and Scott, 1981) for details of this argument.

trothed himself for better, for worse.''[9] In this thumbnail sketch of Paul's kerygma (which owes much, in my view, to a traditional piece of soteriology on which Paul is drawing, especially in his citation of the appeal "Be reconciled to God" addressed to Christians at Corinth) there are several important items left without an explicit mention. Fortunately we can supply the "missing" teaching by referring to several other places where the concept of reconciliation is found in the Pauline "library."

In Romans 5:1-10 Paul places a double emphasis on divine love as the originating force behind the reconciliation of the world. God's love is poured into human lives by the Spirit, thus effecting a life-changing renewal and not simply a legal acquittal (the normal sense given to "justification"); and that love is shown in all its strength and depth in what God did for us as sinners—Christ died for us (v. 8). The stately piece in Colossians 1:15-20 adds yet another dimension to reconciliation. The work of the cosmic Lord is seen not only in the world's creation and preservation in holding it in being; it is displayed in the universal redemption by Christ's cross. By that one death God and the world, torn asunder by the world's submission to alien and demonic powers, are reunited and so "reconciled," with no part of creation, angelic, human, or demonic left outside the scope of God's grand design. The same picture of Christ's lordly control of all that is dominates the Ephesian letter but with a special relevance to a pressing situation in the church. The "enmity" that kept men and women from God is overcome in Christ; and the author sees a pointed illustration or dramatization of cosmic salvation in the fact of a new society of the church wherein barriers of ethnic superiority and racial disharmony melt away before the emergent reality of "one new people" (Eph. 2:11-22). These people are neither Jews nor Gentiles, but make up a third race of men and women in union with Christ, reconciled to God and to one another, and offering a new form of worship as God's holy temple. The barrier that kept Gentiles at a distance from Israel's God, symbolized in

9. A. M. Hunter, *Interpreting Paul's Gospel* (London: SCM Press, 1954), p. 92.

the wall around the inner court of the Jerusalem sanctuary, is now done away in Christ. Henceforth worship is set on a fresh base as freely available to all peoples and freely rendered by a transnational, multiracial community in the Spirit. The net result of these different applications of Christ's work as reconciler is to show how Paul's gospel had a much wider range than is normally associated with "the kerygma." The proclamation of Christ that is Paul's forte reached out from its basis of forgiveness by the cross and resurrection to embrace cosmic and ethnic realms where the same uniting work of Christ is seen at work alongside his concern to bring men and women back to the family and fellowship of God.

One other side needs mentioning, since it is hardly less important for Paul. With all his concentration on the final achievement of Christ's reconciliation of the world, Paul still leaves room for human response in his use of the kerygmatic formula "Be reconciled to God"; otherwise the grace of God seemingly goes for nothing (2 Cor. 6:1). To demonstrate the role of the preacher who in his person brings God and humankind together by the kerygma he is charged to make known, Paul holds up himself as a reconciling agent, notably at Corinth (see 2 Cor. 2:5-11), and builds his gospel—as far as its application to the situation at Corinth is concerned—on the ground that he had already extended in Christ's presence and name his forgiveness to the offending party. A concrete illustration of Paul's intermediary role underlies his connections with both Onesimus and Philemon; in that delicate network of personal relationships Paul acts as a link-person, uniting both estranged parties of master and slave; and he does so *in loco Dei,* as the representative and exemplar of how God deals with erring men and women.

Various Types of Preaching

The New Testament lexicon is replete with a lot of other terms for what is generally labeled "preaching." We have noted the primacy of the kerygma as the offer and demand on the "good news" that came with Jesus Christ and which he in turn embodied in his person and ministry (Mark 1:15 contains several nuances of understanding where the word *euangelion,* good news, is concerned). If the epitome of the *euangelion* is God's concern for his creation, sadly alienated and in distress, and all he has accomplished to restore human integrity, dignity, and freedom in his family as he now welcomes them back as pardoned and renewed children, then there is not a great deal of difference between Jesus' message and ministry and Paul's explication of it in terms of redemption, justification, and new life. A common term uniting these several idioms would be salvation, or better, reconciliation. We find here some easing of the dilemma that faces the thoughtful modern preacher who wonders how he or she is to preach the gospel from the Gospels. Are we delivered over to R. W. Dale's solution that "While He came to preach the gospel, His chief object in coming was that there might be a gospel to preach"?[10]

No such answer seems viable, or necessary, once we detect lines of continuity that run from Jesus' call, "Follow me," and his concern for the outcasts, the despised, and the "sinners" in Israel by way of the cross and the resurrection—where that message is "played out" in the drama of God's love in action making concrete in one focal point its strength and victory—on to Paul's kerygma.

The foundation laid by this "good news" has already built into it the promise of new life and how that life-in-Christ is to be worked out. The remaining terms, most of them technical expressions, simply unfold how the first believers understood and applied their "receiving Christ" (Col. 2:6) and "walking in him" (Col. 2:7).

1. "Teaching" (Greek *didachē*) is a term self-evidently indicating the way that discipleship took on an added meaning. The initial response to the call "Follow me" led naturally to an enrollment in and membership of the school of Christ. "Come to me" was quickly followed by "learn from me" (Matt. 11:28, 29); and "the law of Christ" (Gal. 6:2) became a new norm of Christian living in a context that magnified the office of the teacher (Gal. 6:6). An even higher dignity is seen in 1 Corinthians 12:28 and Ephesians 4:11 where "pastors and teachers" refers to one function.

10. R. W. Dale, *The Atonement* (London: Congregational Union of England and Wales, 1900), p. 46. On the contrary, see G. R. Beasley-Murray, *Preaching the Gospel from the Gospels* (London: Lutterworth Press, 1956).

Thus, the role of the teacher was highly regarded in the Pauline churches whose life we encounter in the Pastoral epistles (2 Tim. 2:2), and Timothy is himself to exercise the gift of instructing others in the faith (1 Tim. 4:6-16).

2. The other side of the coin that extolled the merits of the teaching office speaks of the value of training new converts in their life as members of the body. The Greek word is *katēchesis,* which produces the English "catechism," "catechumen." The term has to do with the education and discipline of those who were under the teacher's authority and control, as those "being taught the Christian message" (Gal. 6:6). Interested enquirers and seekers were given instruction in Christian belief and practice in anticipation of the day when they would be ready to accept full privileges and responsibilities as church members. There is a Jewish precedent for this procedure, as interested Gentile converts were trained in preparation for proselyte baptism. Several parts of the New Testament reflect the existence of a rudimentary catechumenate (Acts 8:32-37; 18:25; 20:20; Col. 1:6; Eph. 4:20f.; 1 Peter 2:2; 5:1; 1 John 2:12-24). The most notable example of a person "under instruction" is Theophilus, who is spoken of in Luke 1:4 as "being taught" as a catechumen.

3. *Paraklēsis* is an omnibus word covering a wide range of meanings, with its basic sense being "exhortation."[11] The most revealing "job description" of the prophet in the Pauline mission churches is given in 1 Corinthians 14:3: "The one who proclaims God's message [Greek *ho prophēteuōn*] speaks to people and gives them help [lit. "upbuilding"], encouragement [Greek *paraklēsis*] and comfort." The Pauline prophet was evidently a charismatic figure, endowed with some authority to lead the congregation into a deeper understanding of the divine mind and will. This enterprise was carried through in reliance on the Spirit as much as in the case of the glossolalic's ministry with a "tongue"; and in both instances Paul's chief concern was to secure the growth and well-being of the assembly according to its needs. There were prophets who discharged a ministry of prediction, such

11. See David Hill, *New Testament Prophecy* (Atlanta; John Knox Press; London: Marshall, Morgan and Scott, 1979), pp. 128, 129.

as Agabus (Acts 11:27, 28; 21:10) and the seer of the Apocalypse (Rev. 1:1-3; 22:9). But Paul's main emphasis lay on a
clear-sighted address to the congregation who by these
prophets were both instructed and stimulated to the action of
doing God's will. The gift of prophecy was a *charisma*, to be
sure; for Paul it was best exercised with the good of the entire
church in view. Perhaps its modern counterpart is "preaching" when it is "done" at its highest level. The bishop in the
pre-Nicene church is called a "prophetic-teacher" (*Martyrdom of Polycarp* 16), a title parallel with the way the minister
functions today.

4. The Greek word *paraenesis* is not found in New
Testament vocabulary, although the corresponding verb
appears once or twice in a nonsignificant context (Acts 27:9,
22; Luke 3:18 as a secondary textual reading) meaning "to
advise, recommend, urge." The noun speaks of "moral instruction with a dash of exhortation," a definition that neatly
combines elements of a patient unfolding of truth and an
earnest plea that such facts should become factors in encouraging young Christians to action and endeavor. One of the
characteristic features of New Testament *paraenesis* is that the
teaching is set in an eschatological framework. Christians are
exhorted to live in a way pleasing to God (1 Thess. 4:1) in the
light of the Lord's presence both in the congregation and at
his parousia or expected return in glory (1 Thess. 4:15-18; 1
Cor. 7:29-31). With the waning of the hope of an imminent
parousia, Christian instruction became more codified and for-
malized into "regulations for the household" such as we see
in Colossians 3:18-4:1 and in the Pastoral Epistles. These
"house-codes" (*Haustafeln*, a term borrowed from Luther)
show how Christian ethics is coming to terms with a less
enthusiastic, world-denying type of Christianity and learning
to accommodate itself to continued life in the social order.
Doubtless the teaching of these "station codes" (i.e., let
everyone live worthily according to his or her "place" in
society), was often enforced by preachers in the congregation.

5. The ingredient of "witness" (Greek *martyria*)
should not be left out when we ask what were the constituents of early Christian preaching. T. F. Glasson's insistence
that early preaching included this note, which is frequently

sounded in the speeches in Acts, is well argued.[12] The personal endorsement of the preacher's own experience ("This very Jesus [God raised from death], and we are all witnesses to this fact," Acts 2:32) would add a telling verisimilitude to what was proclaimed as historical truth with claims on the hearers' attention and allegiance. While we should not say that the apostles proclaimed their own experience as a ground for the acceptance of their message, that inalienably personal and yet impressively corporate witness could not fail to lend weight to their argument and appeal—as we see Paul maintaining in the list of resurrection witnesses (in 1 Cor. 15:1-11).

> What we have felt and seen.
> With confidence we tell,
> And publish to the sons of men
> The signs infallible. (Charles Wesley)

6. A word akin to "witness" is "confession" (Greek *homologia*). It has associations of a credal character, as can be seen from the introduction to 1 Timothy 3:16: "The mystery [or divine secret] of our faith is *confessedly* great." The adverb prepares the way for a stately six-line creed of the incarnation and triumph of the one who appeared on earth and is now elevated to glory. Scattered allusions to the "faith we confess" (Rom. 10:9; 1 Tim. 6:12; 1 John 4:2f., 15; Heb. 3:1; 4:14; 10:23) show that such statements were evidently learned in a catechetical setting as part of a believer's training and preparation to understand what his acceptance of new life in Christ meant on its doctrinal side. And that implies the presence of an instructor to tell him. What he learned would help him to render a "good confession," especially when persecution for the faith put Christians on their guard.

We have combed the documents of the New Testament church to see how varied was the ministry of preaching. The logical starting place was preaching in a context of initial evangelism with its opportunities to make known the good news and call hearers to the "obedience of faith." Thereafter

12. T. F. Glasson, "The Kerygma: Is our Version Correct?" *Hibbert Journal* 51 (1953), pp. 129-172. See also A. A. Trites, *The New Testament Concept of Witness* (Cambridge: University Press, 1977).

in some kind of "training sessions" young converts were edu-
cated in the school of Christ in what later became a "preparation class" leading to baptism, first communion, and church
membership. Learning to live in society and accepting
behavior patterns in the household were prominent items in
the curriculum. As Christians stepped out into a hostile world
they were encouraged to witness boldly and if need be to
"confess the faith" when they faced the prospect of trial and
martyrdom.

The Historical Shape of the Sermon

In the history of preaching several "shapes" or "styles" the
sermon can take on have been observed and studied. The
most obvious kind of sermon is the *expository*. It aims to
"expound" or explain a passage of Scripture, usually with an
application to make the incident or teaching relevant to
present-day concerns.

This style of preaching may claim a long pedigree going
back to Justin whose account of worship in the mid-second-
century Rome is one of the earliest on record. He describes it
this way (in *1 Apology*, 67):

> On the day called Sunday there is a meeting in one place of those who
> live in cities or the country, and the memoirs of the apostles or the
> writings of the prophets are read as long as time permits. When the
> reader is finished, the president in a discourse urges and invites [us] to
> the imitation of these noble things. Then we all stand up and offer
> prayers.

The Sunday *synaxis* described here included a reading of both
Old and New Testament passages, followed by an exhortation by the leader who urged the people to follow the example of what was contained in the Scripture lections. This
seems to convey precisely the idea behind "expository
preaching." In a later development, at a time when the
church became concerned that preaching was degenerating
into an exercise in rhetorical skills (after the Constantinian
"settlement" in the fourth century), it sought to keep its
preaching tied to Scripture by introducing a fixed pattern of
biblical lessons called pericopes, in the hope that preachers'
sermons would follow these in a liturgical setting. But this
device was not altogether successful, and "on Saints' Days
there was a tendency to forsake expository preaching for

topical preaching.''[13] A good example of such "liturgical" preaching is to be seen in Melito of Sardis' homily *On the Passion*, recently published in an accessible English translation.[14] The Serapion liturgy (*c.* A.D. 340) instructs the bishop to pray for the Holy Spirit, that he may be helped in his proclaiming the message of the Scriptures in expository fashion to the congregation.

Expository ministry of the word declined in the long period from Augustine to Luther, and the sermon ceased to be an essential part of the liturgy.[15] If credit goes to any single individual for the recovery of this type of sermon, it must be to Luther whose practice and example of pulpit exposition stand out as eminent. For the Reformer the sermon came to hold the central place in the liturgy, and Luther the commentator on Scripture cannot be dissociated from Luther the preacher and pastor. Calvin too is known as a preacher with rare gifts of clear exposition, a legacy handed on to the Puritans such as Perkins (died A.D. 1602) and Thomas Goodwin (1600-1671). On the American scene expository preaching has never really taken hold, though Jonathan Edwards in the early eighteenth century sought to apply Luther's teaching on justification by faith but in a context of the divine severity. The growing interest in twentieth-century British preachers (men like G. Campbell Morgan and more recently John R. W. Stott) indicates that American audiences do appreciate this method of preaching, even if there seems no exact counterpart to preachers such as C. H. Spurgeon, Joseph Parker, Alexander MacLaren, and D. M. Lloyd-Jones—all expositors par excellence—in the history of the American pulpit.

Second, the *doctrinal* content of a certain kind of preaching has marked it as distinctive. The aim here is to instruct hearers and in an affirmative way to be stating "the truth of

13. D. W. Cleverley Ford, *Ministry,* p. 67.

14. Gerald F. Hawthorne, "A New Translation of Melito's Paschal Homily," in *Current Issues in Biblical and Patristic Interpretation*, ed. G. F. Hawthorne (Grand Rapids: Wm. B. Eerdmans, 1975), pp. 147-175.

15. DeWitte T. Holland, *The Preaching Tradition* (Nashville: Abingdon Press, 1980), traces the decline in preaching to the following: (1) the rise of asceticism in the church; (2) the dependence on liturgy; (3) the emergence of Christianity as a state religion; and (4) the growth of the secular power of the church (p. 27).

the gospel." But also, by adopting a combative stance the doctrinal sermon serves to expose, answer, and repel "errors." There is thus an element of topicality in this engagement since the errors in question have tended to be those current and menacing in the preacher's own time. Nor is this type of preaching done in isolation from a solid exposition of Scripture appealed to as a set of proof-texts as though they were ammunition in the arsenal of the faith. An apologetic motif also has run through some modern examples of doctrinal preaching; and just occasionally the sermon of this order has reached a lofty tone, as evidenced in F. W. Robertson's sermons on Christian doctrine, sometimes regarded as the finest pulpit utterances in the English language.[16]

Doctrine utterances have come down to us from the era of the great christological and trinitarian disputes, especially in the case of the eastern theologians, Basil of Caesarea (330-379), Gregory Nazianzus (330-390), and Gregory of Nyssa (335-395). In this period must be placed John Chrysostom (374-407), the most eloquent and moving preacher of his day and period, and Augustine (354-429), whose doctrinal emphases appear in his sermons.

The Scholastic movement, seen in Thomas Aquinas (1225-1274), placed a heavy emphasis on the intellectual weight of the sermon; but not all in this era lacked the warm mystical approach derived from Bernard (1090-1153) and seen in Bonaventura (1221-1274). Doctrine was wedded to fiery reform in John Wyclif (1330-1384), John Huss (1369-1415), and Savonarola (1452-1498)—all of whom challenged the papacy whose claims were frequently supported by heavily apologetic sermons coupled with emotional appeals to popularize the sale of indulgences and the relics of the saints.

After the first generation of Luther's reform movement, a polemical spirit set in. The consequence was a heavy-handed insistence on correct doctrine, an abstractness and pedantry in the sermon's content and, alas, a parade of scholastic learning that effectively ousted Luther's declared intention:

16. "Frederick W. Robertson is considered to be the most influential preacher in the English language," writes Edmund A. Steimle in the preface to *The Preaching of F. W. Robertson*, ed. G. E. Doan, Jr. (Philadelphia: Fortress Press, 1964).

I endeavor in my sermons to take a text, and to keep to it, and so to show it to the people and spread it out before them, that they may say, *"This* is what the sermon is about."

The Pietist movement in seventeenth-century Germany revitalized the pulpit and stanched the flow of the movement into arid scholastic and orthodox deadness. We can appreciate this new life of Pietism today by reading Bengel's *Gnomon* (1687-1752), which are comments on the New Testament, and Zinzendorf's hymns (1700-1760).

In England the coming of the friars in A.D. 1224[17] kept doctrine in the pulpit from leading to dull preaching. Charles Smyth illustrated an intensely felt desire for more simple preaching and supplied the need, chiefly through the use of *exempla* or anecdotal illustrations, to light up dark places with wonderful tales. Latimer (1485-1555) is notable in his recourse to these *exempla.* More rigorous in his view of the sermon as a teaching vehicle was Cranmer (1489-1556), whose penchant for limpid prose and telling phrase joined to doctrinal seriousness found its outlet in *The Book of Common Prayer* of 1549.

In terms of a single motivation to produce a sermon that lacked all frills and concessions to human weakness and was a methodical appeal to reason, John Tillotson (1630-1694) stands without peer. He may be called the father of the moral essay set in the ambience of the Christian pulpit. As every action of this thoroughgoing sort produces a reaction, so it is not unexpected that with the revival of the early Methodists, Wesley's and Whitfield's (1703-1791, 1714-1770 respectively) stirring sermons, indoors and in the open air, would see the pendulum swing, while not losing contact with basic Christian doctrine.

The Tractarians did not value preaching overmuch, but placed its role within the sacramental life of the Catholic church. Yet pulpit utterances of John Keble (1792-1866) and John Henry Newman (1801-1890) are marked by solid teaching and serious intent.

Doctrinal concerns of a different stamp continue to be voiced in the twentieth century as D. M. Lloyd-Jones' up-

17. Charles Smyth, *The Art of Preaching* (London: SPCK, 1940), pp. 55-62.

dated Calvinist theology, David Read's articulation of Christian essentials, similar to James S. Stewart's earlier expositions which are basically doctrinal, if not obtrusively so, and Paul Tillich's plea for a religion suited to modern man, a "system" that some have charged excludes "the gospel."

Third, a broad spectrum of pulpit specimens is covered by the term *topical preaching*. The raison d'être of this type of sermon is the insistence that we must address our audiences within the intellectual, social, and personal context of their lives and the society around them. What has engaged their attention during the previous week should set the agenda for the pastor's Sunday deliverances: political upheavals, economic pressures, social disturbances, moral questions, family and work problems. These are the stuff out of which sermons are meant to be made, while the preacher tries to bring "the mind of Christ" to bear on matters of immediate and existential interest and challenge.

In the first five centuries doctrinal debates were topical, so there may well have been an overlap in our neat categories. We can see more clearly the relevance of preaching to current abuses in the Renaissance period (in Huss) and Reformation era (Luther's animus against indulgences and the Peasants' Revolt). Savonarola's bid to enthrone Christ as king of Florence was "topical"—and illfated. The Puritans and Independents in seventeenth-century England boldly spoke out against abuses, both religious and political; and in Cromwell a political reformer emerged to redress the wrongs of a monarchy that, as Paul Johnson remarks, was "in rebellion" and thereby treasonable.[18]

We must move on to the century nearer our own to see how "topical" or "social" preaching came to real power. The 1840s produced the Christian Socialist group, led by preachers of the order of F. D. Maurice and Charles Kingsley. The popular appeals of G. A. Studdert-Kennedy in World War I and Dick Sheppard (1880-1937) were signs of the church's growing involvement with social issues, a trend that found vocal expression in Walter Rauschenbusch and Reinhold Niebuhr in a later decade.

18. P. Johnson, *The Offshore Islanders* (London: Weidenfeld and Nicolson, 1972), pp. 192, 193: "The King's responses [to Parliament] could in legal terms be construed as an act of rebellion."

The general low esteem in which the sermon came to be held between the world wars did not prevent some preachers with a "topical" approach from rising to national eminence: Leslie D. Weatherhead in London who sought to marry the insights of the "new psychology" to the Christian life, Donald Soper with an open-air message of Christian socialism, and Norman Vincent Peale whose sloganeering or epigrammatic versions of the gospel have had considerable vogue, aided by radio and TV.

The evolution of the pulpit's appeal in the social setting is interesting. The so-called "nonconformist conscience," which found powerful expression in Hugh Price Hughes (1847-1902) demanding on moral grounds the Irish politician Parnell's resignation in 1890 from the platform (note, not pulpit) of the Methodist West London Mission, has been largely muted. In its place comes a new sort of "topicality," stressing moral values in a context of right-wing politics, which takes precedence over personal ideals.

A Synthetic View

The place of the sermon in the structure of Christian worship is assured, a conclusion history, theology, and human need join to establish. Opinion is divided, however, over whether a recovery of liturgical "order" as expressed, for instance, in the Liturgical Movement of the late nineteenth century and on has contributed to consolidating the secure place of the sermon in the order of worship. From one point of view the sermon has come to be understood once more as an integral part of the liturgy in which the word of God read in the Scripture lections is proclaimed as a prelude to thanksgiving (see Vatican II's reforms at this point).[19] On the other side, it has been alleged that, granted that the word in preaching and in sacrament go together in complementary fashion, it becomes an uneasy partnership when the eucharist is treated as the focal point of the worship. It is impossible to sustain a congregation's high view of the sermon if all the tangible evidence of, for example, a minister's enrobing with different vest-

19. Vatican II, "Constitution on the Sacred Liturgy" IV. 35 (*Documents of Vatican II* [Grand Rapids: Wm. B. Eerdmans, 1975], p. 12), cited by R. H. Fuller, "Sermon," in *The Westminster Dictionary of Worship*, ed. J. G. Davies (Philadelphia: Westminster Press, 1972), p. 345.

ments for the eucharist, points in the direction of the eucharist, as the primary focus of the people's worship.[20] In this area a call is heard for improving the quality of preaching—a trend seen in post-Vatican II Catholicism and the Episcopalian communion as much as in those other denominations that have a long history of appreciation for the sermon as *the* central act of the liturgy.

To be sure, there may be variations of what may be called the traditional mode of preaching, namely, "one person elevated above the congregation, delivering a speech without interruption, and appealing chiefly to the cerebral." Discussion sermons, dialogue formats of a question-and-answer type, dramatic presentations with or without visual aids, enacted sermons based on a sacred dance or mime—all these have been and are still being tested, with varying results. Nonetheless, the time-fashioned role of the pulpit in terms of a single voice, articulating God's word in modern idiom and intentionally seeking to move the congregation to action is still with us, and its future seems as certain as that of institutional Christianity.

With that concession made, the question is raised, What kind of sermons are predictably appropriate to Christian worship, given our previous discussion of what such public worship is and aims to accomplish? In the setting of "mass" or "crusade" evangelism the sermon sets out to communicate the gospel message—as Billy Graham and others have done with a worldwide fame; but the sermon *in this context* is not part of worship. Its role is more one of religious propaganda in the best sense.

In the overall structure of the divine service the sermon plays another role; and that precise function will shortly be considered. Here we suggest that the minister is not called to choose one type of sermon to the exclusion of others. The call "preach the word" (2 Tim. 4:2) summons him or her to an opportunity that can be grasped in several ways. By way of summary these dimensions are:[21]

20. D. W. Cleverley Ford, *Ministry*, pp. 134f.

21. See J. Daniel Baumann, *An Introduction to Contemporary Preaching* (Grand Rapids: Baker Book House, 1972), p. 206 for the terminology that follows.

1. *Kerygmatic* or *evangelistic*. This term means the public offer of the gospel as the announcement of a town crier or herald who brings good news, and seeks a verdict. The New Testament knows the office of "evangelist" (Eph. 4:11), but it also has a broader understanding of the functional role of a pastor who is called to be an evangelist as well as to fulfill his other duties (see 2 Tim. 4:5). To preempt "evangelism" as belonging exclusively to one individual and so to deny its importance to the pastor-teacher is a mistake. Philip "the evangelist" was at work in Samaria (Acts 8:26-40) and elsewhere, but when he settled at Caesarea with his family—and presumably exercised a ministry in the church there—he was still called "the evangelist" (Acts 21:8), just as he commenced his Christian service as "one of the seven" deacons (Acts 6:5) charged with social responsibilities.

2. *Didactic* or *teaching*. We have noticed already the value of those persons who enjoyed the gift of teaching (Rom. 12:7). In a word, they were commissioned and endowed with the Spirit in order to clarify God's will for the congregation and then apply it to concrete situations.

3. *Therapeutic* or *healing*. This word reminds us that there is a close semantic tie-in between salvation and health; both ideas derive from "wholeness." In Acts 3:6, 7, 16 and 4:22 Peter is seen as a man of many parts. He speaks a word of physical healing in the name or authority of Jesus Christ; he is responsive to the lame man's needs and helps him to his feet. The "perfect health" referred to includes both the gracious offer and acceptance of new life from God and the pledge of human friendship and assistance. Word and action on the preacher's part go hand in hand. So it is that preaching and social ministries are not rivals but partners in a common enterprise in making people whole. The banner over the pulpit and the social service agency of the church is one and the same: *shalom.*

4. *Prophetic* or *consciousness-raising*. The biblical prophet looked in two directions. In the popular sense he gazed into the crystal ball of the future and offered oracles of history written in advance as coming events cast their shadows

before them. But this understanding of prophetism in Israel and the infant church is quite inadequate, and even positively misleading. The prophets were not starry-eyed visionaries, but men and women of the Spirit (if we include the Christian prophet, according to 1 Cor. 11:2-16) who saw the future through the prism of God's overarching sovereignty and control of all history—especially the present scene. To be sure, they do peer into the future, but their prime task is that of helping the people of God to make sense of the immediate situation and to be ready for whatever the coming days have in store for them. The accent falls more firmly on *forth*-telling than *fore*-telling.

The prophets see human society under the eye of God, and that perspective gives them a word of social relevance for their contemporaries. One has only to know a little of the historical and cultural background of Isaiah of Jerusalem (chs. 1-39), Micah, Amos, and Habakkuk to see ample evidence of their involvement in the social fabric of the nation and their ability to speak the "word of Yahweh" to discouraged kings, disobedient leaders, false prophets, and venal priests.[22] A reading of Isaiah chapter 7 and Amos 7:10-17 offers a salutary corrective to what passes for "social gospel" in the history of preaching, while supporting the present-day pulpit's responsibility to see justice done in the land and oppression resisted throughout the world.

A desirable result is—and it would be a wonder to behold! —a minister who could blend in one person these diverse parts of a preacher's privilege and duty. He or she would maintain a sharp evangelistic edge at all times, and "preach to reach each" one of the hearers, eliciting a firm commitment to Christ and his cause. The teaching element, based on solid exposition of Scripture, would give strength and substance to his evangelism lest the latter become simply "an appeal extended backwards" to the beginning of the sermon, to use John Stott's dictum. Yet with a maximum concentration on the "word of God written," the preacher-teacher will never lose sight of a deeper meaning of what his office as "minister of the word of God" means. The word was incar-

22. See Richard J. Mouw, *Politics and the Biblical Drama* (Grand Rapids: Wm. B. Eerdmans, 1976).

nate in Jesus Christ who rebuked Bible students in his day with the sad lament: "You study the Scriptures . . . these very Scriptures speak about me! Yet you are not willing to come to me in order to have life" (John 5:39, 40). The most helpful ministry from the pulpit, many people claim, is that which sounds the note of comfort offering to calm our fears and heal our bruised spirits. And finally, the preacher's horizons need to be as wide as life itself. His is a repertoire informed by all that concerns the experience of his fellow men and women not only in his own backyard but across the street and beyond the oceans. This view will involve the sensitive pastor in community affairs and, as he or she has ability, in addressing civic issues, statewide concerns, and the Christian interest in political and social problems and answers decided at the highest levels of government. An upcoming election, an observance of United Nations Sunday, a local referendum on some momentous issue are all heaven-sent opportunities to relate the eternal gospel to temporal matters. Clearly the people will be looking for some leadership from the pulpit that too often in the past has reneged on its responsibility.

Good Preaching Needs Good Listening

The too facile observation is sometimes made that a congregation gets the preaching it deserves. Nor is that remark necessarily true. But it does remain the case that no effective preaching can flourish in an atmosphere of rejection, suspicion, or plain indifference. A bored congregation is a dead hand on the spirit of any aspiring prophet of the Lord.

We close, therefore, with a practical suggestion. It is taken directly from the detailed story, twice repeated, in Acts chapters 10 and 11. Peter eventually has found himself in the home of Cornelius who had anticipated his visit by gathering his family and neighbors for the occasion. Peter's speech is rich in suggestive ideas as to what makes an "ideal preacher." Specifically, he has known the "opened heavens" of revelation and guidance (10:11); he is conscious of his own frailty and humanness, yet cannot shake free the dutiful confidence of God's commissioning (10:26, 34). Above all, it is the risen Lord by the Spirit who is directing this opportunity to speak in his name (10:40, 41, 47).

The flip side of the incident is the presence of an "ideal congregation." They are attentive to hear what Peter has to say (10:33), and have gathered in strength and with a real expectancy and desire to know more (10:33), treating Peter with respect as God's mouthpiece (as Peter himself would later formalize into an admonition, 1 Pet. 4:11, "whoever preaches must preach God's messages"). They have brought others along too (10:24, 27), for good things are meant to be shared. And at a crucial moment, Peter's sermon caught fire and received a divine approbation in a way few sermons do (10:44, 45). The audience is ready with a response in penitence and living faith (11:18), such as would gladden any preacher's heart. A note of warning enters here, however. Richard Baxter's words are salutary:

> Of all preaching in the world . . . I hate that preaching which tends to make the hearers laugh, or to move their minds with tickling levity . . . instead of affecting them with a holy reverence of the name of God.[23]

Baxter quotes Jerome to good effect: "learn to be lifted up not by the plaudits of the people but by their sighs: the tears of the hearers are your praises."

Let Phillips Brooks (1835-1893) have the last encouraging word: "The world has not heard its best preaching yet." Or let us recall Ward Beecher (1813-1887) when he declared, "True preaching is yet to come."

23. Richard Baxter, *The Reformed Pastor*, 5th ed. (London: The Religious Tract Society, 1862), pp. 118, 119.

CHAPTER EIGHT

Baptism and Christian Unity

Crisis for Baptism and Our Agenda

Some recent vivid titles have alerted us that all is not well with the church's practice of baptism. We read of "Baptismal crisis," "The waters that divide," and "The conflict over infant baptism."[1] Right at the outset of our study in this chapter two indisputable facts stare us in the face: one is a historical notice that should give us encouragement, the other poses a problem that does not seem to go away.

On the one side, we must recognize that the use of water in lustrations and washings is an age-old religious custom. Christianity too has followed suit and has incorporated a water rite into its visible expression. Its baptismal practice takes us back right to the beginnings of the faith and the church's life. "Baptism has been an integral part of Christianity from the first . . . and we know of no Christian in the NT who had not been baptized, either by John or in the name of Jesus," comments James Dunn.[2] Unless we are ready to make exceptional cases such as the men and women in the gospel story who professed faith (such as the thief on the cross), this statement may stand. Baptism then puts us into direct touch with the fountainhead of our historic faith, and unites the present-day church with its first-century origins and roots in a way that few religious ordinances can do.

1. B. S. Moss, ed., *Crisis for Baptism* (London: SCM Press, 1965); Donald Bridge and David Phypers, *The Water that Divides* (Downers Grove, IL: InterVarsity Press, 1977); H. Hubert, *Der Streit um die Kindertaufe* (Lang, 1972), cited in G. Wainwright, "Recent thinking on Christian beliefs: iv. baptism and the eucharist," *The Expository Times* 88 (Feb. 1977), pp. 132-137.

2. J. D. G. Dunn, "Baptism," *The Illustrated Bible Dictionary*, vol. 1 (London: Inter-Varsity Press, 1980), pp. 172-175 (p. 173).

But on the debit side, the church's understanding of baptism has constantly been threatened by distortion and several mutually exclusive interpretations. Terms such as "baptismal regeneration"—the notion that the act works in a quasi-automatic way to produce what baptism is supposed to signify—have haunted the pages of baptismal controversy. The rite that, in apostolic times, was treated as the focal point of unity among Christians (1 Cor. 12:12, 13) has become divisive and the occasion of much strife.

The current dispute centers on the theology underlying the practice. Baptism has always been a Christian observance seeking a rationale in theology; it is in the theological justification of baptism that issues must be clarified before we go on to tackle the practical concerns dealing with infant baptism, sponsors or godparents, and the mode of application, whether by much water or little water. To get the sequence right is the first step, and it is not enough to begin with the anomaly of "two baptisms": two ways of baptizing (sprinkling versus immersion), two subjects for baptism (individuals with faith defined as personal, corporate, incipient, or anticipatory: terms which will have to be explained shortly). The burning question is rather: What is meant theologically (i.e., in the total scheme of Christian faith) by the early credal statement: "one Lord, one faith, *one baptism*" (Eph. 4:5)? To address that question we must turn to the New Testament and, running the risk of oversimplification, indicate some pointers to its teaching on baptism.

But first it will be helpful, I believe, if we set down what the agenda of this chapter looks like; and I do that by posing three questions:

1. How normative do we regard Scripture when its teaching (as in this case) is unclear or ambiguous and its "plain" sense is capable of diverse interpretation?

2. Are there several kinds of faith? Granted the centrality of "saving faith" as a personal act of obedience and response, are there other expressions of faith? Do they contribute to our understanding of "saving faith"?

3. Is church history to be made as well as studied? If not, what is the use of delving into the past?—unless we go on

to say that the past can help us to interpret the present and shape the future.

The New Testament Data

1. The coming of Jesus was heralded by the work of his cousin John who is invariably known by the descriptive title "the baptizer." The name suggests that there was something distinctive about John's practice of baptizing men and women in the Jordan river. If John's practice owed much to the precedent of proselyte baptism reserved for Gentile converts to the Jewish faith, then his novelty was that he insisted on baptizing his fellow Jews as a sign of their repentance and amendment of life. He treated them as though they were no different from Gentiles in need of conversion. Or, if his baptism was indebted to the community washings at Qumran, then it was offered to cleanse the people in anticipation of a divine visitation of judgment on the ungodly in Israel. But John's baptism, while it spoke of the call to repentance, carries much more the overtone of doom, as the ax was laid to the root of the trees or the coming one bore the pruning hook and the winnowing fan (Matt. 3:10-12; Luke 3:9, 17) to separate the godly remnant from the mass of the nation. John's baptism, however, had yet another dimension which later New Testament writers never fail to mention. He came to prepare for the arrival of a divine kingdom (Luke 16:16), and to call on his compatriots to get ready for the kingdom's presence in the coming one who in turn would "baptize in the Spirit" (Mark 1:8; cf. John 1:33; Acts 19:4).

2. Jesus consented to be baptized at the hands of his fore-runner (Matt. 3:13-17, which faces at least in part the awkwardness of the question, Why did the sinless Christ need to get baptized? The later fathers of the church wrestled with this difficulty).[3] The most satisfactory answer is that for Jesus baptism became a moment of decision and consecration to the tasks of the public ministry, which in a stereotyped phrase was soon to be dated "from the baptism John preached" (in Acts 1:22, 10:37, 13:24, 25). It was also an act of identifica-

3. See the evidence in W. F. Flemington, *The New Testament Doctrine of Baptism* (London: SPCK, 1948), pp. 26, 27.

tion with the people Jesus had come to save. For that purpose, as heaven's gift to humankind, Jesus needed the Spirit
to "anoint" (the Greek verb gives us the noun "Christ")
him (Acts 10:38). It has been further remarked that Jesus'
practice of baptism—only indirectly referred to and with
some uncertainty in the texts as we can see by reading in succession John 3:22-26 and 4:1, 2—set the use of the action
metaphor on a fresh base. The theme of judgment is continued—but redirected away from the people's doom to the fate
which awaited Jesus himself as the one who would receive a
fiery baptism in his death for sinners. The "baptism" in the
Jordan prepared him for that rugged road that led to Calvary
(Mark 10:38, 39; 14:24; Luke 12:49f.). He reinterpreted baptism as a picture of his passion endured vicariously for his
people, with whom he closely identified himself in both
death and new life. He would save them by his associating
with them in their sin, and would emerge to a risen life,
bringing his people with him. This thought leads us to the
threshold of Paul's baptismal theology in Romans 6:1-11.

   3. The administration of baptism in the early days of
the church is one of the safest and surest conclusions of historical evidence, whatever problems may surround the "great
commission" of Matthew 28:19, 20. The outstanding feature
of the invitation to "be baptized" is the accompanying offer
of the Spirit. Other features of baptismal practice, to be sure,
are clearly in evidence, such as the requirements of repentance and faith (Acts 2:38, 41; 8:12f.; 16:14f., 33f.; 18:8;
19:2; 22:16) making baptism a decisive step that would publicly associate the new convert with his or her fellow believers
and be an open profession; and a passing under the lordship
of Jesus Christ whose "name" (or authority) was invoked in
the rite. To be baptized "in" or "into" his name (Acts 2:38;
8:16; 10:48; 19:5) implied that henceforth the new believer
was called to live no longer for himself but for the one whose
name he now bore. It was the badge of discipleship. Hence
Paul's reluctance to administer baptism lest the superstitious
Corinthians should imagine that they were privileged to
"receive" Paul's name as *his* disciples (1 Cor. 1:12-16), a
possibility not unthinkable if the wording of Acts 14:20 is
taken at face value, and given the fractured state of the
church at Corinth.

Above all, early Christian baptism was a rite of initiation or entry into the company of those who gathered in the name of the risen Jesus, first as a "sect" (Acts 2:41, 47; 4:32; 24:5, 14), and later as a social group with a self-conscious and separate identity (Acts 11:26). They called on his name, first in baptism where the credal recitation was "Jesus is Lord" (Rom. 10:9-14; 1 Cor. 1:2), and rejoiced in that "name" (Acts 5:41), even when they were called on to suffer for it (James 2:7; 1 Pet. 4:14-16). The "name" by that time was clearly that of "Christian" (1 Pet. 4:16).

4. Yet, as far back as we are able to trace "Christian origins," becoming and being a Christian has always been understood as receiving the gift of the Holy Spirit and living in the strength he supplies. Paul speaks for the united witness of early Christianity: "Whoever does not have the Spirit of God does not belong to him" (Rom. 8:9). The Spirit became the hallmark of authentic Christian experience, and receiving the Spirit became the (tangible or sentient) proof of sharing in the new life in Christ. But how was the Spirit received?

This deceptively simple question was given a variety of answers according to the range of New Testament evidence. Acceptance of the good news of Christ was certainly a *sine qua non*, but that phrase only compounds the issue. What was involved in "acceptance," which is the language of trust and obedience and confession? Paul's position (in Gal. 3:2-5; 1 Cor. 12:1-3) is situationally slanted, for he wants to mark off a true receiving of new life from what he regarded as a delusive and dangerous counterfeit. In one other place Paul talks of the initial Christian experience as God's gift in confirming believers in Christ and "anointing" them by applying the seal of the Spirit upon their lives as a first installment of final salvation (2 Cor. 1:21, 22). It is a nice question whether Paul thought of baptism as part of this process; and sometimes Luke's witness in the various accounts in Acts is appealed to as showing that he (Luke) was convinced of a close connection, if not an actual cause-and-effect relationship between repentance, faith, and the receiving of the Spirit in baptism, with or without the imposition of hands (see Acts 2:38; 8:17; 9:17; 19:6 for these diverse traditions dealing with Christian initiation. There was evidently no one set pattern known to Luke).

5. Paul's teaching on baptism built upon what he inherited as part of the tradition he had received at his entry upon new life in Christ. He can speak of baptism and its meaning as a well-known piece of *paradosis* (tradition), while at the same time he assumed that all his readers, even those unknown personally to him, had been initiated into Christ's fellowship in this way (Rom. 6:1-14). The key to Paul's teaching, however, is his describing baptism as a new creation rather than as a washing from sin's stain, as C. F. D. Moule remarks.[4] The central exposition in Romans 6 turns upon the shared experience of having been buried-and-raised with Christ, involving a death to the old life and an awakening to a new experience of life akin to a resurrection, though that is still set in the future. Possibly Paul's argument is polemical here, opposing those who thought that their "baptismal resurrection" did away with the promise of a future raising from the dead (so E. Käsemann).[5] The "dying with Christ," moreover, was the start of a lifelong process even if it took its dramatic beginning in a renunciation of old ways at the time when the drama of baptism was enacted. Then the "old life" was hidden out of sight under the water—the mode of immersion seems required by the sense of the passage—and buried from view as a symbolic act of rejection and renunciation.

The call is thereafter to live as those "aroused from death" and enlightened by Christ's radiance, as the baptismal chant recalled:

> Awake, you sleeper,
> Arise from the dead;
> And Christ will illumine you. (Eph. 5:14)

4. C. F. D. Moule, *Worship in the New Testament* (London: Lutterworth Press, 1961), p. 57. The terminology of baptism is much more emphatic in describing "death leading to life" than cleansing: see J. Ysebaert, *Greek Baptismal Theology. Its Origin and Early Development* (Nijmegen: Dekker & Van de Vegt, 1962), p. 53.

5. E. Käsemann, *Commentary on Romans* (Grand Rapids: Wm. B. Eerdmans, 1980), p. 161.

Sometimes the metaphor is one of the exchange of clothes, suggesting a putting off of an old suit and donning a new set of garments (Gal. 3:27). The summons "put off/put on" then became part of the parenetic call to abandon old life-styles and associations and to accept the regimen of new ways (e.g., in Col. 3:9-12; Eph. 4:22-24). Yet another metaphor is seen in Colossians 2:11-13 where "circumcision," "burial," and "resurrection" are a cluster of ideas to make clear what was in Paul's mind when he reflected on the Colossians' new life in the Spirit (Col. 1:8). The point in common is that his readers have known the "spiritual" counterpart to (Jewish) circumcision, which by definition was physical and outward (Rom. 2:28f.; Phil. 3:3). That counterpart is Christ's baptism (i.e., redemption by his death) in which they have come to share by faith. The addition of faith is important since it establishes the fact that Paul set a disjunction between Jewish circumcision as a token of their admission to the national covenant of Israel, and Christian baptism which rests on a set of different bases altogether. Entry into God's family and covenant in Christ is by personal decision and a public faith-response, directed to God—not to the rite. It includes all who come by way of faith, male and female alike (Gal. 3:28, 29), now called the family of Abraham; and Christian initiation is regenerative in a way that the Jewish puberty rite could never be, since the latter ceremony involved only an unconscious infant in the first week of his life.

It is not out of character, therefore, for the apostle to regard baptism as the gateway to membership in Christ's body, the church. This is exactly the train of ideas in 1 Corinthians 12:12, 13. The human body is composed of many parts, yet it is "one body"—as in our phrase "everybody" meaning everyone. In a surprising twist to his thought Paul proceeds: "so it is with the Christ," where the logic of his argument would expect "the church." But that is precisely his conclusion: he calls the church Christ, says Calvin. And how do the members become that "one body"?

All of us, whether Jews or Gentiles, whether slaves or free, have been baptized into the one body by the same Spirit.

This overview of Paul's teaching arose directly out of his pastoral responsibilities, as we can well imagine from all we know of church situations in his various communities. Baptism highlights the new life in Christ, with the claim to serious ethical endeavor; it presupposes faith yet it confirms it, and has no magical or superstitious value; it marks a transition point dividing the old life from the new; it is the focal point of the church's unity as one entity in Christ, canceling out inveterate hostilities and age-old fears such as the Colossians knew when they lived under the power of the ''elemental spirits'' (Col. 2:8, 20; 3:3). Baptism was thus a dramatic symbol of the new life, akin to burial and new life or a disrobing of old clothes and an arraying oneself with new apparel. Yet it was more than a picture or metaphor; there was a reality behind the drama, and the vividly portrayed action of entering the water and emerging therefrom accomplished the effect thus symbolized, with the operative mode God's action released by faith.

6. Later baptismal theologizing in the Pauline school and elsewhere came to give this even stronger emphasis, while not surrendering the basic insights of the apostle. ''The bath of regeneration'' (Tit. 3:5) sees the transition from the old life to the new under the powerful figure of a new birth, akin to Johannine thought (John 3:3-8). But the new birth is not confounded with baptism since (a) not all the ''new birth'' language requires a baptismal frame of reference (e.g., James 1:18) though some certainly may (1 Pet. 1:3, 23; 1 John 3:9); and (b) the gift of the Spirit in regeneration is not exclusively linked with water baptism (they are distinguished in John 1:33), though here again there are places where the tie-in is firm (John 3:5, ''born of water and the Spirit'' is one such apparently clear case). What, however, prevents the Christian teaching of baptismal regeneration from being treated the same as pagan mystery-cult initiations that conferred automatic salvation is the requirement of personal faith that united the convert with the living Lord and ensured that his or her response entailed a commitment to Christ as Lord and an allegiance to him (1 Pet. 3:21: ''an appeal to God for a clear conscience'').

The Place of Faith in Baptism

1. The way the church's baptismal ceremonies have evolved makes fascinating reading. We have seen how the

"simple" administering of a water rite—either by submersion (the Greek verbs *baptō* and *baptizō* mean "to dip")[6] or by pouring over the candidate's head as he stood up to his waist in a pool and allowed the water to saturate him, as in the Roman catacomb pictures and the evidence of church architecture;[7] the latter "ducking" is similar to proselyte baptism—was associated with other explanatory or interpreting or accompanying ceremonials. For instance:

a) Some form of words was asked for, both as an authorizing formula ("in the name of [the Lord] Jesus [Christ]" in Acts, or in the triune name, according to Matt. 28:19 and *Didache* 7) and as a profession of belief. That confession is summarily heard in the credal cry "Jesus is Lord" (Rom. 10:8-13; 1 Cor. 12:2, 3; Phil. 2:11). The context is one of the proclaimed word that describes the events of salvation-history, which in turn evoked a believing response. Invariably in the nine reported cases of baptism in Acts "believing" and "baptizing" go together. The first signs of a longer credal affirmation appear in Acts 8:37 where the western text describes a dialogue of a question-and-answer type between ministrant and the person to be baptized. As we observed, this pattern laid the groundwork for later and lengthier baptismal professions and declaratory creeds ("I believe in . . .") with thrice repeated actions of baptism. The point to notice is how indispensable the early church thought was the linkage between an attestation of faith and the performance of baptism as an entrée to church membership.

b) The imposition of hands, a Jewish rite usually associated with rabbinic ordination and (maybe) with the healing of the sick, may have been brought over into Christian initiation (see Heb. 6:2). The data in Acts are obscure, and each pericope poses its own problems. We refer to Acts 8:4-25 where G. W. H. Lampe's interpretation, which sees in the laying on of apostles' hands a sign of a special phase of Chris-

6. I. H. Marshall, "The Meaning of the verb, 'to baptize,'" *Evangelical Quarterly* 45 (1973), pp. 130-140.

7. J. G. Davies, *The Architectural Setting of Baptism* (London: Barre and Rockliff, 1962), pp. 23-26.

tian outreach in mission, seems the best one;[8] Acts 9:17 where Ananias' hands on Saul's head are more an index of friendship and a performative act of acceptance than any more significant action; and Acts 19:5, 6 where Paul's laying on of hands may well mark the transition point from a Johannine baptism (presupposing only partial faith) to a messianic baptism and a full Christian status. The evidence of glossolalia and prophecy that follows certified that these men of Ephesus were regarded as bona fide believers in the Lukan-Pauline sense.

c) "Anointing" may well relate to the baptismal experience, linked with the "sealing of the Spirit" (2 Cor. 1:21; 1 John 2:20, 27). At the subjective level this suggests a work of the Spirit who "confirmed" new believers in their faith and gave his witness to them, rather like the promise of Romans 8:16. No actual use of "oil" is intended here, any more than in Acts 10:38 (God anointed Jesus with the Spirit), nor does a hiatus between "conversion" and the (subsequent) "gift of the Spirit" conditional on anointing or imposition of hands by apostolic leaders or sign of glossolalia seem warranted by the evidence. "Sacramentalist" and "Pentecostal" attempts to set a disjunction between the items in the chain—hearing the message, believing the kerygma as God's good news, confessing faith in baptism, and receiving the "seal of the Spirit" come to grief on the hard rocks of the questionable exegesis of "difficult" texts and rare episodes. To change the metaphor, the attempts equally fly in the face of some unobscure data such as Ephesians 1:13, 14; 4:30; Galatians 4:4-6; Acts 2:38; and above all the clear witness of Acts 10:44-48; 11:15-17. The case of Cornelius' friends illustrates how the Spirit's immediacy of action waited only on the response of faith (as Acts 11:17 makes evident), and the initiatory rite was water baptism once they had given evidence of faith in the glossolalic praise of God.

2. When we enter the period following the "apostolic age," beginning roughly at the mid-point of the second cen-

---

8. G. W. H. Lampe, *The Seal of the Spirit*, 2nd ed. (London: SPCK, 1967), pp. 66-70 against J. D. G. Dunn, *Baptism in the Holy Spirit* (London: SCM Press, 1970), pp. 55-68.

tury, we see a bewildering assortment of practices associated
with the rite of initiation. The "primitive" complex of
"preached word—believing response—baptismal act" becomes a kernel around which "in the course of history, many
other words and ceremonies with preparatory or explicatory
significance"[9] gathered. It must be sufficient to mention just
the most important of these ceremonies.

Beginning with postbaptismal anointing, the laying on of
hands, and "signing" with the cross as acts preparatory to
admission to first communion—a sequence found in part
(maybe) in 1 John 5:8 but clearly in Tertullian (A.D. 200) and
The Apostolic Tradition of Hippolytus (A.D. 215), other rites
followed.[10] They are: fasting and exorcism—as negative preparations for baptism—and *apertio*—the opening of the ears
and nostrils of the candidate to hear and savor the bishop's
word, which in turn enabled the candidate to recite properly
the creed, followed by the Lord's Prayer. Elaborate rituals
dealing with a renunciation of Satan, the stripping off of
clothes to leave no part of the human body unexposed to the
water, and the receiving of a white robe as a sign of righteousness, the kiss of peace, a crowning of the initiate as an eschatological promise (Rev. 2:10), the offer of a lit candle as a
symbol of "enlightenment" (as Heb. 6:4; 10:32, and Justin,
Apol. 61 call baptism), the partaking of milk and honey as
the gifts of inheritance in the promised land, and even a hair
cut shaped in the image of the cross—these are practices that
grew up as a part of the baptismal initiation.

More important for our purpose is to observe the rise of a
catechumenate to replace the early New Testament pattern
of "believe—be baptized" seen as two sides of a single coin,
in James Denney's phrase (Acts 8:35-38; 16:25-35).[11] Modern
liturgical studies have given much discussion to the question
whether the origins of the "catechumenate" (i.e., a period of
elementary instruction candidates were to receive before baptism) are traceable to the New Testament era. Certain New
Testament references may indicate such baptismal instruction

9. G. Wainwright, "The rites and ceremonies of Christian initiation.
Developments in the past," *Studia Liturgica* 10 (1974), pp. 7, 8.

10. G. Wainwright, "Rites and ceremonies," pp. 10-14.

11. J. Denney, *The Death of Christ* (London: Hodder and Stoughton,
1907), p. 185.

or catechesis (Heb. 6:1f.; 1 John 2:12-14, and parts of 1 Pet. which may owe their genesis to a set of baptismal homilies). By A.D. 215 *The Apostolic Tradition* had lengthened the period between the initial decision to be enrolled as a cate- chumen and the actual initiation to three years. This period was regarded as a time of learning, particularly in such mat- ters as the Lord's Prayer, the creed, the decalogue, and other matters that pertained to a climactic exorcism conducted by the bishop on Saturday evening prior to baptism on Easter Sunday. With the rise in popularity of infant baptism, the catechumenate in the West shifted in significance away from being a prelude to baptism and became the proving ground of instruction that led to "confirmation" and first commu- nion. As bishops came to hold large dioceses and became pre- occupied with civil affairs, the task of infant baptizing was left to presbyters, and the length of time between such bap- tisms and episcopal confirmations was enlarged. Children were regularly admitted to communion before they were con- firmed. But when in the Middle Ages a more "numinous" character was given to the eucharistic bread and wine and fear of "abusing" them by accident was great, the cup was with- held from the laity and the communion of infants ceased to be practiced. The period leading up to confirmation and first communion was correspondingly lengthened.

3. At the Reformation two diverse solutions to what was evidently an unsatisfactory state of the matter came on the scene. The Protestant Reformers in the main used the delayed confirmation to place fresh emphasis on instruction, beginning with the baptismal interrogation required at infant baptism being directed to and answered by sponsors in the name of the infants. Thereafter the children were admitted to the "school of Christ" in anticipation of their receiving con- firmation after catechetical classes. At the left wing of the Reformation in A.D. 1524, Anabaptists in Europe and Baptist Independents later in England withdrew baptism altogether from infants and reserved the practice of the rite to those who could and did make profession of faith, even if it involved a "second baptism" (hence ana-baptism).

The emergence of sponsors/godparents who answered for the infants raises the question of the role of "faith" in baptism. The Lutherans and Calvinists were concerned to clear away the numerous side issues that the medieval church had introduced into the rite of initiation—especially items such as the blessing of the font, the use of oil, candles, salt (placed on the baptized's lips as a substitute for the eucharist to symbolize healing and the gift of wisdom), and spittle (as part of exorcism). Martin Bucer in his *Censura* dealt drastically with existing rituals and advocated bringing the baptism inside the church (away from the church door) so that all could hear. Most significantly, he questioned whether inanimate objects such as water could be "blessed," and sought to clear away superstition from the rite.[12]

The Reformers' heavy emphasis on "faith" as the sole requirement of a believing person's response to the justifying act of God's grace led them into a dilemma, faced by Zwingli who for a time would have preferred to postpone baptism until children arrived at an age of discretion—but the "anarchical" threat from Anabaptists, along with his further reflection, meant that he seemed to bow to the pressure of political events and retain infant baptism. He was candid enough, however, to omit the baptismal interrogations. Luther, however, inserted the idea that infants *do* make responses through their believing godparents, and even based the rationale of infant baptism on the sacrament's power to "evoke" faith, though he professed not to know how it did so.[13] The Anglican liturgies of 1549 and 1552 left the question in abeyance, but in the 1662 Book of Common Prayer the promise made on the infant's behalf was proleptic "until he come of age to take it upon himself." The net effect was to accentuate the importance of confirmation as a "rite of completion" when initiation was fully carried through. The Baptist view, on the other hand, is that "faith" by definition is personal and incorporates a consciously made decision; hence the refusal to baptize any but professed "believers," irrespective of age. "*Adult* baptism" is therefore a misnomer and should be dropped.

12. J. D. C. Fisher in *The Study of Liturgy*, ed. C. Jones, G. Wainwright, E. Yarnold (London: SPCK, 1978), pp. 124, 125.

13. On Luther's teaching see the evidence referred to in E. J. R. H. S. von Sicard, "Baptism, Lutheran," *The Westminster Dictionary of Worship*, ed. J. G. Davies (Philadelphia: Westminster Press, 1972), pp. 54, 55.

4. So far we have described the expedients devised to relate "faith" to infant baptism: an incipient faith mysteriously engendered by the act of baptism itself or anticipatory faith which is made by sponsors in the hope that one day the child may claim the promise for himself and so enter upon his heritage. We should add here the idea of corporate or congregational faith, which pictures how a believing parent or group may "believe" on behalf of infants who, having entered into a covenantal relationship (an Old Testament idea) at their baptism, are admitted to a believing atmosphere in which they are nurtured and encouraged to exercise faith as "children of promise." The scriptural warrant sought for this last-mentioned proposal (Mark 2:5: *"their* faith" is spoken of men who assisted the helpless paralytic; 1 Cor. 7:14) has never seemed cogent to Baptists who have countered that New Testament faith is inalienably personal and reflects a "decision" to transfer one's allegiance from "the world" to the Lord—an act that perforce requires a public and prior commitment to Christ before the baptism may rightfully be administered. A denial of the central role of individual responsibility seems to strike at the heart of New Testament religion, which has antiquated the Old Testament notion of family or corporate solidarity and set the "personal element" in religion as the controlling factor in understanding both Old Testament anticipation of a new covenant (Jer. 31:31-33; Ezek. 11:19, 20) and the *new* covenant in Christ (2 Cor. 3:6-18). Any other conclusion smacks of a rejudaizing of the gospel, from the Baptist side. From the paedobaptist position it is imperative to insist that "the one covenant is fulfilled and remains" to support the contention that "the children of Christians . . . indeed enjoy covenant status. But if baptism is not a covenant sign [i.e., to God's dealings in both testaments and his "mode of operation"], all this has no relevance to the question of its proper subjects." It is seen rightly that "it is here if anywhere that the ways of those who baptize infants and those who do not diverge."[14]

---

14. See G. W. Bromiley, *Children of Promise. The Case for Baptizing Infants* (Grand Rapids: Wm. B. Eerdmans, 1979), p. 25 for these citations in the text. He goes so far as to remark: "This, perhaps, is the crux of the debate."

*The New Testament Doctrine
and Today's Needs*

The debate over baptismal practice has run into an impasse.[15] The reasons are not far to seek. From the standpoint of the New Testament evidence the exegetical confrontation of argument and counterargument has reached a stalemate, since on both sides extraneous matters get dragged in, such as, did Lydia's or the jailor's households (Acts 16:15, 31-34) contain infants? What about the way Jesus received children in Mark 10:13-16? Surely the Christian parents of children would want to see their offspring share in the eschatological benefits of redemption (an argument offered partly on sentimental grounds!). What of the evidence of archaeology which has exposed the graves of Christian infants? Were they not baptized in infancy? Polycarp, at the ripe age of eighty-six, said he had served the Lord all his life. Surely that implies infant baptism! And so on.

The antipaedobaptist position usually makes much of these arguments from silence and scorns the strained "exegesis in depth"[16] that professes to see at deeper levels a covenantal theology at the heart of the paedobaptist practice. A favorite riposte is to issue an appeal to history. That appeal takes one of two forms.

On the one hand it is said that there is no undisputed evidence of infant baptism until Tertullian who knows of the practice but is opposed to it (*de Baptismo* 18), Hippolytus' *Apostolic Tradition* (ch. 21:4 contains the rubric, Baptize the little ones first. All those who can speak for themselves shall do so. As for those who cannot speak for themselves, their parents or someone from their family shall speak for them) and especially Cyprian (A.D. 246-258), in whose day infant baptism was becoming increasingly common. But the practice is not universally attested even in the patristic period as we can infer from the existence of the "secret doctrines" of the

15. See E. C. Whitaker, *The Baptismal Liturgy* (London: SPCK, 1981), p. 29.
16. A phrase used by the *Interim Report of the Special Committee on Baptism* by the Church of Scotland (1955), p. 4. The term "depth-exegesis" is attributed to William Manson.

church *(disciplina arcani)* made public to the candidates for
the first time at baptism. "Obviously the *disciplina arcani*
could flourish only at a time when infant baptism was not
normally practised. If children were let in on the secret, it
could not remain a secret for long."[17]

The other historical circumstance that led to the revival of
infant baptism involved a serious theological issue. In the
middle of the fourth century, it seems, infant baptism, apart
from emergency baptisms of children mortally sick, lost
ground, and was replaced by the normal practice of postpon-
ing baptism until "actual" sins could be confessed and forgiven in baptism.[18] Indeed, it was maintained that baptism
should be postponed until near the hour of death to ensure a
full pardon covering the entire life's wrongs. But toward the
end of the fourth century the practice of baptizing infants
returned to the scene, a revival that is mainly explained by
Augustine's theological justification. Tertullian had earlier
maintained that the baptismal cleansing was unnecessary
since little children are sinless and do not require forgiveness;
now Augustine in the early fifth century argued precisely the
opposite. Little ones inherit birth-sin *(peccatum originale)*
and enter upon life handicapped with the guilt *(reatus)* of
Adam's disobedience and their share in his fallen nature. It is
imperative that the stain of birth-sin should be cleansed at
the earliest opportunity and that baptism should not be
delayed, since the unhappy corollary of the strict Augustinian
teaching (which the Reformers rejected) is that unbaptized
infants are destined for hell.[19] No more powerful incentive to
promote and secure the theological rationale for infant baptism could be imagined. What was started with Origen who
first introduced the notion of baptism as a cleansing from
birth pollution was given a dark cast by Augustine in terms of
inherited guilt and remained as a shadow over the church's
baptismal practice until A.D. 1525, when Conrad Grebel effectively challenged the entire practice of infant baptism at

17. E. J. Yarnold in *The Study of Liturgy*, p. 110.
18. So J. Jeremias, *Infant Baptism in the First Four Centuries*
(Philadelphia: Westminster Press, 1962), pp. 11-18.
19. G. Wainwright, "Rites and ceremonies," p. 17.

Zollikon, near Zurich, and made real a "radical reformation."[20]

5. Appeals to history are ambiguous, however. There
are three remaining considerations that have decisively influenced our understanding of baptism in the modern church.
All of these suggestions get us to the heart of the matter.

a) How far does the New Testament practice reflect simply
a first generation missionary situation that no longer faced
the church with the same urgency after its recognition by the
state by Constantine and its establishment by Theodosius?
When Christian families appear on the scene and the concept
of a "Christian nation" makes its presence felt—as in Angli-
canism in England and her former colonies—will not this circumstance radically affect the understanding of baptism and
give an impetus to the practice of receiving the offspring of
Christian parents into the church's fold *as though* they were
in an identical position to Jewish children admitted to Israelite theocracy and its covenant? This seems to be the theological reasoning behind the wording, found since the eighth
century, of the bishop's prayer offered over the newly baptized infants:

> Almighty God . . . who has regenerated thy servants by water and the
> Holy Spirit . . . .

"Regeneration" takes on meaning in this context of admission to the church's family with the promise of a future
fulfillment that the pledges made by "their sureties" will be
performed when the infants come of age, as the Anglican
Catechism explains. That future realization involves the
church's provision of a catechumenate to ensure that children
admitted (unconsciously) to their privileges (being "a member of Christ, the child of God, and an inheritor of the kingdom of heaven") at an age of discretion when they present
themselves for confirmation. But, as we saw, the New Testa-

20. Dale Moody, "The Origin of Infant Baptism," in *The Teacher's
Yoke. Studies in Memory of Henry Trantham*, ed. E. J. Vardaman and J. L.
Garrett (Waco, TX: Baylor University Press, 1964), pp. 201, 202. For a
discussion of the events of January 1525, see G. H. Williams, *The Radical
Reformation* (London: Weidenfeld and Nicolson, 1962), pp. 120-127; cf.
Fritz Blanke, "The First Anabaptist Congregation, Zollikon: 1525," *Men-
nonite Quarterly Review* 27 (1953), pp. 17-33.

ment praxis is at once more simple and addressed to a different cultural context. The immediate appeal "Repent and be baptized" makes sense in a missionary setting—and yet poses a set of thorny problems when the service books written on the assumption of infant baptism are carried over to the church's mission in unevangelized fields. But what of adapting the ideas and the language used to express them to a *post-*Christian world, such as the one we confront in western Europe today? The charge of "baptismal disgrace" arises exactly here when only a fraction of the numbers of infants presented for infant baptism ever submit to training leading to a service of confirmation—or more importantly, to a personal commitment to Christ and his cause.

b) This sad "break-down" of baptismal justification, showing only too clearly the disparity between traditional paedobaptist theology and pastoral experience, raises the questions of which is the lesser of two evils and how best does the church cope in a new missionary situation, whether by a reverting to believers' baptism or by a more cautiously framed offer of baptism restricted to the children of Christian parents. A more drastic way out of the impasse is that proposed by Geoffrey Wainwright[21] who notes that the only satisfying way of regarding "faith" in baptism is to give it a sense of future promise. The "forward-looking" aspect is now generally part of modern liturgies: that the child may one day come to profess his own faith.

With this clearly demarcated limit of faith—and so of what happens in baptism—Wainwright asks whether it would be more honest and adequate to admit infants to the catechumenate in hope of their future baptism at such a time when they can voluntarily ask for it. His ruling concern is with the definition of the church: are baptized infants included, given the nature of the response they were able to make only through their sponsors at the "rite of initiation"? "Initiation" to what? is the big question.

As far as the "boundaries" of the Church are concerned, I would rather have the "positive" indefiniteness brought by the idea of a provisional

21. G. Wainwright, *Doxology. The Praise of God in Worship, Doctrine and Life* (London: Epworth Press; New York: Oxford Univ. Press, 1980), p. 141.

place for the children of believers than the "negative" penumbra of baptized unbelievers resulting from the failure of many millions baptized in infancy to arrive at personal commitment. In other words, any fringe had better be composed of those hopefully "on their way in" than of those apparently "on their way out."

c) The definition of the church and its perimeters lies at the heart of the baptismal debate. This issue cannot be discussed, moreover, apart from the matter of the church's unity. All will agree that the oneness of the body of Christ is less obviously apparent if those who profess the same name of their allegiance adopt, practice, and defend (often ebulliently) two quite diverse modes and theologies of initiation to that "one body." Are we doomed to "two baptisms" in modern christendom, or is our pious gesturing toward "our unity in Christ" only a facade to hide the deep divisions over this central concern: How are Christians made and ingrafted into Christ and his church?

In this concluding section let us review the strengths of both positions and recognize the values that both baptismal practices seek to conserve.

1. The Baptist insistence on baptizing only those who consciously profess faith in Christ is able to appeal first of all to the centrality of conversion in the New Testament Christianity based on a personal decision and witness to the world. Second, the dramatic nature of conversion is powerfully and pictorially displayed in the mode of immersion, based on Romans 6:1-14 with its movements of burial under the water and rising from the water playing out the call of death to the old life and a summons to new life in Christ. Third, there is a confessional value in this public ceremony, making possible the dynamic meaning of baptism as an acted parable, an effectual sign, and a profession of Christ's lordship, with a pledge of future allegiance.

2. Infant baptism, on the other hand, emphasizes the covenantal dimensions of faith in which God respects the family unit of "believers and their children." The theology informing infant baptism stresses divine initiative in salvation, that God acts prior to human response, and his action does not wait on our movement to come to him. Indeed, our

coming as helpless sinners is pictured in what God has done in baptism in coming to us in our helpless condition. "For of such (i.e., powerless infants) is the kingdom of God" suggests that no one enter the divine realm unless he or she is childlike; conversely, the children of the gospel story are exactly those whom Jesus welcomed.

> Forms of service which will hold together these divergent views on baptism and yet avoid ambiguity and confusion are obviously not easy to devise.[22]

This admission may appear to foredoom any attempt to unify christendom's diverse understanding of what baptism is and does. But there have been valiant attempts made to bring the two baptismal theologies together, for instance, in the scheme of union in the church of South India and more recently in revised service books published by the Lutheran and Methodist churches. The Anglican document *Christian Initiation: Birth and Growth in the Christian Society* (1970) also prepares the way for elements in a revised liturgy that will accentuate "confirmation" as a necessary complement to "baptism," and give the full rite of initiation a more decisively "personal" side in calling for the candidate's free response in later life.

One other liturgy for initiation has been proposed in the last decade and as an experiment in "baptismal ecumenicity" it deserves attention.

The North India and Pakistan Plan

This liturgical "compromise" made for use in 1974 seeks to unite "former" Baptists and adherents to the practice of infant baptism in the new united church of North India and of Pakistan. The document in question is really (as its title states) an "Order of Confirmation," which is at the heart of the episcopal act in laying hands on the candidates. The emphatic declaration is that they have come to the service publicly to declare their faith[23] and freely to assent to the pledge made in their name at infant baptism. With solemn emphasis it is made plain that confirmation is *not simply a recall of*

22. P. Hinchliff in *The Study of Liturgy*, p. 145.
23. See E. L. Wenger's note, "Indian Baptists' 'Covenant,' " *The Expository Times* 92 (Feb. 1981), p. 149.

promises made by their sponsors, but a public avowal on their part: "You have come to declare your faith in the Lord Jesus Christ, your acceptance of him as your Saviour, and your commitment to him for ever"—language that Baptists and others associate with personal conversion. The bishop's three questions, including "Do you accept Jesus Christ as your Lord and Saviour?" put a sharp focus on the matter of "profession of personal discipleship."

Yet infant baptism is acknowledged as an initiatory rite with validity seen in introducing the child to God's family and church. Prayers at confirmation look back to what was done at baptism, and invoke the fullness of the Spirit to complete in confirmation that gracious work begun in baptism. The effect of the bishop's confirming actions in the imposition of hands is to stress that the rite is completed as candidates increasingly experience the grace and power of the Holy Spirit; but every effort is made to bring baptism and confirmation together into a unitary rite that hinges on conversion as its fulcrum.

If a way forward out of the current baptismal impasse is to be sought and implemented, may it be that the North India scheme points in the most encouraging direction?

CHAPTER NINE

The Table
of the Lord

Sacrament of Unity

If baptism is still a center of disagreement and disunity within christendom, happily the indications are that deep controversy over the communion service is a thing of the past. The sad tale of church history is only too full of instances when the "sacrament of unity"—as Paul so declares it to be (1 Cor. 10:17)—was precisely the opposite. The eucharistic debates excited all kinds of bad feelings, and four hundred years ago Christians were misunderstood, persecuted, exiled, tortured, and killed in the name of a "correct" understanding of the Lord's Supper. Mercifully these times have passed and a new day of mutual understanding and tolerance has dawned. But there is more than just a desire to live together with our diverse eucharistic principles and practices. The last two generations have seen a remarkable coming together of Christians, a sharing of insights, and a cross-fertilizing of traditions that has sought to go back to a more firmly rooted biblical understanding, coupled with a recognition that in the sixteenth century both the Reformers and Trent were needlessly facing one another in adversary roles.[1] "It is the tragedy of

1. This account of the matter has been challenged by Francis Clark, *Eucharistic Sacrifice and the Reformation* (London: Darton, Longman and Todd, 1960; 2nd ed. Oxford: Blackwell, 1967). He maintains that the Reformers rejected—in full awareness of what they were doing—the late medieval doctrine of the "eucharistic sacrifice." This agrees with Peter Brooks's more recent contention that Cranmer's teaching is of the Zwinglian-Calvinistic type *(Thomas Cranmer's Doctrine of the Eucharist* [New York: Seabury Press, 1965]).

See, however, the rejoinder to Clark's thesis by Nicholas Lash, *His Presence in the World* (London: Sheed and Ward, 1968), pp. 126-137. Cf. G. Wainwright, *Doxology. The Praise of God in Worship, Doctrine and*

English Church history that the Reformation developed as a reaction and not as a positive movement," wrote Gregory Dix.[2]

By way of an introduction to this subject we should review the various ways the eucharist has been at the heart of a growing common understanding of the church's teaching and how that teaching has in turn reacted on recent studies of the theology behind the celebration of the communion.

1. *Sacramental theology has explored fruitfully the idea of signs* as part of our general perception of the nature of Christianity. Truth is apprehended under "signs" that point to actions which in turn (Christians believe) "reveal" God. Since there is no direct revelation available for us to inspect and experience, we are dependent on intimations of the divine presence in the form or shape of symbols. Such "signs" or "symbols" convey meaning through word (language is a sign par excellence) and deed. The eucharist involves both aspects of human activity, based on what Jesus said and did in the upper room. The force of both parts of the Lord's Supper scenario is to change drastically the role played by the elements of bread and wine which Jesus "took" and over which he "spoke." A remarkable meeting ground has resulted as Roman Catholic interpreters have drawn away from the notion of a physical change (implied in transubstantiation), and Protestants have explored what the elements become when the word is spoken over them and they are received by the believing community; in some sense they have power to convey and actualize the reality, Christ's body and blood, that they point to and represent.

The common ground is seen in terms such as "transsignification" or "trans-finalization." Either word suggests a change of purpose or intent, so that the bread is no longer as

---

Life (London: Epworth Press; New York: Oxford Univ. Press, 1980), pp. 271, 272; C. Buchanan, *What did Cranmer think he was doing?* (Bramcote: Grove Books, 1976).

2. G. Dix in *The Parish Communion*, ed. A.G. Hebert (London: SPCK, 1937), p. 137. The mutual suspicions and recriminations of the Continental Reformers are well known: see Basil Hall in *A History of Christian Doctrine*, ed. H. Cunliffe-Jones (Edinburgh: T. and T. Clark, 1978), pp. 369, 370.

it came from the baker's oven but receives a new *"significa-tion"* as pointing to a new reality it now em*bod*ies, that is, the *bod*y of Christ given for us. B. Welte's[3] illustration of a piece of cloth really illumines this discussion. Once woven into a preset pattern of color and design, it is no longer just a piece of fabric but a flag conveying overtones of national honor and patriotic fervor (or the opposite, depending on how it appears to the eye of the beholder).

2. Biblical theology has come to the aid of a sister discipline in regard to *the meaning given to "memorial"* (Greek *anamnēsis*). Zwingli is usually thought to have refused any meaning of "This do in remembrance of me" other than the plain sense: we are bidden to recall an absent figure. A parallel was proposed by the Catholic O. Casel who, in the heyday of the history-of-religions school, drew on the parallels offered by the mystery religions to argue that the Christian sacraments shared in the same world view.[4] The eucharist was above all a ritual "mystery" involving a memorial of a cult hero. Now a study of the Hebrew thought-world behind "remembrance" has antiquated both previous views. There is a dynamic sense of "memorial," which suggests life not death, and is based on the evocative power of the "memory" of Israel in its cultic worship of God. Hebrew worship was dramatic and vital, reliving the past through its creed and liturgy, and calling Yahweh's past deeds out of their "pastness" into a living "present" where their saving benefits were newly appreciated and experienced. Gregory Dix exploited this discovery of the power of memory to evoke action, and concluded that since "re-calling" in biblical thought and teaching has the power to make "a past thing 'present' again, so that it is here and now *operative by its effects,"* the meaning of eucharistic remembrance is drastically altered. "The *anamnesis,* in this active sense, of the Paschal

3. B. Welte in *Actuelle Fragen zur Eucharistie*, ed. M. Schmaus (1960), reported by G. Wainwright, *The Expository Times* 88 (1977), p. 133. This article is most informative and I have drawn freely from it.
    4. O. Casel, *The Mystery of Christian Worship* (London: Darton, Longman and Todd, 1962). On this book see Th. Klauser, *A Short History of the Western Liturgy* (London: Oxford Univ. Press, 1969), pp. 24-30.

Sacrifice of Christ [is] the *'re-calling'* of it before God and man so that it is *here and now operative by its effects.'*[5]

Debate is still going on as to the precise way Christ's sacrifice is remembered "before God." One influential view, championed by J. Jeremias, reads the interpreting words of the Last Supper as though what was meant was "that God may remember me," that is, at the parousia.[6] The traditional way of translating the text (that it is our action of remembering Christ) seems preferable, however; but the issue of how God is affected by the eucharistic sacrifice still remains, and "reminding" God raises the awkward question whether God is ever forgetful or in need of our "recall."

3. What is more certain is *the eschatological dimension* of the church's supper since that meal expresses a gospel that is hardly understandable except in terms of the new age that has dawned with Christ's coming. The church stands at the "turning point of the ages" or in the interval where the old order and the new eon intersect or overlap (1 Cor. 10:11). The eucharist began its long history with the prayer-call *marana tha* ("Our Lord, come,"[7] 1 Cor. 16:22; *Didache* 10:6), and both the Synoptic Gospels and Paul concur in attaching a forward-looking side to the meal: we break bread and take the cup "until he comes" (1 Cor. 11:26) in his final kingdom, of which the eucharist is a continual foretaste and "ante-donation" (as Jeremias calls it), a pledge in advance of a final gift of messianic blessedness and joy in the banquet of

5. G. Dix, *Parish Communion*, p. 121 (his italics).

6. J. Jeremias, *The Eucharistic Words of Jesus*, 2nd ed. (New York: Scribner's, 1966), p. 252. Jeremias' argument has been effectively opposed by H. Kosmala, "Das tut zu meinem Gedachtnis," *Novum Testamentum* 4 (1960), pp. 81-94 on three grounds: (1) the verse (1 Cor. 11:24) is a unit, and must not be split in two: "Do this" and "in remembrance of me" go together; (2) the "remembrance" aspect is a veiled prayer for Christ's parousia, offered by Christians; (3) an alternative term for "remembrance" is *koinonia* (10:16), and that word requires to be taken as the church's relationship to the heavenly kyrios.

7. This division of the Aramaic term, which comes over into Paul's Greek as *maranatha*, is all but finally proved by some recent discoveries from Cave 4 at Qumran (i.e., in the Middle Aramaic period). See J. A. Fitzmyer, "The Aramaic language and the study of the New Testament," *JBL* 99 (March 1980), pp. 5-21 (p. 13).

the ages. The "sign" language of eucharistic action (eating, drinking, communing) translates into the picture of the church's ultimate hope, so appealingly given in Revelation chapter 19. Meanwhile the church is reminded forcefully at the table that it is a pilgrim community, living "between the times" of the first and final advents and sustained by the pilgrims' *viaticum* of "heavenly" food and "supernatural" drink (see 1 Cor. 10:1-5 for these images, as well as John ch. 6). Here we have no lasting city nor permanent rest (Heb. chs. 4, 13).

4. *The doctrine of the church* comes directly under the influence of this kind of eucharistic discussion. Appropriate to its calling as an "exiled people" journeying *in via*, on the road, and not yet having reached its heavenly home *in patria*, the church's meal is a constant reminder of the destiny that is not yet attained. The character of the church as an assembled company and more pointedly of a family gathered around a common meal-table is powerfully illustrated in this way. The stress on "fellowship" (Greek *koinōnia*) may be claimed as the unique contribution of Paul since he expounded his eucharistic doctrine in the light of a situation at Corinth where this "oneness" of the congregation had broken down and the nature of the church, in his view, was seriously impaired. The meal character of the eucharist delivers it from a too ethereal and too other-worldly status, and grounds its significance in the nature of the church as a fellowship of believers who together make up the *familia Dei*. So both the essential unity and the basic "shape" of the church are alike measured against the table of the Lord at which his people sit down together.

5. The communion service never allows the sharers to forget one other wholesome dimension of their faith: *the church lives in the world*, and in that world "bread" is a concern for millions who eke out their existence on the threshold of poverty, starvation, and malnutrition. The eucharistic bread is thus a silent call to the church's mission to enter into the service of Christ who fed the crowds in Galilee and died in loneliness and despair at Calvary. The offertory in which

the people brought their gifts to the table/altar for consecration is a tradition that takes up a second idea, namely, that what is presented at the eucharist represents man's labor in the field and orchard. Daily work is brought under the aegis of divine blessing and man's cooperation with nature and nature's God. And man's unity with the created order of which he is called to be steward and custodian is further exemplified, with an indirect rebuke of our misuse of nature when we selfishly keep her bounties to our own greed and exploit those who labor in her fields and farms at poverty levels. The eucharist can function as an effective socializing instrument, recalling the oneness of all members of the human family who, if they do not live by bread alone, certainly have basic needs that the rich nations cannot refuse to concede and then eat the Lord's Supper with clear conscience.

> The rich and the poor meet together;
> the Lord is the maker of them all. (Prov. 22:2)

From Last Supper to Lord's Supper

"Our Passover Festival is ready, now that Christ, our Passover lamb, has been sacrificed. Let us celebrate our Passover" (1 Cor. 5:7, 8). This statement, set in a context of apostolic admonition to a grievously failing community at Corinth, has the distinction of being the first recorded comment on what the church's holy meal-rite meant. The unusual feature, found in so many of Paul's allusions and enforcements, is that he is writing to a motley collection of men and women in Greco-Roman society who nevertheless are expected to catch his subtle undertones of meaning drawn from the Scriptures of the Jewish people. The case in point is the Hebrew Passover, which commemorated the past deliverance of the nation and anticipated its future blessedness in the messianic age. Already ethical teachings had gathered around the Passover with its various dishes, cups, and sauces. In particular, "leaven" was banned from Jewish households during the days of the feast, and a symbolic meaning was attached to the yeast. It stood for what permeates the batch of dough and makes it "rise," that is, pride. Paul exploits precisely this notion and warns against cherishing the presence of blatant evil (1 Cor. 5:6-8). At the center of his ruling he set the celebration of the meal—the Christian "Passover" since the lamb

has been sacrificed, even Christ. Paul's christianizing procedure receives here one of its most obvious examples. Both the
death of Jesus and the meal-rite that commemorates that
death are boldly interpreted in Old Testament–Judaic categories, and the significance of both are drawn out.

To this first illustration of the Christian "take-over" of
Jewish festal categories we must add the fact that there was
ample justification, going back to the Gospel tradition. Even
if it was written down at a time later than the sending of 1
Corinthians, we may believe that oral recitation of the "Last
Supper" meal, in the framework of the early church's practice of breaking bread, recalled the Passover time at which
Jesus and the disciples gathered in the upper room. There are
some problems about the precise nature of the meal they
shared, but Théo Preiss's comment is apropos:

> Everything leads us to believe that Jesus and the men of his time were
> less smitten with the passion for historical precision than ourselves and
> saw rather in the stories of the Exodus a totality which, because of their
> liturgical customs, was simply a development of the theme of the Pass-
> over.[8]

Jesus, in his final meal and looking back in part to meals
shared in Galilee, invested *this* meal with a solemn significance taken directly from the Passover. Ever since Gregory
Dix's initial discussion it has been customary to refer to the
four-action "shape" of the eucharist: Jesus took bread; he
gave thanks; he broke the bread; he gave it to the disciples.
As Dix applies these four actions and finds in them the four
momenta of the patristic and pre-Nicene eucharist,[9] namely,
Offertory, Thanksgiving Prayer, Fraction, and Communion,
the conclusion is unexceptionable. But the danger is that the
real point may be overlooked. The novelty of what Jesus did
in the upper room lay more with his words than with his
deeds.[10] And Jeremias and others have rightly called our

8. Th. Preiss, *Life in Christ* (London: SCM Press, 1954) p. 90.

9. These acts "constituted the absolutely invariable nucleus of every
eucharistic rite known to us throughout antiquity" (G. Dix, *The Shape of
the Liturgy* [Westminster: Dacre Press, 1945], p. 48). See also K. W.
Stevenson, *Gregory Dix—Twenty-Five Years On* (Bramcote: Grove Books,
1977). ch. 5.

10. This sentence does not overlook the importance of *actions* that are
interpreted by the accompanying word: see James F. White, *Introduction
to Christian Worship* (Nashville: Abingdon Press, 1980), pp. 207, 208.

attention to the importance of the "interpreting words" *(Deuteworte)* as pointing us to the heart of the matter. We may now analyse these:

    1. *The words spoken over the bread and the cup* have come down to us in several ways:

> Take; this is my body. . . . (Mark 14:22)
> Take, *eat;* this is my body. . . . (Matt. 26:26)

> This is my body which is *given* for you. Do this in remembrance of me. (Luke 22:19)
> This is my body which is for you. Do this in remembrance of me. (1 Cor. 11:24)

> The bread that I will give him is my flesh, which I give so that the world may live. . . . (John 6:51)
> Do this for my remembrance, this is my body. . . .
>   (Justin, *1 Apol.* 66.3)

> This is my blood of the covenant, which is poured out for many. . . . (Mark 14:24)
> Drink of it, all of *you; for* this is my blood of the covenant, which is poured out for many *for the forgiveness of sins.* . . .
>   (Matt. 26:27, 28)

> *First Cup:* Take this and *divide it among yourselves* . . . .
>   (Luke 22:17)
> *Second Cup:* This cup *which is poured out for you* is the new covenant in my blood (Luke 22:20)
> This cup is the new covenant in my blood. Do this as often as you drink it, in remembrance of me. . . . (1 Cor. 11:25)

> Whoever eats my flesh and drinks my blood has eternal life; and I will raise him to life on the last day. For my flesh is the real food; my blood is the real drink. Whoever eats my flesh and drinks my blood lives in me, and I live in him. (John 6:54-56)

> This is my blood; and gave it to them alone. . . .
>   (Justin, *1 Apol.* 66.3)

All this body of data is confusing, to say the least, and flies in the face of the general assumption that the church was anxious to preserve the words of the Lord as sacred *ipsissima verba.* One would have supposed it might have been otherwise; but plainly the evidence points in the opposite direction. For whatever cause we are faced with a bewildering array of traditions in which the Lord's words over the eucharistic elements have been handed down.

Yet, even when we grant this wide diversity—and there are even more complications arising from different textual traditions that give to Luke's account either the presence of two cups (Longer Text, in the order cup-bread-cup) or one cup but in the order cup-bread (as in the Shorter Text, mainly western)—there is still a way in which to claim certain features as part of Jesus' *ipsissima vox,* his authentic intention, even when we can never be sure of what he actually *spoke.* Set within the paschal framework (at least in the Synoptic and Pauline versions), the emphatic tones of his recorded sayings, were heard as follows:

a) "This *is* my body"//"This *is* my blood"—the most elemental version we have seems to put all the stress on the verb "is"; but this cannot be so, since Aramaic has no verb "to be" and the copulative often has an "exegetical" or explanatory force. Hence the rendering has to be "this stands for, represents *(significat)* . . . ." The clearest Old Testament background is Exodus 24:1-11 with verse 8 ("This is the blood that seals the covenant which the Lord made with you") offering a striking parallel. The bread-wine matches the thought in Deuteronomy 16:3 where the old Aramaic paraphrase has "This is the bread of suffering our fathers ate in the land of Egypt" (A. J. B. Higgins).[11] There is, in both instances, a representative identity between what *is* now on the table (both paschal and Christian) and what *was* then shared in the patriarchal story. The dynamic equivalence gives significance to the action undertaken to make the past live again—but with some obvious distinctions. The "bread of affliction" is now transformed into Jesus' own "person" ("body" = "I myself," as in the English "every-body" = "everyone"; the Aramaic link-term is *gûph).*[12] The "blood of the covenant" is now that which is given to seal a new agreement.

b) The *"new"* covenant may be suspected as being a Pauline addition, since we know how he exploits the idea of newness in his discussion (2 Cor. 3:1-16) of two contrasting ages

11. A. J. B. Higgins, *The Lord's Supper in the New Testament* (London: SCM Press, 1952), p. 53.

12. E. Schweizer, *The Lord's Supper According to the New Testament* (Philadelphia: Fortress Press, 1967), p. 17.

or economies that are, in this chapter, antithetical and exclusive. The whole midrash in 2 Corinthians 3 is based on Ezekiel 11:19; 36:26 but more particularly on Jeremiah 31:31-34 with its oracle of a coming new age and a fresh start made in God's relations with Israel. At this point the Lord's Supper takes over from the "model" of the Last Supper in the upper room, and adds in some transforming dimensions, namely, the "new covenant" is not revamped Judaism or the "old covenant" altered or improved (Käsemann's argument is sound here);[13] it bespeaks a new relationship between God and the world inaugurated by the universal man Jesus Christ whose people are neither Jews nor Gentiles but a "new creation" (1 Cor. 10:32; Gal. 6:16; Eph. 2:11-22).

c) The tokens of this new people living in a new age of eschatological fulfillment are already there in the Gospels as part of Jesus' announcement that the kingdom is "at hand." The command "to repeat" ("Do this in remembrance of me" in Luke-Paul)[14] may equally be a liturgical "afterthought," but it may well claim the sanction of the Passover ritual that Jesus apparently utilized with some care and attention. The Passover annual celebration is made in memory of the departure out of Egypt, according to the rabbinic authorities, based on Exodus 12:14 ("to remind you of what I, the Lord, have done") and 13:9 ("it will remind you"). The manward direction of the reminder is clear and straightforward. Lest Israel should become a forgetful and wayward people—a frequently heard complaint among the prophets—they need a certain prodding. This is the function of the way

13. E. Käsemann, "Paul and Israel," in *New Testament Questions of Today* (Philadelphia: Fortress Press, 1969), p. 185.

14. This saying is claimed by G. F. Hawthorne, "Christian Prophets and the Sayings of Jesus: Evidence of and Criteria For," *SBL Seminar Papers 1975*, vol. 2 (Missoula, MT: Scholars Press, 1975), pp. 105-129, as "a concrete example of a word received from the risen Lord, transmitted to the Corinthian church by the prophet Paul, which found its way into the gospel narrative as a word of Jesus through Paul's close associate, Luke" (p. 114). This suggested origin of Luke 22:19b is agreed to by J. D. G. Dunn, *NTS* 24 (1977-78), pp. 175-198. See also David Hill, *New Testament Prophecy* (Atlanta: John Knox Press; London: Marshall, Morgan and Scott, 1979), ch. 7.

that holy days such as sabbath and feast days gain in significance. They were to make the people vividly aware—by a dynamic retelling and reliving of Israel's past heritage in history—of all they owed to Yahweh the God of their fathers and their present status as his chosen and ransomed people.

Jesus stood in this historical stream. Whether or not he actually said, "Do this," the commission to "remember him" is implicit in the paschal setting and also in the promise of a future reunion in the Father's kingdom when he will be once again present with his own; the inference is clear that they were to expect him to reappear at any time in the interim. Hence "remember" and "watch" are linked.

2. *Paul enriched the eucharistic teaching he had received* (1 Cor. 11:23) in a number of directions. We may itemize these:

a) By common consent the key term of Paul's understanding of social ethics and its dimension of "partnership" that unites believers with the Lord and with one another is *koinōnia,* ordinarily translated "fellowship." The breadth and range of this word may be seen from the many uses of it that appear in Paul's writings. Our interest focuses on one particular aspect. Paul teaches a dual aspect of "fellowship" as it is seen at the Lord's table. Of first importance is the statement:

> The cup we use in the Lord's Supper and for which we give thanks to God: when we drink from it, *we are sharing in* the blood of Christ. And the bread we break: when we eat it, *we are sharing in* the body of Christ. (1 Cor. 10:16)

The italicized verbs are really nouns *(koinōnia),* with the verb "to be" understood. Both cup and bread are [a means of] participation in the realities they represent; and in a dynamically real way they convey to faith the substance of what they signify. They "convey" the Lord's own passion—his body given for and to us, his blood poured out for our sakes—to our experience. As we "bless" the bread and the wine, that is, thank God, we enter into the "good" of that for which we are grateful.

The horizontal plane of *koinōnia* is just as vivid for the apostle. Indeed, his argument reasons from the "one loaf"

(1 Cor. 10:17) to the unity of the "one body," the church. Outbreaks of social strife and selfish disorder that disrupted the church's life at Corinth (11:17-34) had no more serious or destructive effect than to put the church's *koinōnia* at risk. These malpractices served only to indicate to Paul how little the congregation thought about the nature of the "sacrament," a proper term in the light of their assumed protection from harm (in 10:1-13). Their despising one another, in an unholy contest between the rich and the poor, and their internal bickering over leaders and groups, led to a complete denial of the *Lord's* Supper (11:20), and their incurring only his displeasure and chastening. So Paul has to show the people how the manward aspect is indissolubly linked to the godward reference. No communion with the Lord apart from fellowship with one's neighbor in love and concern is possible—that would be his plain speaking in the drift of these verses. "One baptism, one table" (1 Cor. 12:13) are for him the ground plan of a doctrine of the church that is foundational in its essential oneness in Christ; and unity-in-fellowship is an integral part of its life in this world, with the eucharist its focal point.

b) The statement in 1 Corinthians 11:26 *("you proclaim the Lord's death until he comes")* is Paul's way of expressing the prospect of a future reuniting in the kingdom as offered in the Synoptic Gospels. Paul's choice of the word "proclaim" (Greek *katangellein)* is interesting; it otherwise connotes the public proclaiming of the kerygma, and in 1 Corinthians 2:1; 9:14; Romans 1:8; Philippians 1:17f. the apostle clearly saw no great distinction between the kerygma as preached in his public evangelizing mission and the same gospel as presented to believers at the Lord's table. The eucharist for him was "sacramental" in the same way that his preaching conveyed and actualized "the word of God" in human experience; and both types of proclamation rest on a basis determined by God's free grace, and evoke the response of faith (Rom. 1:5; 1 Thess. 2:13). Both ordinances are effectual within the encompassing field of God's prior action in "using" earthly means (words, bread, wine), and determined by the way they are "received," "believed," and "applied." The parallel is even closer when we press the question: *How* does the "sacrament"—whether of the word or the eucharist—"work"? Our understanding is helped by the mutual interplay between the two situations.

Paul's word is always his—it is the word of a man, but it becomes the divine word once it is uttered in faithfulness to his apostolic calling, and with a desire to communicate the saving truth of God. God then takes it up into his purpose, and so joins it with that purpose that it becomes no longer Paul's word but God's: "God making his appeal through us" (2 Cor. 5:20), "not . . . man's message but as God's message, which indeed it is" (1 Thess. 2:13b). In a very real sense this is for Paul the only rationale he offers for his striking conclusion: "God is at work in you who believe" (1 Thess. 2:13c). "The hearing that leads to faith" (Gal. 3:5) is the human response to the word of Paul, now owned by God.

So it may be said of the eucharistic action. The bread and wine remain what they were "created" to be, food and drink—until they are offered to God to be employed in his service. Their being caught up into the divine purpose "makes" them more than just what came from the baker's oven or the vineyard. They "change" in this dynamic sense of "becoming" Christ's body and blood under God's sovereign control, as expressions of his free grace, and operative only within the encompassing relationship of grace and faith, just as Paul's words take on the added dimension of meaning only where they are received in trustful acceptance. In both cases the issue turns on "control": both the word of the preacher and the use of elements are always subject to God's overriding. We do not "use" either words or species; God "uses" both, which is the essence of the debate between Luther and the medieval Catholics, as Hans-Christoph Schmidt-Lauber and R. P. C. Hanson have recently noted:

> "The difference between Luther and Rome does not lie in the real presence, but in the fact that Roman Catholic theology brings the atoning sacrifice of Calvary with all its effects and fruits *under our control, to use* and to claim it according to our desires and our pious devotion for this and that aim, for the living and the departed." (Quoted from A. E. Buchrucker, italics added)[15]

15. Hans-Christoph Schmidt-Lauber, "The Eucharistic Prayers in the Roman Catholic Church Today," *Studia Liturgica* 11 (1976), pp. 160ff.

Professor Hanson puts it in a slightly different way:

> This type of priest [allegedly empowered *to control the eucharistic sacrifice*] has in fact elbowed out the believer in eucharistic worship. He is not representing him, he is a substitute for him. (Italics added)[16]

In sum, we are trying to take seriously the meaning behind the verb in the twin sentences:

> This *is* the word of God.
> This *is* my body, my blood.

In both cases literal identity or transferred qualities seem ruled out of the question. Paul's words remain his, and by his "words" he stands self-revealed. Christ's body and blood are not there on the table in any transubstantiated or consubstantiated form. Yet the action of God in sacramental power turns the earthly into what is savingly effective: so under God's sovereign hand Paul's words become kerygmatic, and the bread and cup become soteriologically the Lord's body and blood in which believers are permitted a share (exactly in 1 Cor. 10:16, 17). The link-term is "proclaim," since the kerygmatic transformation turns the human into the divine, not magically nor automatically as though it were a conjuring trick working willy-nilly, but rather fideistically, as human faith meets and matches divine grace in a grateful response to the kerygma proclaimed alike from pulpit and table.

c) The eschatological sign under which the eucharist stands reappears in Paul in the words "until he comes" (1 Cor. 11:26). The context is manifestly polemical. The teaching is directed chiefly against the realized eschatologists at Corinth who imagined that they were already "raised with Christ" and had entered the full reality of the kingdom (1 Cor. 4:8). The net effect was to deny two aspects of the Christian message precious to Paul: the nerve-center of the cross (1 Cor. 1:18-2:2), and the future hope of the believers' resurrection. The Corinthian enthusiasts were basing their faith on an experience of baptismal resurrection that lay in the past. Already "risen with Christ" (a Pauline conviction, to be sure), they drew the unwarranted inference that theirs was now a charmed life on earth, set free from earthly constraints,

---

16. R. P. C. Hanson, *Eucharistic Offering in the Early Church* (Bramcote: Grove Books, 1976, 1979), p. 26.

moral restrictions, and mundane responsibilities. They were the corps d'élite of the new kingdom, unencumbered by such "petty" controls as sexual and marriage obligations (1 Cor. chs. 5-7), neighborly concerns (1 Cor. chs. 8-10), and the need to think of the non-Christian outside (1 Cor. 14:23-25; 15:33, 34) if only their private religious satisfactions were met (1 Cor. 14:12). Paul faults this community chiefly for their lack of love (1 Cor. 8:1) and their absence of that *koinōnia* that builds up the entire congregation. But his rationale is more than pragmatic and superficial. He goes to the heart of the theological aberration, and he does so by setting an "eschatological proviso" and a kerygmatic banner over all the Corinthian spiritual exercises and practices.

The "eschatological" dimension—"until he comes"—is meant to remind the church of its destiny as a pilgrim people not yet arrived at its heavenly goal and still under the discipline of its earthly toils. The eucharist points ahead to the ultimate homegathering of God's people, and prepares for the "banquet of the blessed" in the future messianic kingdom, and the resurrection of the dead. The following paragraphs (1 Cor. 11:27-34) extend this theme with their notes of judgment and warning. Either take yourself in hand *now,* says Paul, or face the prospect of God's judgment, already experienced proleptically in certain unhappy scenes at Corinth, at the last day. The intermediate term has once again to do with "the body" (11:29).

"Not recognizing the body" is best taken to refer to the corporate nature of the church.[17] It is hardly the eucharist loaf that is in mind here, as though the Corinthians were guilty of undervaluing it (by profaning it) or overstressing its importance by treating the bread superstitiously. The "body" is the church (as in 10:17; 12:12, 13), but the church seen as an eschatological society living in this world with all its snares and hazards and awaiting its final glory. The foretaste of that glory is given now as Christians share together after the pattern of Jesus' hospitality to "publicans and prostitutes" at

17. G. Bornkamm, "Lord's Supper and Church in Paul," in his book *Early Christian Experience* (London: SCM Press, 1969), pp. 127-129. See also H. Conzelmann, *I Corinthians,* Hermeneia (Philadelphia: Fortress Press, 1975), p. 202. See later p. 183.

meal tables in Galilee.[18] He promised them a share in the
future kingdom (Matt. 21:31, 32)—an aspect of the good
news the Corinthians had willfully overlooked with their
social snobbery and blatant disregard of the common life in
the body of Christ.

d) The Lord's table was for Paul an occasion of self-
examination (1 Cor. 11:28-32), as we have seen. The church
came to see its true status as a "fellowship of believers"
there, and to exercise that mutual caring and concern that
arise directly out of its oneness as Christ's body with many
members. Paul will go on to work out this theme in 12:12-27.

He enters a solemn warning here (in 11:28-32) based on
the experience of Israel in Egypt. We refer back to 5:6-8;
10:1-13, from which we learn of Paul's fascination with these
stories of his nation's fortunes at the time of the oppression
and the rescue operation undertaken by Moses. He is well
aware of Israel's deliverance and passage through the Sea of
Reeds, preceded by Yahweh's feast of Passover; and he sees
profound significance in the Christian version of "celebration" at the eucharist, at which God's redeeming mercies to
the new Israel are rehearsed and dramatized with a fresh content and connotation.

But Paul also knows how God's acts in history have a double edge. The Jews, secure in their houses and joined to the
people of God, celebrated Passover as an occasion of deliverance: "it is the sacrifice of Passover to honor the Lord,
because he passed over the houses of the Israelites in Egypt"
(Exod. 12:27). There is, however, an obverse side: "He killed
the Egyptians, but spared us" (Exod. 12:27), since that nation stood outside the covenant and was joined to its idols
(Exod. 12:12; Ezek. 20:8).

Idolatry was a prevalent sin at Corinth (1 Cor. 10:14), and
in typical Hebraic manner Paul reasoned that idolatry
brought with it a crop of evil associations (immorality, de-
bauchery, murder). What happened at the Lord's table illustrates and enforces the judgment power present at the exodus
and inflicted on Pharaoh and the Egyptian deities. Those
Corinthians who fail to "examine themselves" (as 2 Cor.

18. O. Hofius, *Jesu Tischgemeinschaft mit den Sündern* (Stuttgart:
Calwer Verlag, 1967).

13:5 warns) range themselves on the side of the unbelievers and eat the sacred meal in an unworthy fashion. It becomes to them a fearful sign of impending doom, akin to what happened to faithless Israel in the desert, even if they did have their sacraments (1 Cor. 10:1-13). Their behavior disrupted the unity of Christ's body and was tantamount to a denial of the church's claim to be the new Israel "without leaven" (1 Cor. 5:7), that is, pure from the defilement of the outside world to which the incestuous man is exiled (1 Cor. 5:12, 13) and which Paul thought still lay under the apocalyptic judgment of God (1 Cor. 11:32).

This midrashic background helps to throw a little light on the severity of Paul's ruling in the chapter that began with "instructions" to regulate the Corinthians' "coming together" for worship (11:17). His great fear was that their *synaxis* actually did more harm than good. His admonitions, therefore, were designed to promote that self-"mirroring" and awareness of corporate identity and calling that would neutralize divine displeasure (11:34: "you will not come under God's judgment as you meet together"). The solemn notes of these warnings are impossible to miss. It is thus an oblique tribute to the "occasional" nature of Paul's letters and so to the contextualized setting of Christian theology in the New Testament church that "had it not been for some irreverent behaviour at Corinth, we might never have known what he [Paul] believed about the Lord's Supper," as James Moffatt observed.[19]

Some Eucharistic Paradoxes

The development of the church's understanding of the supper rite has proceeded largely in response to past controversial discussions and dialogues, as we have noticed. Statements about the nature of the eucharistic sacrifice and debates centering on the "real presence" have been answered by counterstatements and opposing points of view with corresponding fresh emphases and new practices. We can see this feature clearly in the adaptations to the eucharist rite made by Cranmer from 1547 to 1552, the Prayer Book of 1552 re-

---

19. J. Moffatt, *Grace in the New Testament* (London: Hodder and Stoughton, 1931), p. 157.

flecting suggestions made by the Continental Reformers Bucer and Peter Martyr. Yet Cranmer's theology of the eucharist remained what it had been—substantially Calvinist,[20] and he seems to have been largely indifferent about rubrics.[21] The revision of 1662 hardly changed the matter, except that certain safeguards were introduced to ensure greater stress on the "reverent" behavior of the participants, and items such as the offertory, thanksgiving for the faithful departed, the singing of the creed and the sanctus were added, to give a fuller "body" to the service. From 1662 to 1980 (the date of the definitive Series IV) Anglican liturgy remained virtually unchanged, but repeatedly there have been shifts of emphasis (as in the 1928 Prayer book, and the later Series I-III). What follows in our concluding section is an attempt to state that which (in one person's judgment) needs to be conserved, and how our understanding of and approach to the Lord's Supper may be practically related to congregational worship. I propose a set of discussible points in paradoxical fashion.

1. *The presence of Christ is* at *the table, not* on *the table.* This sentence is intended to draw attention to what the species of bread and wine signify rather than the elements themselves. The bread and cup function as signs, pointing beyond themselves to him whose body and blood they represent and mediate to faith. Any substantial change in the elements seems to us to import an alien category into the biblical-theological understanding of "signs" as effectual symbols, as we illustrated earlier. (The piece of cloth remains what the designer and weaver intended, but once hoisted on a pole it becomes a flag unfurled at the masthead.) The "change" is in the use to which the object is put and how it is perceived by the beholder and user.

The "presence of Christ" is most real *at* the table as the elements thereupon direct our gaze not to themselves but to the one who came "in flesh and blood" offered for the life of the world (as John 6 phrases it). John Knox (based on his

20. So Peter Brooks, *Thomas Cranmer's Doctrine of the Eucharist.*
21. "Anthemes, respondes, invitatories, and such like thynges as did breake the continuall course of the readyng of the scripture"—these Cranmer eliminated (James F. White, *Introduction*, p. 123).

Form of Prayers and Ministration of the Sacraments, 1556)
helps us here:

> . . . to the intent that our eyes and senses may not only be occupied in
> these outward signs of bread and wine . . . but that our hearts and
> minds also may be fully fixed in the contemplation of the Lord's
> death . . . .[22]

As far as we can enter into the mystery of the "real presence" we may agree that Calvin expresses an indispensable
truth in his teaching on "worthy reception" or virtualism, a
tradition the Anglican Reformers—like Ridley and Cranmer—and Presbyterians were content to follow. The appeal is
to the divine promise and the believer's faith-attitude to that
promise, itself made possible by the Holy Spirit. Calvin
maintains that Christ is present as "before our eyes," and his
body and blood assure us that he is "one substance with us";
and even more, that he is "for" us, since both elements are
"given and shed for you." The union of Christ and his people is interestingly made part of the Roman rite. J. Jungmann
comments on the mingling of water with the eucharistic
wine:

> The mixing of the water with the wine symbolizes the intimate union of
> the faithful with him to whom they have bound themselves in faith;
> and this union is so firm that nothing can separate it, just as the water
> can no longer be separated from the wine.[23]

In the 1969 mass the ancient prayer is updated:

> By the mystery of this water and wine may we come to share in the
> divinity of Christ who humbled himself to share in our humanity.

It is doubtful if this version expresses the kerygmatic and in-
carnational truth as adequately as the 1570 Tridentine prayer:

> Grant that through the sacramental use of this water and wine we may
> have fellowship in the Godhead of him who deigned to share our man-
> hood, Jesus Christ thy Son.

---

22. See #36 in *Prayers of the Eucharist. Early and Reformed,* ed.
R. C. D. Jasper and G. J. Cuming, 2nd ed. (Oxford: University Press,
1980), pp. 179-181; J. M. Barkley, *The Worship of the Reformed Church*
(London: Lutterworth Press, 1966), pp. 22-26.

23. J. A. Jungmann, *The Mass of the Roman Rite. Its Origins and
Development* (London: Burns and Oates, 1959 ed.), p. 333. Cyprian *(Ep.*
63) emphasizes the symbolic sense of commingling the water and the wine.

How can we partake of and share in Christ's own divine-human life? Calvin's reply emphasizes the mystery of the promise, related to faith and activated by the Spirit, so that our eyes are directed both upward to heaven where Christ reigns and inward to quicken our souls and nourish them to eternal life. To see only the outward symbol is to partake in an unworthy manner; the communion is an inward experience conditional on faith and resting on divine promise. So it is not simple experience, but a most real communication of God's life within our lives. But it is essentially "spiritual" in its manner "because the secret power of the Spirit is the bond of our union with Christ."[24] Hence all eucharistic liturgy should include an epiclesis, an invoking of the Holy Spirit to come upon the worshiping company to give them sensitivity to the Lord's "real presence," and (for many Christians) on the elements, to set them apart for holy use. The new Roman mass (1969) has two epicleses directed to both the elements and the community of faith.

2. *The Lord's Supper is the supper of the Lord.* Cranmer's rewording of the service will make our point admirably. The material drawn up in 1548 was carried forward to the 1549 Prayer Book, but with the new main title "The Supper of the Lord, and the Holy Communion."[25] Bernard Lord Manning, from the standpoint of the Independents, sees much significance in a change from a ritual service to a supper meal. "The Lord's Table, for us, is the Table of the Lord. It is not the table of Congregationalists or of bishops. The union that we want is, first and most, a union that recognizes and expresses and proclaims our religious unity in the faith of the Gospel."[26] R. P. C. Hanson has also drawn into his discussion of the eucharistic offering the question of what kind of meal it is the Lord's Supper is supposed to commemorate. His fivefold cord of argument against the idea of a priestly offering of Christ is not easily broken:

24. Calvin, *Institutes* IV.xvii.33.
25. See #34 in *Prayers*, pp. 166-174.
26. B. L. Manning, *Essays in Orthodox Dissent* (London: Independent Press, 1939), p. 141.

(a) the priestly offering of sacrifice is not consistent with Scripture's witness; (b) historically Christians did not claim to be offering material sacrifices and their religion was distinctively noncultic; (c) the rationale of the priest acting for Christ is ill considered for he is really acting only for the whole church, Christ's body; (d) the eucharistic sacrifice can find no justification for affecting the state of the departed in the next life; and (e) this teaching leads, perhaps more than anything else, to the formation of an hierarchical caste within the church, giving rise to a sacerdotal system which on other grounds is out of favor today.

Professor Hanson, whose arguments we have summarized, may be permitted to give his conclusion in his own words:

> [The offering of Christ's sacrifice in the eucharist] contradicts Scripture, reverses the proper relation of the believer to Christ, leads inevitably to doctrinal and ecclesiastical developments which history has shown to be disastrous for the welfare of the Christian Church, and obscures the authentic, original, entirely sound early Christian doctrine of sacrifice.[27]

One positive way to set this corrective to work in a practical manner would be to suggest a retitling of the Lord's Supper. By a change of nomenclature we would be acting performatively, putting the stress where, it may be claimed, it rightly belongs: the Lord's Supper is *the supper of the Lord,* a meal shared by the congregation-in-fellowship, and expressing above all its common life as a gathered assembly, a people of the Lord, and a family of God.[28]

There is a practical point to our discussion. It is always a nice question to choose the correct verb—the *mot juste*—to accompany the subject, the Lord's Supper/the eucharist. In a public announcement is it: the service will be "held" (too plain), "administered" (too pompous, smacking of priestly propriety), "celebrated" (too grand perhaps for most congregations, though certainly a vast improvement),—or "spread," which has at least the distinction of reminding all present that it is the *table* of the Lord and his supper at which we are gathered as privileged and invited guests, and he is both "host and sustenance."[29] The "spreading of the table"

27. R. P. C. Hanson, *Eucharistic Offering,* pp. 25-27.
28. On the domestic character of the early eucharist, a feature lost from the fourth and fifth centuries onward, see G. Wainwright, *Doxology,* p. 327.
29. Cf. Zwingli's designation *hospes et epulum* ("he himself is both our *host and* our . . . *food,"* *Epicheiresis,* 1523).

has a common ring about it, and it keeps the eucharistic service on the right track of a rendezvous with the Lord and his people who are our people, all bound together "in the bundle of life."

3. *The Lord's Supper is a special means of grace, not a means of special grace.* The relocating of the adjective effectively does two things at a single stroke: first, it denies to the service any quality that savors of magic or superstition. That means that whatever the Corinthians may have imagined in terms of the sacraments conferring protection, or whatever Ignatius may have taught about the potency of the eucharist ("break one loaf, which is the medicine of immortality, and the antidote which wards off death but yields continuous life in union with Jesus Christ" [*Ephes.* 20:2]), the remembrance of the Lord in his death and risen life acts only within the network of lively faith and personal commitment to Christ and his demands of discipleship.

Yet there is, on the other side, the undisputed place of the communion service in the Christian life and the church's ministry that no other aspect of worship can rival or displace. C. T. Craig puts it well:

> The sacraments did not make faith unnecessary, but Paul would not have understood an expression of Christian faith apart from a community in which the Lord's Supper was celebrated.[30]

The relation between eucharist and grace is a much debated theme; but to us it seems that the issue turns on one central pivot, described in John's writing:

> whoever accepts my commandments and *obeys* them is the one who loves me . . . whoever loves me will *obey* my teaching . . . whoever does not love me does not *obey* my teaching. . . . (John 14:21, 23, 24)

> If we *obey* God's commands, then we are sure that we know him . . . . Whoever *obeys* his word is the one whose love for God has really been made perfect . . . . (1 John 2:3, 5)

> For our love for God means that we *obey* his commands. And his commands are not too hard for us. . . . (1 John 5:3)

The upshot of this teaching lies in the phrase "the grace of obedience." It recalls that while all God's dealings with his

30. C. T. Craig, *First Corinthians*, Interpreter's Bible, vol. 10 (Nashville: Abingdon, 1953), p. 145.

people are rooted in his grace, there is a way in which his especial pleasure is directed to those who abide in his love and walk in his way; in a word, those who are obedient receive the assurance of God's free favor and are permitted to rejoice in it as their privilege.

The Lord's table is as far removed from legalistic religion as one could imagine. Yet it is observed in fulfillment and pursuance of the one dominical command: "Do this." As our faith responds to and our love accepts such a gracious summons, God's favor rests upon the observance in a way that goes out to every demonstration of human responsiveness. Christian experience confirms what Scripture and theology teach. Here is a "simple" act, as customary as breaking bread and sharing a cup of wine, yet invested with a significance far outreaching the motions of taking, eating, and drinking. They are acts of obedient love and loving obedience; and the act conveys and actualizes the divine presence-in-grace as no other act can do, or in fact does.

Queen Elizabeth I was perhaps intent on cutting through the technical debates that surrounded the eucharistic controversies of her reign in an attempt to get to the heart of the matter; perhaps too she was being astutely political and noncommittal when she wrote:

> 'Twas God the Word that spake;
> He tooke the bread and brake;
> And what the word did make,
> That I believe, and take.

But at least she was expressing what the supper is all about: obedience to Christ's command.

4. *The real presence is made possible by the real absence.* One of the features that characterized the traditional Lord's Supper rite was its solemn accents, emphasis on sacrifice and oblation, and its mournful atmosphere. Undoubtedly there is a place for all these reminders as we are bidden to reflect on the cost of our redemption. The attitude of the worshiper as onlooker and attender with the priest functioning as celebrant and chief actor, usually with his back to the people, chimed in with this kind of eucharistic practice. The Liturgical Movement that began late in the nineteenth century had as one of its avowed aims a more active

part for the laity to play, an enterprise enthusiastically caught up in the Constitution *De Sacra Liturgica* (1963), the first of the Vatican II manifestos to be published and a sign of coming reforms. The 1969 mass increased the role of the lay worshipers, and lifted the rite out of a trough of mournful contemplation to a new plateau of joyful participation. The church was now the main celebrant: "Mother Church greatly desires that all the faithful may be brought to take that full, intelligent, active part in liturgical celebrations which the nature of the liturgy requires" *(De Sacra Liturgica,* sec. 14). The eschatological dimension was restored, giving the church its cue to celebrate as a pilgrim people and as sharers in "the heavenly liturgy . . . in Jerusalem towards which we are wending our pilgrim way" (sec. 8). One further item was an enhanced appreciation of the resurrection of Christ who as living Lord comes to greet his people. The mass began to lose the character of a passion play—like Oberammergau—intent on reviewing the past; it portrayed more vividly the fact that Christ is alive in the present. The 1969 Roman rite, the Anglican Series III, and the Methodist service all agree in the wording of one of the memorial acclamations:

> Christ has died,
> Christ is risen,
> Christ will come again.

Justification for this central affirmation is seen clearly in Luke 24:13-35. The Emmaus road disciples were aware of the Lord's risen presence as he took and broke the bread (24:30, 31); the climax of the story is written in editorial language: "how they had recognized the Lord when he broke the bread" (v. 35). Postresurrection appearances thereafter are fixed usually but not exclusively within the setting of a meal (Acts 1:4 [RSV marg.]; 10:41; John 21:10-13; cf. Mark 16:14). W. Rordorf's thesis that the origin of the Lord's day is to be traced here to the postresurrection meal theophanies[31] has much to commend it, though it has recently been attacked.[32]

31. W. Rordorf, *Sunday: The History of the Day of Rest and Worship in the Earliest Centuries of the Christian Church* (Philadelphia: Westminster Press, 1968).

32. R. T. Beckwith and W. Stott, *This is the Day* (London: Marshall, Morgan and Scott, 1978).

The important point here is that our holding together in a paradox both real absence and real presence prevents us from stumbling into several pitfalls. "Real absence" may suggest a withdrawal of Christ's presence from the world and the church, which is manifestly untrue; yet in one sense he is thought of as localized in the heavenly regions, "at the Father's side" or "right hand" or exalted above all (these are common liturgical motifs found in Ephesians and other liturgical texts such as 1 Pet. 3:22). Nothing should imperil the character of Christ as enthroned and triumphant, at least as the exalted one in the *Regnum Christi* (the witness of Rev. 5 is clear). To that degree he is removed from his people on earth. The Lord's Supper does not imprison him nor bid us think of him as a hapless, immolated victim.

The eucharist is the occasion of his royal coming (Greek *parousia*). The cries of Hosanna and *Benedictus qui venit* ("Blessed is the one who comes") are appropriate in the eucharist prayers of invocation as well as in the earliest prayer specimen, *marana tha* ("Our Lord, come").

The "real presence" is equally a valid statement, reminding us that he who is thus exalted is still our brother and kinsman; and he pledges to greet his people as they invoke his presence. Yet his coming is not under their control—a fateful error, earlier referred to—nor the result of priestly manipulation or contrived liturgical action. *He comes in grace,* that is, in his own unfettered way, yet in accord with a promise he has given (Matt. 18:20).

The Lord's Supper is no memorial service, given its setting on the right side of Easter and the celebratory tone that runs through its proclamation of Christ's triumph. The eucharist traces the *Heilsgeschichte* themes from creation to the new world of God's ultimate rule over all creation. The great Eucharistic Prayer of Hippolytus ranges from

> [Thanks for] your inseparable Word,
> through whom you made all things

to

> [He] might break the bonds of the devil, and tread down hell, and shine upon the righteous and fix the limit, and manifest the resurrection.

The God of salvation-history is one who is always "coming"—to heed his people's call, to deliver them in their distress and save them from their sins and their consequences, to lead them forth as his covenant people, and to establish his rule in their midst. The Christian eucharist picks up and carries forward these noble ideas of election, salvation, new life, and guidance until the end is reached in a perfected kingdom of God.

Meanwhile, Christ "comes" at the eucharist in anticipation of his final parousia at the eschaton. The church is thus bidden to welcome him now, as one day it will greet him in the consummation, at the "banquet of the ages" (Rev. 19:7-9). To erect a memorial in honor of a dead leader or revered hero is an understandable human and patriotic gesture; but it has no place in the liturgy of the church of the risen one. Eucharist is not a wistful backward glance in nostalgia, but rather:

> Journeys end in lovers meeting,
> Every wise man's son doth know.

CHAPTER TEN

The Holy Spirit in our Worship[1]

Introduction

We have now completed our study of the chief constituents of Christian public worship. Our main data-resource has been the life and experience of the apostolic church as reflected in the pages of the New Testament. The pattern that emerges there, sometimes only in embryo, grew and developed across the centuries of church history, and we have plotted some notable landmarks on the way. Now is the time to look back, and in three final chapters to offer some assessments partly to do with the nature of the evidence we have at our disposal and partly in regard to the practical bearing of that evidence for church life today.

You may recall that we began our thinking about Christian worship with two observations regarding the nature of the enterprise that goes under that name. The first has to do with the essentially *theocentric character* of worship, since worship by implied definition is the *celebration and praise of God*. By this term we mean that our worship involves an activity undertaken not primarily to satisfy our needs, nor to make us feel better as a direct consequence, nor to minister to our aesthetic taste or social well-being. All these notions have crept into a modern understanding of worship and have tended in varying degrees to corrupt it. The truth is that the opposite of these apparently laudable aims may result as an immediate consequence of our engaging in worship. Richard John Neuhaus states this uncompromisingly:

---

1. On the theme of this chapter see J. J. von Allmen, "Worship and the Holy Spirit," *Studia Liturgica* 2 (1963), pp. 124-135.

The celebration that we call worship has less to do with the satisfaction of the pursuit of happiness than with the abandonment of the pursuit of happiness.[2]

Nor is there a foolproof guarantee that any of these desirable ends will ever be achieved. The goal of worship is the adoration of God for his own sake, since he alone is worshipful and the "end" of all worship. We acknowledge this claim he makes on our worship in the familiar language of the Westminster Catechism:

> Q. What is the chief end of man?
> A. Man's chief end is to glorify God, and to enjoy him for ever.

The road to that "end" (both as its terminus and its purpose) may well bring us through unpleasant and bitter experiences as we enter troughs of painful self-examination, an awareness of our sinful state, and a challenge to forsake our lesser loyalties at the behest of the highest of all calls that reach us, "Follow me." The path of worship in its ultimate approach to the Most High God often runs by way of repentance and renewal, an introspective trauma that may hurt us before it promotes our final healing. Paul knew that the painful process of repentance sometimes cannot be avoided but is part of the attainment of a desired end (see 2 Cor. 7:10 for a reference to a letter that both cost the writer much [2 Cor. 2:4f.] and led to the bruising of the Corinthian readers on their way to a full recovery). T. S. Eliot's lines spring to mind:

> The wounding surgeon plies the steel
> That questions the distempered part;
> Beneath the bleeding hands we feel
> The sharp compassion of the healer's art
> Resolving the enigma of the fever chart.[3]

The second observation we offered earlier was that because God is "fit to be praised" and "worthy"—a term implied in "worship"—the person who addresses him will want to *offer his best* in terms of a "sacrifice of praise" (Heb. 13:15) that makes demands and represents the best he has to offer. This is not, of course, a Pelagian desire to please God in one's own

2. R. J. Neuhaus, *Freedom for Ministry* (New York/San Francisco: Harper and Row, 1979), p. 126.

3. *The Four Quartets,* East Coker, ll. 147ff.

strength or to gain his approval by dint of "one's best" as though we could, if we needed to, influence God to act on our behalf. The call for our wholehearted attention and self-giving (heard in Ps. 96:8: "Bring an offering and come into his Temple") underscores the serious intent of the true worshiper who, while relying wholly on the divine grace and compassion, knows that only our full commitment to God really matches the degree of gratitude and appreciation with which we receive his gifts to us. At least this element is part of what "worship in spirit and reality" (John 4:24) involves; and the Father, we are told, seeks such serious practitioners of worship.

Faced by these several complementary faces of worship— God is holy, yet he seeks our communion; God is great, yet in some way he is enriched by our praise; God is love, yet he desires his love to be acknowledged and enjoyed and shared by us—we are presented with a momentous task. How can we offer to God a sacrifice pleasing before him? How can we aspire to be both solemn and glad in his presence, since his holiness requires a due sense of awe and his grace frees us from anxious fears? R. Otto's picture of God as *mysterium tremendum ac fascinans*—a mystery both terrifying and appealing—simply places the two paradoxical strains side by side.[4] In practical terms, the dilemma of worship is to know how to unite the solemn and the joyous, remembering that solemn does not mean mournful, for God is not dead and Jesus is the risen Savior, and that joyous is not another word for flippant, for God is holy and Jesus is Lord. Somehow we have to strike a balance between an access to God that fatally lies in the direction of being too sombre and rigid, and an approach whose path is lit up with ceaseless smiles and grins and equates worship with an unfeeling bonhomie.

The Spirit is the Answer

But what is the question? Precisely, we submit, the dilemma of worship is posed by *our* inability to bring together, when we are left to our own devices and resources, the twin requirements that lie at the heart of Christian celebration. To focus on God as central to all life, and to be delivered from that

4. R. Otto, *The Idea of the Holy* (London: Oxford Univ. Press, 1923).

egocentricity that is the plague of the human condition—
these are our prime needs. The Westminster formula sets out
the high ideal: ''to glorify God and to enjoy him for ever,''
while Luther as a theologian of grace knows his own inner life
so well that he can identify the human predicament exactly as
the heart ''turned in upon itself'' *(incurvatus in se).* This
''incurvation'' that ''turns all [God's] gifts to poison''[5] or
uses them for selfish aggrandizement and arrogant pride
means that we cannot and do not want to worship God for his
own sake but seek refuge in ''using'' worship for our own
ends. ''Join Us For Worship. You Will Feel Better For It!''
proclaims the church notice board, reported by Neuhaus.[6]
But the advertised promise is beguiling, as we have seen,
since it offers more than it can deliver, and if it were to suc-
ceed, it would still fail. For worship takes on its authentic
meaning when God is at its heart, and our self-centered interests and fussy concerns are kept under proper control.
What the worshiper needs above all is a reminting of the debased coin that will enable worship to shine in its own light as
an exercise calculated to direct us unerringly to God and permit us to view all else *coram Deo,* as he sees it. *Exactly at this
point we need the Spirit.* He is the answer to the church's
agenda for worship. For he alone can lead the people of God
to their true source of being in the lordship of God as the central factor of their life, and can turn us away from self-
oriented ways and works to that ''place to stand'' from which
we enjoy a God-related perspective. Such a ministry of the
Holy Spirit is, I submit, what Paul has in mind when he
claims: ''we worship by the Spirit of God'' (Phil. 3:3).

The lingering question or set of questions is, How does the
Spirit do it? To that matter we devote the balance of the
chapter.

The Holy Spirit in Action

1. *The Spirit promotes and inspires the Christian confession of saving belief.* As a preface to this rubric we should

5. Benjamin Drewery in *A History of Christian Doctrine,* ed. H.
Cunliffe-Jones (Edinburgh: T. and T. Clark, 1978), p. 325 on Luther's
phrase in turn drawn from his *Lectures on Romans,* Weimar ed., vol. 56,
p. 356.
6. R. J. Neuhaus, *Freedom,* p. 123.

freely admit that the offices of the Holy Spirit in the church are organized, in a New Testament setting, only in a loose fashion—there is no systematic statement. Our task is to draw together the various threads that hang down from a number of passages in the hope of weaving them into a tapestry.

The overall impression we gain by doing so is that the first Christians had a vivid awareness of the Spirit's presence and power, and their worship—to use the expressive phrase of W. C. van Unnik—stood within the "magnetic field of the Holy Spirit."[7] Our first observation emerges directly from that picturesque description even if the precise details are somewhat obscure. We begin with a well-known pericope:

> You know that while you were still heathen, you were led astray in many ways to the worship of lifeless idols. I want you to know that no one who is led by God's Spirit can say, "A curse on Jesus!" and no one can confess "Jesus is Lord," unless he is guided by the Holy Spirit. (1 Cor. 12:2, 3)

The context of Paul's writing is that of the exercise of spiritual gifts (Greek *charismata*, v. 4) in the church, and it is likely that the cry "Jesus is Lord" first echoed in a meeting for congregational worship when at Corinth also the enthusiastic ejaculation "Jesus is damned" was heard. Notice that Paul prefaces this description by recalling the pagan ways of his readers when they were drawn away to the cult of those deities which Paul the Hebrew regarded as "dead" and "lifeless" (literally "dumb" in Ps. 115:4-8). We need to enquire what we may learn about the historical and cultural circumstances in which such a series of cries, "Jesus is cursed"/ "Jesus is Lord" would effectively match each other in a context where the inspiration of the Spirit was being claimed for both of them. Several suggestions have been made, each of them with varying plausibility and offering a distinctive contribution to our theme.

a) The way Paul refers back (v. 2) to the pre-Christian experience of the Corinthians suggests that the anathema invoked on Jesus was part of the same uncontrolled enthusiasm as the readers knew when they were "led away" (a strong

---

7. W. C. van Unnik, *"Dominus Vobiscum:* The Background of a Liturgical Formula," in *New Testament Essays in Memory of T. W. Manson,* ed. A. J. B. Higgins (Manchester: University Press, 1959), p. 294.

verb) to a corybantic worship such as Euripides describes in the *Bacchae*. (Paul's argument here runs parallel with a similar appeal in Gal. 4:8, 9.) What is in view is a scene where Corinthian enthusiasts have allowed themselves to be so imbued with "spirit"—akin to the devotees of the Cybele religion or the Dionysus cult—that they are uttering sentiments such as "Jesus is cursed," which Paul can only reject as unworthy and wholly mistaken.

Perhaps also, as W. C. van Unnik has maintained,[8] they had a lopsided view of the cross as Paul preached its message. Hearing the news that Jesus died a sinner's death and bore the divine curse (as in Gal. 3:13), they imagined that this was all-important and the sole saving truth. Paul reproaches them for embracing this half-truth, and goes on to insist that the lordship of Christ, attested in the resurrection, is what really matters (as in Rom. 10:9, 10). But there are some residual difficulties with these interpretations.[9]

The most we can say under these views is that Paul was confronted with a situation of unbridled enthusiasm at Corinth, and in response he appealed to the Holy Spirit to restrain excessive and exuberant ecstasy which claimed an origin in the "Spirit," much as he inserts a cautionary reminder that God is not the author of disorder and confusion in the worship of the assembly (1 Cor. 14:33).

b) Another influential way of understanding the scene in 1 Corinthians 12:1-3 is championed by Oscar Cullmann.[10] He

8. W. C. van Unnik, "Jesus: Anathema or Kyrios (1 Cor. 12:3)," in *Christ and Spirit in the New Testament. In Honour of C. F. D. Moule,* ed. B. Lindars and S. S. Smalley (Cambridge: University Press, 1973), pp. 113-126.

9. They are touched on in R. P. Martin, *The Family and the Fellowship: New Testament Images of the Church* (Grand Rapids: Wm B. Eerdmans; Exeter: Paternoster Press, 1980), p. 129.

10. O. Cullmann, *The Earliest Christian Confessions* (London: Lutterworth Press, 1949), pp. 28ff. A variation of this view is offered by J. D. M. Derrett, "Cursing Jesus (1 Cor. xii.3): the Jews as Religious 'Persecutors,' " *NTS* 21 (1975), pp. 544-554. Derrett argues that the formula "Jesus is accursed" stems from the context of the Jewish persecution of Christians.

S. Kim, *The Origin of Paul's Gospel* (Tübingen: J. C. B. Mohr, 1981), p. 50 wants to regard the phrase as an indication that this curse on Jesus was part of Paul's own repressive activity when *he* persecuted the church on the basis of *his* understanding of Deut. 21:23.

sees the problem as one of witness under trial by appealing to the later head-on confrontation between the Roman magistrate and the Christian bishop of Smyrna, Polycarp. The test was whether or not the old man would say "Christ is accursed" by acknowledging that Caesar is lord; and his *Martyrdom* tells the heroic story of his fidelity under fire. The Holy Spirit thus aided the witness and gave him the strength to confess Christ boldly and not to renounce him in order to gain freedom. In this interpretation, the sayings of Jesus that promised the Spirit for exactly this purpose are appealed to (Mark 13:11; Luke 12:11, 12). The chief difficulty here is that there is no evidence of persecution raised against the Corinthian church, though it is true that Paul and others had been called to the magistrate's bench in Corinth, according to the record in Acts 18:12-17.

c) Yet one more way of explaining the setting in the cry "Jesus is accursed/Lord" is current.[11] This view proposes that the cursing of Jesus relates to the earthly figure who was held in disdain by Gnostic Christians at Corinth; they allegedly used this disavowal of the human Jesus as a foil to set forth their hope in the heavenly, exalted Christ, and they claimed the Spirit as their present possession. Paul retorts that no such dichotomizing is possible, that the Holy Spirit may only be known in a wedding of the human Jesus and the enthroned, heavenly Lord, and that what we confess in worship joins together both our present experience of the exalted Christ and the historical past-ness of what God did in the earthly Jesus. Paul wants to protect worship from losing contact with concrete realities, lest these become lost in a mist of ethereal speculation. There is something to be said for this third view, since the data elsewhere in the Corinthian correspondence point to the presence of precisely such a gnosticizing tearing asunder of the past and the present, and specifically regarding the earthly and the exalted states of existence (see 2 Cor. 5:1-10; 11:4). Paul's reply is clearly in an exposition of "the theology of the cross" over against a belief in realized eschatology that held the resurrection to be a present actuality and minimized the hope of the church's future (1 Cor. 15:12).

11. The most influential exponent is W. Schmithals, *Gnosticism in Corinth* (Nashville: Abingdon Press, 1971), pp. 124-135.

Paul's theology of Christ's present lordship starts from the cross (1 Cor. 1:18-21) and points to the "first installment" of the Spirit (2 Cor. 1:22; 5:5) whose inner witness is ever to stay within the bounds of experience set by the forgiveness of sins and reconciliation to God; and that experience rests on the death of Jesus for sinners (Rom. 5:1-10; 2 Cor. 5:18-21).

Perhaps for our purposes there is no need to choose one of the above interpretations to the exclusion of the others. The Spirit, we read, does safeguard our worship from unseemly and indecorous manifestations that lead only to confusion and disorder. He inspires the confession of Christ's sole lordship in the credal forms we have noted, and in both baptism and times of testing the believer is known as one whose life is set under the kingly authority of Jesus Christ. No anticipation of future glory, however well glimpsed at worship, can forget the way of the cross in this world, and our confession is one that joins the exalted Lord and the humiliated servant as alike eminently praiseworthy, as in the "canticle to Christ" (Phil. 2:6-11). Charles Wesley has captured these several ideas in his noble stanza, addressed to the Holy Spirit:

> No man can truly say
> That Jesus is the Lord,
> Unless Thou take the veil away,
> And breathe the living word;
> Then, only then, we feel
> Our interest in His blood,
> And cry, with joy unspeakable,
> Thou art my Lord, my God!

Our offices of worship take on meaning as they are focused on God whose loving design is revealed in Christ—and in Christ crucified and exalted. The Spirit's work is to make that focusing possible and to keep our gaze fixed there, whether the temptation to avert it comes in the form of a luxuriant emotionalism, a fierce call to compromise, or an etherealizing of our faith whose contact with history is made tenuous. The Holy Spirit is the great safeguard against all such tendencies; he promotes the lordship of the crucified and recalls the errant church to its one hope, "Jesus is Lord," a confession we make as often as we assemble for worship on his day and with his presence among his people.

2. The offices of the Spirit are exercised in the several ways worship takes shape. *He energizes and controls the various configurations* that together go to make up all we understand about Christian liturgy. The following list sets down what these items are, chiefly for convenience's sake, since we recall that Christian worship is a seamless robe, and every single part needs to be seen within the pattern of the whole. But it is remarkable how, even when the list is given, the ministry of the Spirit is prominent throughout.

a) He inspires the church to pray, helping believers in their weakness (Rom. 8:26, 27) and, in a mysterious way that Paul does not pause to explain, interceding for Christians by apparently interpreting before God the hidden secrets and unspoken requests that we find hard to articulate in words.

The above statement is the usually accepted view of Paul's teaching in Romans 8. Christian prayer remains "under the sign of this not-knowing, of real ignorance, weakness and poverty, and that even in their prayers they live only by God's justification of sinners," who are assisted by the enabling Spirit of God (so C. E. B. Cranfield).[12] Ernst Käsemann, however, has proposed a different way of regarding Paul's words here and has set the teaching in a polemical vein.[13] In this view Paul has in his sights a wrong understanding of glossolalic speech (called "sighs too deep for words") when it is regarded as a freedom from earthly things and a profession of the church's advanced spirituality. Paul protests that this is not so. The glossolalic utterances betray the church's kinship with the rest of creation that groans in travail and expectancy of final deliverance; they need an interpreter as the charismatics at Corinth were told; and those who cry out in this way are only too acutely conscious of their own infirmity and not-yet-accomplished redemption. The Spirit comes to the rescue of the church at worship. He is (only) the first installment (Greek *aparchē*) of the final salvation, and acts as an interces-

---

12. C. E. B. Cranfield, *The Epistle to the Romans,* The International Criticial Commentary, vol. 1 (Edinburgh: T. and T. Clark, 1975), p. 422.

13. E. Käsemann, *Commentary on Romans* (Grand Rapids: Wm. B. Eerdmans, 1980), p. 241. But see A. J. M. Wedderburn, "Romans 8.26— Towards a Theology of Glossolalia?" *Scottish Journal of Theology* 28 (1975), pp. 369-377.

sor/interpreter needed to make prayer meaningful just as the glossolalic speech at Corinth was restricted to the presence of an accompanying interpreter to give it sense and significance (1 Cor. 14:13, 26ff.). The "unspoken sighs" are therefore a sign of the church's lot in this world and of its utter dependence on the Spirit to fashion a mode of worship that is pleasing to God. The polemical thrust of Romans 8:26f. is to be seen when we move on to Romans 12:1, where Paul offers his corrective. That which is agreeable to God's will is a "living sacrifice" of the entire person, offered as "rational worship" and involving the whole social life of the Christian in the church and the world, as Colin Brown observes.[14]

Whether the passage under review is to be taken positively or polemically, Paul's emphasis remains. The Spirit's work is to make such an addressing of God in petition and praise a reality in the first place (since we do not know *how* to pray as we ought) and then a meaningful exercise *("what* to pray for" follows on). The life of prayer is set within the orbit of the will of God, and it is the Spirit's help we invoke in making our approach to God a means of our understanding and doing that will.

Paul is clear that the Spirit gives life and so places the believer within the family and fellowship of God's people (see 2 Cor. 3:6; Rom. 8:2, 11; Gal. 5:25). As part of that experience of "new life in the Spirit," Christians were able to gain and enjoy access to God through Christ the divine son and the vivifying ministry of the Spirit. In terms that are implicitly trinitarian in structure and content, the limpid statement of Ephesians 2:18[15] expresses the conviction, rooted surely in Christian experience gained in worship:

> Through him [Christ] we both [Jews and Gentiles, now one in the new man, the body of the church] have access in one Spirit to the Father.

b) Worship especially in the Pauline mission communities had three sides, as far as we can judge. The *charismatic* ele-

14. C. Brown in *The New International Dictionary of New Testament Theology,* vol. 2 (Grand Rapids: Zondervan, 1976), p. 885.

15. G. Wainwright, *Doxology. The Praise of God in Worship, Doctrine and Life* (London: Epworth Press; New York: Oxford Univ. Press, 1980), p. 91 comments on Ephesians 2:18: "This verse from Ephesians expresses exactly a classic pattern in the history of Christian worship."

ment was prominent.[16] By this term we understand the offering of enthusiastic and exuberant praise and prayer under the direct afflatus of the Holy Spirit, whether in intelligible speech (what Paul calls "speaking . . . with my mind," 1 Cor. 14:9) or ecstatic utterances (what he refers to as the gift of *glossolalia,* 1 Cor. 14:2, 6ff.). While Paul does not condemn the latter practice, he is sensitive to its apparent danger of exhibitionism and meaninglessness (1 Cor. 14:20-23). He knows how easily such an exalted experience can get out of hand (1 Cor. 14:32, 33). He warns against allowing this type of worship to predominate in such a way that it cancels the concern for the upbuilding of the entire fellowship (1 Cor. 14:12).

Paul, in fact, sets some controls on *glossolalia* by channeling the use of the gift into the realm of the Christian's private devotion (clearly in 1 Cor. 14:2, 18, where Paul's *own personal communion* with God using "a tongue" is in view). But whenever the gift is practiced "in church worship" (14:19, 28) where believers come together in public assembly (14:23, 26) it is a different matter—and evidently *glossolalia* then has a different purpose. No longer is it a question of a person speaking solely to God; rather, it is a matter of a message directed to the assembled company. So there must be a corresponding interpretation in order to explicate the tongue and make its meaning clear and plain. The overriding consideration is that everyone must be edified, not just the speaker of *glossolalia* (14:5). "Interpreting" the esoteric utterance is itself a gift of the Spirit (1 Cor. 12:10); and when "tongue" and "interpretation" are linked the apostle's chief pastoral concern is satisfied: "To each is given the manifestation of the Spirit for *the common good*" (RSV) or "for the good of all"; and that means that "the whole church may be helped" (1 Cor. 14:5).

Congregational worship in the Pauline churches also has its *didactic* side. This term covers a wide ministry involving the spoken word that aimed at clarifying the will of God for the

16. Books—popular and technical—on the so-called "charismatic movement" are legion. Fundamental is W. Hollenweger, *The Pentecostals* (London: SCM Press, 1972); but more related to the concerns of worship is Colin Buchanan, *Encountering Charismatic Worship* (Bramcote: Grove Books, 1977).

people. Various verbs are used to show how seriously Paul took this ministry of instruction and Christian education: teaching (1 Cor. 12:8; 14:26; cf. Eph.4:11; 1 Tim. 3:2; 4:13; 5:17), instructing (1 Cor. 2:13; Col. 3:16), prophesying (a term that from 1 Cor. 11:4, 5; 14:3, 31 looks as though it signified what we today call preaching);[17] and discerning the truth and testing the content of prophetic oracles (1 Cor. 14:29; 1 Thess. 5:21). The ability to speak the word of wisdom and knowledge, to prophesy, and to distinguish the genuine prophetic message from the spurious utterance (see 1 John 4:1)—all this ministry is made possible as the men and women who engage in it "are inspired by one and the same Spirit" (1 Cor. 12:11). The Spirit is Christ's gift to the church (Eph. 4:7), and through him Christ's bestowal of ministry (Eph. 4:11, 12) is made effectual.

The Pauline model of worship placed increasingly heavy emphasis on didacticism as an integral part of worship, and there is a developing line from "free participation"[18] (1 Cor. 14:26) to a more orderly and structured sequence, as we shall see. Yet the Pauline motifs remain: an awareness of the Spirit's activity in teaching and training believers, and his insistence that "everything must be of help to the church" (1 Cor. 14:26).

The third feature of corporate worship strikes the note of praise, for which the term *eucharistic* conveys the exact sense. From the Greek verb "to thank" or "praise," this description applies equally to prayers of thanksgiving (referred to as "blessing [God] in the Spirit," 1 Cor. 14:16), to prayers of "general thanksgiving" (1 Tim. 2:1-4) with one special focus, namely, "grace over food" (1 Tim. 4:3-5), to hymns of praise inspired by the Spirit (Eph. 5:19, 20 = Col. 3:16, 17), and to the occasion par excellence when believers met to celebrate with grateful spirits the festival of redemption at the Lord's table. At Corinth party rivalries and selfish behavior

17. So I interpret David Hill's conclusion in *New Testament Prophecy* (Atlanta: John Knox Press; London: Marshall, Morgan and Scott, 1979), pp. 128-131. The entire scope of Hill's chapter five merits careful study.

18. Paul may well have been disapproving of this type of worship because of the dangers leading to confusion and disorder inherent in it (so A. Robertson and A. Plummer, *A Commentary on 1 Corinthians*, The International Critical Commentary [Edinburgh: T. and T. Clark, 1914], p. 320).

marred the assembling for the Lord's Supper (1 Cor. 11:20). The very objective that the eucharist gathering should have achieved, namely, a true fellowship *(koinōnia)* between believers, was never attained. The purpose of edification and mutual enrichment within the body of the Lord was frustrated. To that extent the relation of the Spirit to the eucharist was not possible, for the reason Paul had given earlier.

In 1 Corinthians 10:16, 17; 12:13, Paul had drawn lessons from the oneness of the eucharistic loaf and the unity of Christ's body to remind the divided church of its sorry condition. Above all, the Corinthians had failed to see the connection between the "one Spirit" (in which they rejoiced) and the "one body" of Christian community. The intermediary- or link-term is the "one bread, one cup" symbolism, recalling how Christians have a share in the one loaf and have been "watered" by the one Spirit.[19] The thrust of the Pauline argument is a powerful incentive to a unity whose focal point is the table of fellowship as the Spirit makes its eucharistic occasion a meaningful reality. Otherwise the sad conclusion stands: (a) the fellowship meal fails completely to live up to its name (1 Cor. 11:20: it is not the *Lord's* Supper that is eaten; rather, the Corinthians are simply taking their agape meals in selfish disregard of their fellow believers), and (b) more seriously, "your meetings for worship actually do more harm than good" (11:7). There is a "judgment theme in the sacraments" (C. F. D. Moule's title),[20] and all manner of evil results flow from the root cause of "not recognizing the Lord's body" (11:29). The last term has been taken to refer to the eucharistic species that the Corinthians were treating as ordinary bread. But this is unlikely, given the high value of sacramental efficacy the Corinthians already had displayed (1 Cor. 10:1-13). Other scholars refer the Corinthian fault in 11:29 to their taking a magical view of the elements and so disdaining the need for a corporate sharing of the meal. Probably we should see here an allusion to the "body" (of 1 Cor.

19. Or baptized, as G. J. Cuming has recently argued, suggesting that the verb in 1 Cor. 12:13 means just that *("Epotisthēmen:* 1 Corinthians 12.3," *NTS* 27 [1981], pp. 283-285).

20. C. F. D. Moule, "The Judgment Theme in the Sacraments," in *The Background of the New Testament and its Eschatology,* ed. W. D. Davies and D. Daube (Cambridge: University Press, 1956), pp. 464-481.

10:17, looking ahead to 12:12, 13), which is the church. What the Corinthians failed to discern was the unity of the Spirit that the eucharist was designed to promote and exemplify. There was a massive breakdown of *koinōnia* at Corinth and Paul offers some strong advice to set matters right. Their "not recognizing the body" means, in effect, a denial of the Spirit's unifying action. For all their talk of the Spirit and their claims to be "spiritual" (lit. "people of the Spirit," *hoi pneumatikoi,* 1 Cor. 14:37), they had lamentably failed to see the Holy Spirit in the most obvious and telling of all his actions, namely, in bringing the one people of God to a common place of mutual interest and selfless caring for one another, even in sickness and bereavement (1 Cor. 11:30), at the one "table of the Lord."

Our conclusion, based on the above survey, leads to one important result. Whatever the outward forms or expressions of worship, at least in the Gentile churches of Paul's foundation, the work of the Holy Spirit was there to promote the well-being and highest good of all participating members of the one body in Christ, and to build up that body in its true oneness and fullness. The thought of the church at worship as an accidental convergence in one place of a number of isolated individuals who practiced, in sealed compartments, their own private devotional exercises is utterly alien to Paul's mind. The picture thus held up to the mirror for condemnation may well have represented the idea of a Gnostic conventicle, perhaps favored by the Corinthian enthusiasts. It is quite the opposite of Paul's understanding of "one body, one Spirit."

3. The Spirit *keeps Christian worship on the right track so that elements that are inalienably personal and distinctively corporate are not lost.* We have seen the historical example of what went wrong at Corinth. Notions of sacramental magic (in 1 Cor. 10:1-22) and gnosticizing individualism (1 Cor. 14:26-40) were the plague spots of the Corinthian assembly. Paul counters these false ideas with clear statements about these two problems.

He meets the false confidence in sacramental efficacy with a forceful reminder of the ethical dimension of response to the new life in Christ. He calls for restraint, good order, and a clear-sighted awareness that sharing the body and blood of Christ is a token of commitment to the high standards of Christian living in both personal and social behavior. If the Spirit is not explicitly named in this regard, his activity is never far away from Paul's mind, as we see from Galatians 5:16-26.

The other aberration relates to the practice of individual piety that leads so easily to selfishness and the gratification of personal whims. Paul's check is to reinforce the communal interest (1 Cor. 14:26) wherein all the members have a part to play, yet not all have the same part, just as not all Christians have the same charismatic gifts (the questions in 1 Cor. 12:29, 30 expect the answer No: all do not practice these *charismata*).

Paul's pastoral theology is at its best in his handling of delicate situations relating to the church at worship. Into the framework of his insistence on good order, social decorum, sensitivity to one's fellow Christian, and a desire to offer "rational worship" with a curb on excesses and excrescences that disfigure the image of the church as Christ's body fall the two vexatious matters in 1 Corinthians: the role of women (1 Cor. 11:2-16; 14:33-35) and the presence of the angels (1 Cor. 11:10). Both strangely worded sets of rubrics are governed, it seems, by one dominant concern. Paul at all costs needs to keep Christian worship on that narrow track where it neither loses its distinctive element of "liberty in the Spirit" and the joy of celebration that the new age has dawned, nor falls into a morass of riotous excess that flouts all social conventions and permits Christians to imagine that they are under no constraint whatever, probably on the mistaken assumption that the new age had come in its fullness (1 Cor. 4:8). The healthy *via media* is the Pauline path; and the Holy Spirit offers direction to keep unwary feet from straying too far to either side.

Conclusions

Some general observations may suitably round off this chapter in the light of the ground we have traversed.

1. The centrality of God-in-Christ in Christian worship represented in the New Testament emphasizes the func-

tion of the Spirit's ministry to enable us to emerge from the straitjacket of our emotional introspections and oversensitive preoccupations with our "feelings" at any given time. Such "liberation" will permit us to rise into the presence of God through a contemplation of him in his goodness, beauty, and truth, and especially in his redeeming acts. Helping us to achieve this is the role of Christ's "remembrancer," the Johannine Paraclete, the divine Spirit (John 16:13, 14).

2. Our reliance on the "helper" (one meaning of *paraklētos*) to arouse in us a desire to worship worthily will mean that we will then want to offer our best. This implies a resolute turning from an indifferent, casual, and mechanical observance of the holy office of praise.

3. The gifts of the Holy Spirit are all personal, and this reminds us that an epiclesis of the Spirit is most adequately understood as his coming not on objects (water, bread, oil) but *on persons*. He respects our personalities made by God and for God. Therefore true worship will disown any practice that suggests a manipulation of people, a cajoling of them to accept what the priest offers or the preacher says, or an unhealthy play on the emotions, whether through eyegate or eargate.

4. The charismatic gifts, which derive from the Spirit within the congregation, are imparted not to a spiritual élite or a ministerial caste or a professional guild of leaders but *to the entire body*. This fact, rediscovered at the Reformation in the phrase "the priesthood of all believers," gives a dignity to the worshiping company in the exercise of its priestly function to offer up "sacrifices of the Spirit" (1 Pet. 2:1-10). Its reminder also makes real in our modern church life the fulfillment of that ancient promise that God will pour out his Spirit on all people (Joel 2:28ff.; Acts 2:16-21).

CHAPTER ELEVEN

Unity and Diversity in New Testament Worship

In the preceding chapters we have taken most of our examples from the New Testament, and have tried to see what patterns of worship found there have emerged as part of church life. From time to time we have also seen the way those pictures have been filled out and added to in response to the changing needs of the church across the centuries. Perhaps unconsciously we have left an impression of a New Testament norm that is fixed and invariable. If so, we need now to dispel that idea as we apply the tension between "unity" and "diversity" within the canonical documents to the theme of Christian worship.

The Limits of New Testament Practices

We should at the outset respect the developmental process that already has begun within the New Testament books. More particularly, the evolution of Christian worship has proceeded apace both acting upon the development of doctrine and in turn being influenced by the church's growing understanding of its message. Moreover, there are certain all-too-obvious limitations within the biblical literature itself.

While the churches that meet us in the pages of the New Testament are worshiping communities of believing men and women, not all forms of worship are present at any given time and place. Much of the descriptive data gives the appearance of being *ad hoc,* especially in 1 Corinthians chapters 12-14; and some if not most of it is tantalizingly vague. For example, at this time of the church's ongoing life we can have only the dimmest idea of what was Paul's meaning or the Corinthians' intention in 1 Corinthians 15:29: the practice of "baptism for the dead." Perhaps the most recent explanation[1] is the best —at least to date! Nor are we sure what the various meal occasions in the book of Acts mean. Presumably the breaking of bread at Troas was the Sunday eucharist (Acts 20:7-12); but what of the table fellowship in Acts 2:46, or the meaning of the unusual circumstances surrounding the same type of eating in Acts 27:35? The presence of angels who are spectators at both Jewish and Christian worship (according to the Dead Sea scrolls and 1 Cor. 11:10) raises all manner of unanswered—and unanswerable—questions.

Besides which, *our* questions are not always germane to New Testament concerns; and as there are precious few specific details (listed on a double page of the *Interpreter's Dictionary of the Bible: Supplementary Volume)*[2] and no surviving liturgies or service books (which are anachronistic terms in any case), we should refrain from reading out of the text what is not there to begin with!

In the New Testament period we are at the beginning of a long process. Christian worship has grown across the centuries in response to all sorts of stimuli and pressures. One obvious example is the sign of the cross, which emerged as an innova-

---

1. J. C. O'Neill, "I Corinthians 15:29," *The Expository Times* 91 (July 1980), pp. 310, 311. He paraphrases the sense of the verse:
   Otherwise, what do those hope to achieve who are baptized for their dying bodies? If the completely dead are not raised, why then are they baptized for themselves as corpses?
"The bodily rite of baptism was used by people who expected the body soon to die and decay, because they expected that rite to ensure eternal life at the resurrection of the body" (p. 311).
   This interpretation may be clarified and sustained in the light of H. Riesenfeld's earlier suggestion, "Paul's 'Grain of Wheat' Analogy and the Argument of 1 Corinthians 15," in *The Gospel Tradition* (Philadelphia: Fortress Press, 1970), pp. 171-186, that the issue at Corinth was not "the resurrection of the dead," but "death as the presupposition for resurrection" (p. 174), which the free-thinking Corinthians denied (1 Cor. 15:12, 36). They expected that they would never die since they were already celestial persons who had entered upon the life of the kingdom already fully present in time (1 Cor. 4:8).
   2. *The Interpreter's Dictionary of the Bible: Supplementary Volume*, ed. K. Crim (Nashville: Abingdon Press, 1976), pp. 556f.

tion (with some doubtful pre-Christian adumbrations)[3] at a time when a cipher for what was seen as the center of the faith (a staurogram, depicting Christ crucified) was needed to provide a badge for a universally acknowledged religion, at the time of Constantine's settlement in the fourth century. Church buildings that have survived as relics are dated to the third / fourth centuries,[4] replacing the pattern of house congregations we read of in the New Testament (1 Cor. 16:19; Col. 4:15, 16; Philem. 2) and in turn based on contemporary models, as recently investigated by Robert Banks.[5]

Leaders in worship services pose an equally fascinating enquiry. The scene in 1 Corinthians 14:26 suggests, at first sight, a structureless and spontaneous gathering, involving full participation of all present and without oversight. Yet leadership in the Pauline congregations is in evidence (Phil. 1:1; 1 Thess. 5:12; 1 Cor. 16:15, 16), even if the historical worth of the record in Acts 14:23 is under suspicion. By the time of the Pastoral Epistles we are familiar with regular offices in the church. There are overseers/bishops, elders, deacons and deaconesses, and perhaps other functionaries such as the performer of the office of lector (cf. Mark 13:14; Rev. 1:3). Leaders are known in Hebrews 13:17 as well as elders in James, 1 Peter, and the letters of John, while the role of the teacher figures prominently in James (3:1) as in the Johannine communities. These "ecclesiastical" offices are well attested in the so-called Apostolic Fathers (1 Clement, Ignatius, Shepherd of Hermas, *Didache*). The teasing question is whether we are to see the beginning of the process in Acts (e.g., 13:1-3; 20:28) and the later "Pauline" letters (e.g., Eph. 4:11).

Faced with the scarcity of unequivocal evidence, we may well pause before deciding categorically what rite or custom

3. G. W. Buchanan, "Worship, Feasts and Ceremonies in the Early Jewish-Christian Church," *NTS* 26 (1980), pp. 279-297.

4. The earliest, best-attested example is at Dura-Europos in Syria, dated A.D. 256. See Clark Hopkins, *The Discovery of Dura-Europos*, ed. Bernard Goldman (London/New Haven: Yale Univ. Press, 1979), p. 93.

5. Robert Banks, *Paul's Idea of Community* (Grand Rapids: Wm. B. Eerdmans, 1980). But see my review in *Interpretation* 36 (1982), pp. 212, 214 for some questions raised by this book.

belonged to the New Testament church, and say with certainty that we can attribute certain functions to specific individuals. This has sometimes been courageously attempted, as in the theory that 1 Peter reflects a sequence involving an (Easter) baptismal liturgy. But there are too many imponderables to give us confidence about this reconstruction.

One other caution is in order. It is a simple reminder that Christian worship as we know it today has gathered to itself a sizeable encrustation of practices, traditions, and procedures for which New Testament precedent is entirely or nearly completely lacking. Musical instruments, while referred to in liturgical settings in the Apocalypse, seem not to have played any part in house church services; there the music rendered is "in the heart" (Col. 3:16). Candles, too, are so much a feature of Roman, Orthodox, and Lutheran liturgical architecture that we have to remember how their use came in later than New Testament times (the lamps of Acts 20:7 were simply for illumination, and their heavy fumes were not like incense, as the ill-starred Eutychus discovered). The exceptional use of lights at Troas would be explained if we could associate the late-evening service with a Saturday-Sunday vigil, but this is dubious. Most likely the (later) practice, evidenced in Tertullian (A.D. 200) and especially in the fourth century in Constantine's Rome, goes back to the Jewish custom of candle-lighting at sabbath eve and Passover.

The literature of the New Testament church at its worship provides us with a set of principles—not fixed, immutable practices.[6] To be sure, in accepting the New Testament as

6. A brave attempt has been made to "reconstruct" a service of worship in the Pauline congregations, using the data from 1 Cor. 12-14; 16:20-24; Col. 3:16, 17, and the Pastorals, seen in the light of such post-apostolic sources as *Didache* 8:3 (for the Lord's Prayer), 1 Clement 40:1 (the reference to "order" related to 1 Cor. 14:40), Tertullian, *1 Apol.* 65 (common prayer) and *1 Apol.* 39 (hymn-singing). The resulting "Pauline service" looks like this:

Salutation (Grace and peace be with you)
Thanksgiving
Intercession
Bible-reading. Teaching and Admonition.
Psalms (ancient and modern)
Doxology, Kiss of peace
Dismissal (Come, Lord and the Grace)

normative we are obligated to test later developments by the
criteria of those principles insofar as we can ascertain and pin-
point them. Our chief interest now is to observe certain practical features of New Testament times and discover what if
any abiding significance is behind the custom. The examples
we have selected for illustration give the appearance of being
temporary and suited to an environment and culture that is
no longer with us. The cases in point are: the need for women
to be "veiled" at worship; the practice of foot-washing; and
the Corinthian agape meal at which the rich came early and
enjoyed themselves to excess while the poor arrived late when
all the food and drink had been consumed. The delicate matter is to discover the abiding theological principle or "constant" within the variable circumstance that is clearly condi-
tioned by the social milieu of the practice.

   1. The head-covering of 1 Corinthians 11:2-16 is required, says Paul, to preserve good order and as a sign of
authority in the exercise of the prophetic gift. He introduces a
mild form of hierarchical control to buttress his argument and
to place here (as in 1 Cor. 14:32-36) some restraint on the
feminine use of glossolalia, which was evidently in Corinth
(and maybe in Ephesus, according to 1 Tim. 2:8-15) getting
out of hand. At all events, Paul maintains, let there be
respect for social convention based on what he appeals to as a
"natural order" (in the creation story), and let the sexual
egalitarianism he had already adopted (in Gal. 3:28, 29)[7] not
be misunderstood as a movement for emancipation leading to
civic and familial anarchy. The prohibition against "speaking" (1 Cor. 14:34) refers either to women glossolalics or
(more probably) to the way in which their voices were heard
claiming the office of charismatic teacher and professing to
being "in charge" or usurping authority, not as women but

Added items (partly attested): Profession of faith, Lord's Prayer, Sanctus, and Decalogue. Common Prayers.
See G. J. Cuming, "The New Testament Foundation for Common
Prayer," *Studia Liturgica* 10 (1974), pp. 88-105.
   7. The pair "male/female" is omitted from the list in 1 Cor. 12:13,
evidently because Corinthian women members needed no such encouragement to seize upon Paul's charter. See J. C. Beker, *Paul the Apostle* (Philadelphia: Fortress Press, 1980), p. 319.

as *parvenu* charismatic leaders in the congregation (as in 1 Tim. 2:11, 12 and later Montanist prophetesses). Paul's counsel is clearly formulated under pressure from local customs in the hellenistic cities, a distorted view of his own charter of equality, and a concern to maintain the fabric of society while the gospel is proclaimed as a prelude to the end-time.

While these pressures are relaxed for modern Christians, there is still need to heed the warning for "good order," lest worship degenerate into an anarchical distemper of strident voices and self-centered exhibitionism. That, we submit, is the residual theological truth embedded in a wrapping of local convention. And today it has nothing to do with restrictions on feminine apparel or participation in divine service.[8]

2. The washing of the disciples' feet (John 13:1-20) clearly reflects a civilization that knows only unpaved roads, open-toed sandals or bare feet, and a hot climate to tax the weary foot-traveler. The bathing of feet was a mark of needed hospitality for visitors in both Israel and Greco-Roman cities (1 Tim. 5:10). But it is less obvious how anything remotely resembling this practice can have meaning in our urbanized society of the western world in spite of the explicit dominical command that he has set an example for us, "so that you will do just what I have done for you" (John 13:15).[9] "Example"

8. See the most recent discussion of these Corinthian passages by J. B. Hurley, *Man and Woman in Biblical Perspective* (Leicester: Inter-Varsity Press, 1981), especially pp. 185-194. He concludes that the restraint on women means that they ought not to participate in the examination of the prophets, while he concedes that they may exercise the role of prophet (in 1 Cor. 11). Yet that concession raises a serious problem with his exegesis. If women fulfill the role of prophets, why are they prevented from weighing what their fellow (presumably male) prophets have said, and why have they need to ask their husbands at home?

9. For example, the foot-washing ceremony moved from what it was in the early centuries (a bishop's lesson in humility as he washed the feet of a candidate for baptism) to the level of a sacramental act itself. Thus Ambrose taught that just as a person's sins were washed away in baptism, so the *pedilavium* washed away the hereditary sins which are derived from Adam, whose feet were ensnared by the serpent.

"This elevated the washing of the feet from a useful and edifying ceremony to a level on an equality with the sacrament of baptism itself," comments E. C. Whitaker, *The Baptismal Liturgy* (London: SPCK, 1981), p.

here signifies for us surely not the precise detail of a foot-
washing in a church service but the spirit that prompted such
an act in the first place, namely, a disposition of lowly service
on behalf of those who need our practical assistance in a way
they can appreciate. Paul has caught the inner meaning in his
words (Rom. 12:3-8) concerning modest self-esteem and
"showing kindness to others with cheerfulness." Performing
"humble duties for fellow Christians" is the Good News
Bible's legitimate rendering of 1 Timothy 5:10.

   3. The love feast as practiced at Corinth and elsewhere
(2 Pet. 2:13; Jude 12) was originally a sign of partnership between Christians as they sought in this way—by a common
table, based on Acts 2:44-46—to help the poor members and
exemplify the nature of the "common life in the body of
Christ." We have seen what the agape meal became at Corinth, and it deserved and received the apostle's stern rebuke
with advice that led to its abolition (1 Cor. 11:33, 34; Tertullian voices similar objections). But once more it is the
underlying principle enshrined in (but not tied to) the practice that matters. That principle is perceived by the word
koinōnia, which speaks of a united participation in all the
good things we enjoy in a divine-human fellowship and a
desire to share them. The need for such a "common sharing"
will remain when the temporary form of an agape meal has
passed.[10]
   The *exempla* we have culled from the New Testament
suggest a further question. Are not all the ingredients of first-
century worship variables and so negotiable? Why not abandon *all* the culture-conditioned elements and start afresh?
Why not accept seriously the challenge of "experimental worship" (as it is called) and devise a cultus in the tone and style
of our *zeitgeist,* respecting the past only when it has something really significant to pass on to us?
   Part of the reply to this proposal is that we are under

49. The textual history of John 13 (especially v. 10) reflects this change. See
R. P. Martin, *New Testament Foundations,* vol. I (Grand Rapids: Wm. B.
Eerdmans; Exeter: Paternoster Press, 1975), pp. 306-310.
   10. The agape meal was on its way out, even in New Testament times,
according to M. J. Townsend, "Exit the Agape?" *The Expository Times* 90
(Sept. 1979), pp. 356-361.

obligation to conserve the traditions we have inherited for the sake of the future; the other part is because we live in a time of theological and liturgical flux. In a period of transition it becomes difficult to know for certain which forms of innovative worship will survive constant scrutiny and testing in their use. Moreover, we are delivered over to a subjectivism that can find no rationale except the appeal to what is currently deemed "acceptable." That means what is in keeping with prevailing aesthetic taste or happens to line up with the latest piece of theological speculation. Clearly we need some objective criteria by which to evaluate all that passes for "Christian worship";[11] and at least one criterion will need to be found in all that the early church deemed necessary to express convincingly the good news and ensure its responsible transmission. *It is in the distinctives of apostolic worship that the truest "constants" will be present.* So we turn to ask what are such elements of early Christianity that mark it out as offering a worship of God that in turn makes it an exercise in a class by itself. If we can put these "parts" together into a pattern, we shall be looking at a version of Christianity that has an inner coherence and unity. In our day, when the pluriformity and diversity of New Testament thought and life are receiving full exposure, it is well that, while freely granting that the data do not yield a uniform and monochrome picture, we should see if there are underlying considerations that when taken together produce a recognizable pattern. The following sections will address in turn these two parts of the evidence.

The Coherence of New Testament Worship

1. Recent liturgical scholarship has shown the *centrality of Christ* in the New Testament "cult." There are certain "christological constants" that center upon two chief matters. One is the revelation of God as Father that Jesus Christ both brought and embodied. His distinctive appellation is "Abba," dear Father, suggestive of Jesus' intimate knowl-

---

11. This point is well established by G. Wainwright, *Doxology. The Praise of God in Worship, Doctrine and Life* (London: Epworth Press; New York: Oxford Univ. Press, 1980), p. 344: "What must be affirmed at the present juncture is that any liturgy which re-focused the encounter between God and humanity elsewhere than in Jesus Christ, to whom the scriptures bear witness, would be other than Christian worship."

edge of and communion with God; moreover, Jesus gave his
disciples access to this "secret" (Matt. 11:25-30 = Luke
10:21, 22) and epitomized it in a prayer-form, the Paternoster that has ever since remained normative for the Christian understanding of who God is and how we may approach
him in communal prayer and concern.

The other chief factor that stamps the Christian cult as
"one of a kind" in a society known for its syncretism and
religious tolerance is the shared conviction of the first Christians that they worshiped in the name of *the risen Lord.* His
resurrection from death to life was viewed not so much as a
"wonder" as a vindication of the claims of his earthly life and
as placing a capstone on his announcement of the imminent
rule of God. With his coming, sacrifice, and triumph the new
age, already heralded and anticipated in his ministry with
proleptic signs that gave hints and a foretaste of its reality,
the new era of God's reign among humankind had begun.
And the first believers rejoiced in the glory of living at the
"turning point of the ages." The resurrection above all else
gave them immediate, unmediated entry to a new life in
which the exalted Lord was known, loved, obeyed, and
served; he was their life in a way as natural as that in which
Paul can write "Christ lives in me," "life means Christ,"
"Christ is our life" (Gal. 2:20; Phil. 1:21; Col. 3:4).

The implications of the living Lord, present with his people as he came to meet them in worship, are vitally significant. The greetings of "Hosanna" and "Blessed is he who
comes in the name of the Lord" find their appropriate setting
in the anticipation of the risen Christ who drew near to his
own in a manner that assured them that he was no spooky
phantom or invading stranger (cf. Luke 24:18, 31). He was
the Jesus they had known in Galilee and Jerusalem, and the
postresurrection meal-occasions and meal-revelations that run
through all the Gospel sources and into the narrative of Acts
(1:4, marg., 10:41) have links with the feeding stories of the
Gospel tradition. The earliest prayer, *marana tha* ("Our
Lord, come"), takes us back to those days of the Aramaic-
speaking church when his presence was invoked and known.
The fact that Paul can appeal to a foreign-sounding watch-
word in writing to a Greek-speaking church (1 Cor. 16:22)
and that in an early liturgy *(Didache* 10:6) the same invoca-

tion reappears is positive proof that in *marana tha* we are looking at a liturgical formula that conveys powerfully the early Christian confidence in the Lord's personal presence and influence at the table and as an anticipation of his awaited parousia (Rev. 22:20). The replacement of the *marana tha* form by *Benedictus qui venit* (from Matt. 21:9), "Blessed is the one who comes," in the later liturgies only serves to underline the vivid expectation that from the beginning and as an indispensable feature of its cult, Christians understood the eucharist "as the coming of the Lord to His people in a visitation which prefigures the final advent."[12]

The implied claim behind these formulaic statements and in such christological sayings as Matthew 18:20; 28:20 is that early Christianity was boldly incorporating a unique dimension into its worship. But there are anticipations. The promise "Where two or three come together [in worship] in my name, I am there with them" (Matt. 18:20) is a case in point. The idea contained in the pledge of his presence is based on a rabbinic precedent: "If two sit together and the words of Torah [are spoken] between them, the divine Presence [Shekinah] rests between them" (Aboth 3:2).[13] It looks as though the Matthean promise is a bid to supersede the Jewish claim centered in the indispensability of Torah and its power to evoke the glorious presence of Israel's God. On the contrary, Jesus' presence among his chosen people who gather "in his name" is what counts in Matthew's apologetic.

We can broaden this notion of "promise and fulfillment" and suggest ways in which the Christian claim both builds upon and brings to ultimate meaning the motifs that characterize worship in several world religions. Judaism places its main stress on the nature of God as holy creator, a tenet gratefully taken over and incorporated into Christian praise. Submission to the will of God, regarded as numinous omnipotence, is the hallmark of Islam (as its name implies). Inner peace and liberation from an unending cycle of rebirth (nirvana) and self-control are offered in the practice of Buddhism. Cleansing and renewal are among the chief concerns

12. G. Wainwright, *Eucharist and Eschatology*, 2nd ed. (London: Epworth Press, 1978), p. 72.

13. H. Danby, *The Mishnah* (London: Oxford Univ. Press, 1933), p. 450.

of Hinduism with its multiplicity of gods and various rituals. Nor ought we to overlook the links that connect the rise of Christianity, which appeared historically within the world of Greco-Roman culture and religion, as offering a new "cult."

Yet, as was noted long ago, the vital matter is not what religions have in common, but what is their distinctive claim on attention and adherence. Marcion, in the mid-second century, for all his faults saw perceptively the real answer: the "new thing" that Jesus Christ brought into the world *was himself.* And Christian worship is established on the basis of that claim: the risen Lord is present with his believing church, which both expects and experiences his living power as he comes to meet them in the offices of Christian worship. The effect may be tested in a simple way. If Jesus Christ both introduced and "enfleshed" the final revelation of God, here is the touchstone of any worship that would claim his name and sanction: does it unmistakably lead the worshiper to a knowledge of the creator-Father in whom all creation lives[14] and who in his son has drawn us back into his family where we may live as his children? This, we propose, is the litmus test of authentic Christian liturgy, for (we are assured) it is the Father himself who seeks precisely such worshipers (John 4:23).

2. The second outstanding hallmark of the New Testament church at its devotions is, as we have reiterated, *the awareness of the Holy Spirit.* We recall how pervasively he is said to work in and through all parts of the "cult," even in New Testament times. The sequences of praise, prayer, confession, proclamation, and interpretation—all derivable from an Old Testament-rabbinic model in Temple and synagogue—are given a new impetus as the Spirit works conflu-

---

14. Both God as creator and God as Father (or personal, if "Father" today has too many sexist overtones) are needful to combine our understanding of God as "above" and "with" us. As Wainwright puts it in *Doxology,* p. 351:

> In that [God] upholds and transforms, he is transcendent. In that he does it from within, he is immanent. In the terms of personal relationship by which Christian worship is unashamedly characterized, the transcendent immanence or immanent transcendence of God expresses itself as God's love for his creatures.

ently through such exercises and focuses attention on God in
Christ as the goal of the church's adoration and love. The
Spirit draws all Christian energies and efforts to a center
point; and in the sacraments of initiation and remembrance
his works reach their high point.

In baptism what occurred in a special way for Jesus is
renewed in the experience of the obedient people. The Spirit
came upon the divine son whose "consciousness" of filial
adoption rose to a new pitch at his baptism (Luke 3:21, 22:
the western reading which unites allusions to Ps. 2:7 and Isa.
42:1 and has: "You are my son, today I have become your
father" is preferred by some scholars; but it is rejected by
Marshall).[15] Even so, as Marshall goes on to explain, filial
awareness and the call to messianic service go together in the
baptismal accounts of all the Gospels.

It is not difficult to see how, when transferred to the level
of Christian experience, the occasion of baptism could—and
in fact did—replicate the Lord's own special awareness, signi-
fying the gift of sonship, the visitation of the Spirit, and the
beginning of a life of testing and discipleship. Not least is the
dramatic way in which the Lord's baptism ushered him to the
start of a new phase of his messianic vocation. For the first
Christians conversion was indeed a crisis, wherein their old
pagan past was "judged" and rejected, and a summons to a
new "experience" enacted in realistic fashion. Baptism
would powerfully dramatize the transition, and the "coming
of the Spirit" was, from all the evidence we have in Acts, in
Paul, in 1 Peter, Hebrews, and 1 John, no casual or matter-
of-fact description. A life-transforming occasion centered in
conversion-baptism is in view; and the mighty Spirit was the
leading actor and agent in the drama.

The data regarding the eucharistic celebration are less well
attested, but there is no reason to doubt, from the one example we do have (the Lord's Supper at Corinth) that eucharistic
worship, prefaced by glossolalic prayer and hymnic speech
and including a solemn "fencing of the table" and warning

15. I. H. Marshall, *Commentary on Luke,* New International Greek
Testament Commentary (Grand Rapids: Wm. B. Eerdmans; Exeter: Paternoster Press, 1978), pp. 154, 155. He comments on the western text "You
are my son; *today I have begotten you*" that it "is undoubtedly
secondary."

rubrics (1 Cor. 16:20-24), was impregnated with the Spirit's power and grace. The later epiclesis formulas, which call down the Spirit on people and objects, carry forward the way in which Christians have always, whether consciously or not, recognized their reliance on the Holy Spirit for worship offered acceptably to God "in spirit and truth."

3. *Concern for others and the upbuilding (Greek* oikodomē)[16] *of the community* are features of apostolic worship, as far as we can judge from Paul's exposition. We must grant that Paul's emphases may well be colored by local conditions at Corinth, and may be but his immediate *ad hoc* responses to the situations that prevailed there. Against this conclusion we need to set the fact that he seems to be drawing on a body of traditional material as he appeals to the eucharistic and credal *paradosis* (in 5:7, 8; 10:16; 11:23ff., and 15:3ff.). The element that carries all the signs of being Paul's own innovative contribution is the way he relates the liturgical teaching to his acute, pastoral sense of the oneness of Christ's body and the urgent need at Corinth to see that "body-life" built up to maturity by emphasizing *koinōnia*. The precise circumstance of the Corinthians' attempt to turn the church into a hellenistic conventicle may well have spurred on his ecclesiology; what remains as a constant throughout his epistolary instruction is the clear picture of the church as a "body" in which all parts are summoned to function aright by respecting and cooperating with all the other "members." "Members together in the body of Christ" (Eph. 4:25) may stand as the overarching rubric of Paul's doctrine of the church and its congregational worship.

16. This term "upbuilding" needs careful definition. Ph. Vielhauer, *Oikodome* in the series *Aufsätze zur NT,* band 2 (Munich: Chr. Kaiser Verlag, 1979 ed.) concludes (p. 108):

> *Oikodomein* (to build up) is a cultic, kerygmatic, and ethical—and so a soteriological—term. It is not an individualistic idea, but one of fellowship . . . . It has nothing to do with a secular, human fellowship, constituted by human beings but a fellowship "in Christ," "in the Spirit," which is constituted and made normative by love, and related to the church. The logical subject is always God; the logical object is always the church. . . . The goal of divine purpose is not pious individuals but one holy catholic church in the profoundly and radically eschatological meaning of the New Testament. (My translation)

The prevalence of this consideration—summed up in the call "let all be done for edification"—is clear from the two chapters of 1 Corinthians. Let us observe the following:

The Spirit's charisma is given to each person for the good of all . . . . (1 Cor. 12:7)

Prophesying and glossolalic speech with interpretation serve one purpose: that the whole church may be helped [Greek *oikodomē*] (1 Cor. 14:5)

The most useful gifts of the Spirit are those which "help to build up the church . . . ." (1 Cor. 14:12)

The assorted items that go to make up the full list of worship practices at Corinth should "all serve for upbuilding . . . ." (1 Cor. 14:26)

Paul, in writing in the above way, obviously is in a generous mood. He freely grants the variety of the Spirit's endowments; he gently directs attention to what he considers the better *charismata;* and yet he finds a place for a wide assortment of gifts to be exercised in the assembly. The nonnegotiable factor, however, stands: all these enrichments must be directed to the growth of the entire congregation. This altruistic concern of a believer for his or her fellow Christians shines through Paul's discussion, and remains for him the distinctive social responsibility which he makes clear each person must have for one's neighbor (1 Cor. 10:24; see Phil. 2:4 for similar wording).

Patterns of Diversity

We now address a more difficult task. Granted that there are certain indispensable elements of unity or commonality which feature in New Testament worship, what can be said about equally obvious traits of diversity? Such variety, if we may anticipate our conclusion, will be seen more in the presence of complementary parts of the whole rather than rival or mutually exclusive aspects, and the multiformity of such liturgical approaches does not compromise or cancel out what we have earlier noted about some basic worship norms. The centrality of God revealed in Christ Jesus by the Spirit, the Spirit as a leader of corporate praise and prayer, and the interdependence of Christians as parts of a body—these are hardly in dispute wherever we turn. Yet there is some tension. We would expect this in the light of a developing, growing aware-

ness of the church's place in the world and in God's design
for humankind along with the need to build up models of
worship in response to emerging patterns of church life and
the increasing danger of alien teaching, particularly the threat
of the hellenization of Christianity. Four stages of a trajectory
that runs from Paul to the Johannine communities may be
detected. To each we will supply a label, more for the sake of
description than of delimiting the essence of each example
and prejudging its value.

a) *Worship in the charismatic community.* Little further
comment is needed under this heading since we have already
discussed the chief lineaments of Paul's teaching as addressed
to a charismatic community such as the Corinthian church
proved to be. Paul's response to problems at Corinth was on
the one side to acknowledge the work of the Spirit and to rejoice with his readers at the way the Spirit was given full rein
in their midst (1 Cor. 1:4-9; 14:12); and yet on the other
hand Paul entered some pleas for a canalizing of the Spirit's
afflatus and energy into channels that would be fruitful and
wholesome. The safeguards present in the Corinthian correspondence have been suggested by James D. G. Dunn, following H. Conzelmann, under three heads:[17] (i) the close
connection Paul wanted to establish and ensure between the
earthly Jesus and the exalted Lord, lest the church lose its grip
on the historical facts underlying the kerygma; (ii) the
primacy of love *(agapē),* which for the apostle is both a key
term (75 out of 116 occurrences in the New Testament) and a
controlling factor to test the legitimacy of the *charismata*
(1 Cor. 13:1-13: love is not a charism of the Spirit, but the indispensable accompaniment of all genuine charisms); (iii) the
concern for "up-building," whose effective denial at Corinth
resulted only in a break-down of the church's unity and disorder in the congregational assembly that left the outsider in
confusion. One of the powerful antidotes to the Corinthian
malady was Paul's heavy concentration on the ministry of
"teaching," which sought to combine the glossolalic and the
rational elements; that is, Paul wanted an informed and
intelligible approach to worship, under restraint and with

17. J. D. G. Dunn, *Jesus and the Spirit* (Philadelphia: Westminster
Press, 1975), pp. 293-297; cf. H. Conzelmann, *An Outline of the
Theology of the New Testament* (London: SCM Press, 1969), p. 40.

decorum, yet he knew that the Spirit's presence was just as necessary in that type of worship "with the mind" as in the case of the more exuberant and unfettered "abandon" to the Spirit's leading as prevailed at Corinth. The direction for the future was set by these cautionary controls, as we can see from Colossians 3:16 (emphasis on "teaching" and "instructing"); Romans 12:6-8 (the office of teacher is held in high esteem); and the later Pastorals where instruction and training in godliness go hand in hand and the immediacy of the Spirit's work has receded. Interestingly, with a more formal and routine type of worship the scene of "full participation" given in 1 Corinthians 14:6, 26 also disappears from view . . . until it is restored in the Society of Friends and then in the (Plymouth) Brethren movement in the mid-nineteenth century.[18]

b) *The reminiscing fellowship.* We choose this caption to describe the model offered in Luke's writing. He is evidently looking back on the "early years" of the church's life—see, for instance, how he can call Mnason the Cypriot "a disciple since the early days" (Acts 21:16)—from the vantage point of a later period and recollecting with hindsight how it was "in the beginning" when the pristine church came fresh onto the stage of history. Those halcyon days are recalled, not nostalgically, but in order to point up certain "lessons" for the church of Luke's own day, several decades after the events he is rehearsing. The Acts of the Apostles is, to that extent, a book designed to edify the later church, as E. Haenchen notes.[19]

Luke goes about this task by painting several cameo pictures of the church at worship in its earliest days. With variety in the geographical and cultural settings, we are introduced to the Jewish-Christian community with its attachments to

18. F. F. Bruce, "Books, Liturgical: 13. Plymouth Brethren," in *The Westminster Dictionary of Worship,* ed. J. G. Davies (Philadelphia: Westminster Press, 1972), p. 92.

19. E. Haenchen, *The Acts of the Apostles* (Philadelphia: Westminster Press, 1971), pp. 103-110. I. H. Marshall, *Acts,* Tyndale NT Commentary (Grand Rapids: Wm. B. Eerdmans, 1980), p. 33 concurs at this point. The Acts of the Apostles was written as a book "intended as it is to show the Christians of Luke's day what it means to be the church and how they should continue to live according to the pattern established in the early days."

the Temple cultus and ceremonies (Acts chs. 2-5). After Stephen's radical critique of the Temple religion and its sacrificial system (Acts 7), we are made ready to see a Judeo-hellenistic church emerge with a new basis for its cult, namely, the invoking of Jesus as Lord (Greek *kyrios*) and a new freedom and spontaneity as at multiracial cosmopolitan Antioch (Acts 13:1-3). The Spirit is prominent now as the great enabler of Christian worship, and he directs the future progress of the Christian mission based on a Gentile-oriented outreach. At Troas (Acts 20:7-12) we see how the "breaking of bread" service of Acts 2:42, 46 still persists in a Greco-Roman setting but as part of a structure that will later become "fixed" and provide the two-part sequence of the Christian *synaxis* or gathering for Sunday worship. The "liturgy of the word" and the "liturgy of the upper room" are visible in their embryonic forms in the simple house celebration in Troas.

We have no means of knowing how worship was conducted in Luke's contemporary church. What may be surmised is that with tendencies to overinstitutionalizing, his church was meeting problems characterized by a loss of enthusiastic fervor, a stifling of the Spirit with organized church structures, an ecclesiastical overlay, and a growing formalism. The writer of Acts is seeking to meet these challenges and doing so by "telling the story" of how it was "in the beginning" when the Spirit first came. Luke is one of the first Christian authors to raise the cry *ad fontes:* back to the fountainhead of the church's early moments. This "retour aux sources" is not undertaken in a detached way (as though he were the first "historian" recording history for its own sake). He has access, we may believe, to a reliable body of historical tradition and is in touch with at least some eyewitness reporting (Luke 1:1-4). But his ruling interest is to recapture the past as he retells it and make it speak to the present. His successive pictures of the church at worship are arranged to drive home a single point—that worship as his church knows it is in need of a fresh infusion of "power" derived from the Holy Spirit at a time of increasing and insidious formality and deadness. If the *Didache* is a document reflecting worship in Syria at about the time Luke is writing, we can "flesh out" the way

worship was losing some of its vitality and becoming institu-
tionalized on the way of transition from leadership under
"prophets" and "teachers" (cf. Acts 13:1-3) to the regime of
"bishops and deacons" *(Didache* 15:1, 2). Luke pursues
several lines in his attempt to stem the tide of rising ecclesiastical officialdom and institutionalism. Specifically, he
sets forth the church at its worship as (i) under the Spirit's
direct leading (Acts 4:31; 13:1-3); (ii) enthused with a con-
quering newborn joy (Acts 2:46, 47); (iii) faithful to apostolic
standards (Acts 2:42); and (iv) immediately alive to God
(Acts 5:11). But the "historicizing" attitude of Luke was, so
history informs us, a vain effort, since the theological and
cultural pressures were too strong. This "throw-back" to the
days of apostolic purity and dynamism served only to provide
a standard by which to measure the later church's increasing
response to demands for its "settling down" to the world and
adopting formal structures and patterns of worship.

c) *The organized church*. If we want to see the shape of
things to come, we must turn aside from the Lukan model to
the church in the Pastoral Epistles. Irrespective of questions
about their authorship and precise dating, these letters,
addressed on their face to Timothy and Titus, have several
features that place them in a period when the church has concern for ministerial "orders" and structural organization.
This is evident in a number of ways. The church is "defined"
as the "pillar and support of the truth" (1 Tim. 3:15);[20] and
within its framework Timothy fulfills a supervisory role, with
responsibility to ordain bishops, deacons, and (maybe) deaconesses (1 Tim. 3:1-13; cf. the credentials of the bishop/
overseer in Tit. 1:7-9). The pastor is charged to conduct worship in a "proper" manner (1 Tim. 4:11-16) and to super-
intend "elders" who preach and teach (1 Tim. 5:17-22),
having been set apart by the pastor's ordination of them.
"Heresies" must be exposed and denounced by Timothy's
recourse to the church's confessions of faith and credal formulas (1 Tim. 3:16; 2 Tim. 2:11-13); and both Timothy and
Titus are encouraged to remain loyal to the apostolic

20. The church in the Epistle to the Hebrews shares the same designation of a "building" (3:6), but the thought is controlled by the author's
equally emphatic insistence on the church as a "pilgrim people," living
"between the times" of the first and final advents of Christ.

"deposit" (Greek *parathēkē)* entrusted to them and to be handed on by them to others (2 Tim. 1:12-14; 2:2, 15-19; 3:14-17; Tit. 2:1, 15).

In such a setting the church is evidently conscious of the need for consolidation and containment by safeguarding the heritage of the past. Fidelity is a cardinal virtue, and worship clearly aims at conserving the truth of the apostolic gospel lest it should evaporate in the mists of speculative, gnosticizing debate (1 Tim. 1:3-7; 2 Tim. 2:16-18). The Spirit assumes a role of "preserver of the past" and is invoked to validate the right of Timothy, Titus, and their immediate successors in the ministerial office. These men are the church's bulwark for the purity of the gospel, and the worship they conduct and oversee is couched in the form of a confessing yet inward-looking community that needs to close its ranks. This literature has the church itself as an article of its faith (as in Ephesians). We are on the threshold of "ecclesiastical" history, when the church itself is part of salvation-history and sees no incongruity—indeed it rejoices in this—in professing that it believes in itself. "I believe . . . in one holy catholic apostolic church" is a sentence ready to be inserted in the creed.

d) *The "spiritual" fellowship.* In history every action of a momentous kind invites and promotes a reaction. The pendulum was not long in swinging from the increasingly powerful influences seen in the Pastorals, the *Didache,* Ignatius, and First Clement with their fussy concerns over set prayers, regular ministries, orderly worship, and an incipient sacramental system.[21] The reaction set in and became visible in the Asian churches whose inner life we see reflected in the Johannine Gospel and Epistles. If the Pastoral letters (also located in an Ephesian provenance, at least as regards the letters traditionally addressed to Timothy) give direction as heresy encroaches and seeks to dilute the truth of the gospel as Paul had proclaimed and championed it, the Johannine literature speaks to a situation where there are competing emphases, partly christological, partly ecclesiological, in the "community of the beloved disciple" John, to use R. E. Brown's

---

21. 1 Clement 20 is a good example of this insistence on "right order": quite the opposite to the situation described in 1 Cor. 14:26.

title.[22] We are interested in our study in one aspect only of the "threat to worship" as John's disciples feared it. Both Gospel and Epistles raise a warning against the trend to over-institutionalize. "John" senses the danger of suffocating the Spirit, placing too much emphasis on credal orthodoxy, relying too heavily on structural forms, and so placing the church in a new Babylonian captivity. It is a moot issue whether "John's" protest is directed to just such a situation as that seen in the Pastoral epistles.

At all events, for him the way forward is to stress the believer's individual participation in the life of God-in-Christ. We may set down some of the hallmarks of John's antidote. (i) Worship is set "in the Spirit" (1 John 3:24) and is largely independent of outward forms, locations, and ceremonials (John 4:20-24). The "water" of traditional religion is marvellously transformed into the "wine" of the new age where Jesus' glory shines forth as the universal logos (John 2:1-11). (ii) Love of God and the brethren is the real test of authentic Christianity (1 John 3:1-18; 4:7-21), over against credal orthodoxy and a blind trust in "sacraments." The antisacramentalism alleged in the Fourth Gospel by R. Bultmann is a timely protest against the opposite viewpoint of Oscar Cullmann who sees baptism, unction, and eucharist on almost every page of the Gospel.[23] The truth is somewhere in the middle. There is no explicit institution of the Lord's Supper in John chapter 13, which does, however, have an upper room meal; but the evangelist has incorporated a discourse set in the synagogue at Capernaum (ch. 6) as though to stress the "inner" meaning of eucharistic celebration: it is nothing less than feeding on Christ the bread of life, just as John's earlier chapter has depicted Jesus as the giver of living water (John ch. 4).

(iii) It cannot be fortuitous that this body of literature lacks completely the term "church" (Greek *ekklēsia*). For John the believers do form a society under the imagery of a flock (10:1-16; cf. 11:52) and the vine (15:1-11), but inevita-

22. R. E. Brown, *The Community of the Beloved Disciple* (London: Chapman, 1979).

23. R. Bultmann, *The Gospel of John* (Philadelphia: Westminster Press, 1971); O. Cullmann, *Early Christian Worship* (London: SCM Press, 1953), part 2.

bly in such images the important thing is the personal relationship the believer sustains to the Lord himself.[24] As the
sheep hear the shepherd's voice when he calls each by name
(10:3-5), so there is no possibility of life unless the separate
branches are linked to the parent stem of the vine (15:4, 5).
John's view of the church governs his concept of worship: the
church is made up of individual followers who are joined one-
by-one to the Lord, and the worship they offer springs
directly out of an experience of enriched individualism.

Conclusion

Four models of Christian liturgical praxis have been detected
within the church of New Testament times. We can summarize these several "patterns of worship" by expressing
each, if with some oversimplification, in a sentence. Paul is
all for the spontaneity of the Spirit, even if he imposes some
controls so that the essence of his kerygma may not be obscured or distorted. Luke harks back to the "good old days"
when the Spirit came and manifested divine power; and he
sighs for that lost innocence as he seeks to recapture it. The
Pastorals issue a stern call, in the name of Pauline orthodoxy,
for a closing of ranks and consolidating of the inheritance lest
it evaporate and be lost for ever. John is impatient of any corporate expression of worship that minimizes the individual.
So he signals the Asia Minor communities, let each one be
joined to Christ, and let worship be from the heart. He ex-
plores the vertical dimension of worship where Paul's image
of the body is of the horizontal kind.[25]

These are four complementary models. Each is needed
when we today forget their respective emphases and insights,
and exaggerate one or more at the expense of the others.
Christian worship is an exercise in keeping the balance by
refusing to topple over into frenzied enthusiasm to the

24. E. Schweizer, "The Church in the Gospel of John," in *Church Order in the New Testament* (London: SCM Press, 1961), p. 122 (11g): "the more strongly direct union of the believer with Christ is emphasized, the more clearly he is seen as an individual"; p. 124 (11i): "the individual's direct and complete union with Jesus Christ sets its stamp on the ordering of the [Johannine] Church."

25. T. G. A. Baker, *Questioning Worship* (London: SCM Press, 1977), p. 53.

neglect of good order and proper form. Yet we can go astray by succumbing to a deadly conformity to tradition by ignoring the vitality of the Spirit who works in our day with new forms. The church needs these models to supply ''mid-course correction'' as it journeys through history. It will never attain its perfect worship until it reaches its ultimate goal *in patria*, in the eternal homeland, where its feeble voice and imperfect worship will give place to the Jubilee of heavenly worship in a renewed creation. Until then, ''the Spirit and the bride'' live in creative tension, and seek to fashion a model of worship that is as pleasing to God as erring mortals can make it.

CHAPTER TWELVE

Reshaping
our Worship

Retrospect and Prospect
At the close of our studies we begin with a glance backwards. We have sought to clarify what Christian worship is and to extol its virtues as a cardinal Christian theme, trying to rescue it from the Cinderella role it plays in much current church teaching and practice. Worship is a noble word for a noble concept. It represents, as William Nicholls rightly says, "the supreme and only indispensable activity of the Christian Church. It alone will endure . . . into heaven, when all other activities of the Church will have passed away."[1] But worship is more than just a facet of church life. It underlines and informs our understanding of all we believe and cherish concerning God and his design for the church and the world. The focus of that design is Christ in whom authentic worship finds its model and through whom our worship takes on meaning. All we believe and proclaim is affected by how we see the ministry and mission of the church and its agenda in the divine scheme. We submit that no statement of the church's raison d'être comes near to the heart of the biblical witness or the meaning of church history unless the worship of God is given top priority. The church exists for this reason above all else. It is called into being and continues to function in God's providence and grace to offer to the Father the sacrifice of praise and thanksgiving, and to celebrate the mighty acts of God in creation, redemption, and the final triumph of his kingdom in this world and beyond.

1. William Nicholls, *Jacob's Ladder. The Meaning of Worship* (Richmond: John Knox Press, 1958), p. 9.

To put our definition in other terms, Christian worship is
*the adoration and service of God the Father through the
mediation of the Son and prompted by the holy Spirit.*[2]
Three corollaries follow from this statement.

1. *The trinitarian structure* of all worship that is
known as distinctively Christian is apparent. True, the doctrine of the Trinity is only embryonic in the New Testament
literature. That body of writing, reflecting Christian experience gained in worship, provides the raw materials for the
later dogma and ecclesiastical formulation—and there is a
long line of development from the christology of Luke-Acts to
Chalcedon!

The type of trinitarian theology we are offered in the New
Testament has two distinct features. First, it is a theologou-
menon based on experience, and second, it is cast in the liturgical wording of the church's praise of God. We can test the
validity of these two propositions.

Recently Stephen S. Smalley has demonstrated how both
Paul and John agree in associating the three "persons" of the
godhead with the life of believers; and they do so by writing
indiscriminately of the believers "in God" and God "in the
believers."[3] Consider the chart:

You in God	(Col. 3:3; John 17:21)
You in Christ	(2 Cor. 5:17; Rom. 8:1; John 15:4f.)
You in Spirit	(Rom. 8:9; Gal. 5:16, 25; John 4:23f.)
God in you	(Phil. 2:13?; 1 Cor. 6:20 is nearer; John 14:23)
Christ in you	(Col. 1:27; Gal. 2:20; John 14:18-20)
Spirit in you	(1 Cor. 3:16; Rom. 8:9; John 14:16f.)

2. J. D. Crichton, "A Theology of Worship," in *The Study of Liturgy,*
ed. C. Jones, G. Wainwright, E. Yarnold (London: SPCK, 1978), pp. 18,
19. The trinitarian "shape" of Christian worship is well brought out by
P. W. Hoon, *The Integrity of Worship* (Nashville: Abingdon Press, 1971),
p. 115: "The Trinity constitutes a basic morphology which cannot be
violated if liturgical theology is to be Christian."
3. S. S. Smalley, "The Christ-Christian Relationship in Paul and
John," in *Pauline Studies. Essays presented to Professor F. F. Bruce on his
70th Birthday,* ed. by D. A. Hagner and M. J. Harris (Grand Rapids: Wm.
B. Eerdmans; Exeter: Paternoster Press, 1980), pp. 95-105 (p. 98). Some
additional scriptural references have been supplied.

Presumably both apostolic writers can write as they do because they are basing their appeals or statements on facts well attested in human experience. They are not primarily theologizing but rather recounting what they share in common with their respective readers, and bidding them draw conclusions on the basis of a common realization of the life of Father, Son, and Spirit known to these men and women.

The salient verses in which the "persons" are drawn together in a single sentence almost invariably reflect the church's worship practices: Matthew 28:19; Acts 2:33; 2 Corinthians 13:14; Ephesians 2:18; Hebrews 9:14; and 1 Peter 1:2. Finally, Augustine's remark on the baptismal experience of Jesus, attended as it was by the heavenly voice of the Father's attestation and by the Spirit's descent, is apropos: "Go to Jordan, and you will find the Trinity." Christian instinct associated from the beginning access *to* the Father *through* Christ and *in* the Spirit with its own liturgical life and experience; and it may be suggested that the later formalization of doctrine sprang naturally out of this experience of fellowship with God mediated through his incarnate word and made real by the witness of the Holy Spirit.

One additional consequence of this trinitarian sequence is important. If, as we have contended, there is a threefold pattern to Christian worship, the "persons" are not to be played off against one another as though they were in rivalry or even pursuing a "division of labor" as an "economic" Trinity. There is no compromise, as we saw, of the Hebraic insistence on God's unity or unshared monarchy. Worship is most properly addressed to God the Father; there is no countenance given to a false christomonism as though the "cult of Christ" was in competition with the one God, nor any false reliance on the Spirit, as Montanus imagined, to the exclusion of a concentration on the Father as the "fount of deity" and so eminently praiseworthy in and of himself.

2. Christian worship is *salvation-historical in content and context.* The term "salvation history" is used in this connection in a purely descriptive way, as J. D. Crichton uses it when he delimits the scope of worship: "To the Father through the Son and in the Holy Spirit, is the underlying pat-

tern of the history of salvation.''[4] The term is used without a necessary commitment to the scheme of biblical theology under this name that offers a philosophy of history. In the way we are employing it, the designation ''salvation-historical'' *(heilsgeschichtlich)* implies that God's dealings with his people in the world are rooted in *history* and expressed in *salvation.* Two poetic pieces in the Old Testament saga will illustrate this theme. In Judges chapter 5 the song of Deborah, often claimed as one of the most ancient literary compositions in the Old Testament, invites the praise of Yahweh who acted in the events of Israel's past and wrought deliverance. The celebration of victory (Judges 5:11) is set within the framework of praise to God (v. 3). A sharper focus is put on this theme in Exodus chapter 15. There ''the song of Moses'' rejoices in God's saving his people and bringing them to their inheritance in the land (v. 17). The worship of the Temple is the climax of this grand enterprise, as the ''mighty acts'' (v. 11) of Yahweh are rehearsed and relived as both a reminder and a reenactment of all that Yahweh did for this nation, and continues to be and to do on their behalf. History—seen in the exodus and pilgrimage to Canaan—and present experience melt into one act of worship. The past is recalled so that it might be relived, and each succeeding generation feels its kinship and share in what God did for ''the fathers'' of Israel. Deuteronomy 26:4-10, Israel's first credo, expresses this interfacing of ''event'' and ''experience'' in a remarkable way. The narrative that begins with a harking back to the worshiper's forbears (v. 5: ''My ancestor was a wandering Aramean'') quickly loses its objective character as a dispassionate recital of ''deeds long ago,'' steps out of the frame of history, and becomes part of the worshiper's present experience (vv. 6-9: ''The Egyptians treated *us* harshly . . . *we* cried to Yahweh . . . he brought *us* here''). The climactic point is reached as the offering is presented: ''So now *I* bring to Yahweh the first part of the harvest he has given *me*'' (v. 10). This sequence clearly shows the genius of biblical worship spelled out in terms of recollecting the past, rehearsing God's mighty deeds so that they ''live again,'' and entering in a most realistic way into their dynamic mean-

4. J. D. Crichton, ''A Theology of Worship.''

ing for the present generation. At Passover all these motifs
are very much to the fore.

The "song of Moses" finds its natural complement in the
"song of the Lamb" (Rev. 15:3). The cluster of images that
gathers around the mention of the "Lamb" is exploited in
Revelation chapter 5, with its graphic pictures of a sacrificial
yet victorious animal which now stands at the centerpiece of
heaven's worship. The song is directed to this figure, which is
worthy because of its sacrifice and is praised because it has
redeemed humanity to God (5:9, 10). So the song continues:

> The Lamb who was killed is worthy
> to receive power, wealth, wisdom, and strength,
> honor, glory, and praise!

But the final paean of praise is ascribed to God:

> To him who sits on the throne and to the Lamb,
> be praise and honor, glory and might,
> forever and ever!

Old Testament themes are here in profusion, recalling the
sacrifices of Tabernacle and Temple, the Paschal victim, the
servant of Isaiah 53:7, and the horned lamb that leads the
flock in the Jewish apocalyptic writings. New Testament
counterparts to these adumbrations of sacrifice and triumph
are suggested by the twenty-four elders who rejoice in their
common redemption "from every tribe, language, nation
and race." The bounds of Old Testament particularism are
burst, and we confront a worldwide, multinational church as
successor to old Israel. The priestly ministry belongs to all
(5:10); no longer is it reserved to a hieratic caste or favored
nation.

Yet the church of the new Israel has learned well that God
acts in and through history: the scroll that the Lamb alone can
read is evidently the book of human destiny, "the record of
God's judgments and redemption that issue in the kingdom
of glory,"[5] a testamentary that contained the secrets of the
divine plan for this world and the next. The gracious purposes of God for his world are entrusted to the song's central
actor, and with his enthronement the drama reaches its high

5. G. R. Beasley-Murray in *The New Bible Commentary: Revised*, ed.
by D. Guthrie and J. A. Motyer (London: Inter-Varsity Press; Grand
Rapids: Wm. B. Eerdmans, 1970), p. 1288.

point. But he comes to his exaltation—as the New Testament
hymns (Phil. 2:6-11; Col. 1:15-20; 1 Tim. 3:16; Heb. 1:2, 3)
consistently recall—only by the path of obedient suffering,
sacrifice unto death, and submission to his destiny. Out of
this condescension, involving both a descent from glory to
shame and an act of amazing humility, there comes vindication by God in his resurrection and subsequent enthronement. That installation to the seat of authority is a token of a
new age of God's rule. All creatures throughout the universe
(we read in Rev. 5:13) ascribe praise to God as a sign of their
acknowledgment that there is a new Lord and that the day of
their independence is over (as in Phil. 2:9-11; Col. 2:15;
1 Pet. 3:22).[6]

The church's responding "Amen" sets the seal on the new
accession of God's power controlled by love (Rev. 5:5, 6: the
Lion is the Lamb). What happened in history and wrought
the world's salvation is seen now to have cosmic and transcen-
dental significance and to involve the "liturgy of heaven" as
much as the praises of the church on earth. The far-reaching
sweep of "the song of the Lamb" therefore gathers to itself
the paradox of what is and what shall be. In worship the
church reaches out to claim as present experience the universal kingdom of divine sovereignty over all powers that await
the final outworking of history. As in the epistle to the
Hebrews, whose writer knows that we do not yet see all things
in subjection to God (2:9), there is the prospect that the
church at worship sees as a reality already present of a victorious kingdom:

> You have come to Mount Zion . . . the heavenly Jerusalem, with its
> thousands of angels. You have come to the joyful gathering of God's
> first-born sons . . . . You have come to God. (Heb. 12:22, 23)

So Christian worship lives within the tension of the two
ages, between the times of the "already" and the "not yet."
It shares all the frailty and feebleness of its human origin and
character, for its participants are "both justified and sin-
ning" mortals. Yet it looks back to what God has done,
focused in Christ incarnate, atoning, and triumphant; it sees

---

6. For a discussion of hymns and christology, see the present writer's
contribution to *Essays in Christology,* Festschrift for Donald Guthrie
(1982), and his article, "New Testament Hymns: Background and Development," in *The Expository Times* 93 (1982).

Jesus "now crowned with glory and honor because of the death he suffered" (Heb. 2:9), and recognizes in him the one true worshiper, already seeing in a vision the drama of the heavenly host and bringing near that day of God's ultimate triumph by mingling its earthbound celebrations with the themes of heaven's rapture.

3. In the light of the above it is not difficult to believe that essential Christian praise will be *celebratory in tone*. The style of worship under the new covenant is not mournful but joyous; it is a festal gathering to which we are invited (Heb. 12:22, RSV marg.) as the first-born of God's children gather in holy array. The direction of the worshiper's gaze is not inward, but outward and upward—to God the source of all being and blessing. And the mood is not one of reminiscence but of realization of God's presence and grace presently available.

The key term is "remembrance": "This do in remembrance of me."[7] But the church is not engaged in a backward glance and recall as a neutral or detached observer of what happened in the dim past, however inspiring such recollection might well be. John Stuart Mill, we are told, was willing to attend communion service in tribute to a great leader who lived long ago. But that is hardly the spirit behind "in remembrance of me." "Remembering" shares in the dynamic quality of evocation. Past events are regarded as triggering a set of evocative experiences in which those dated events live again; as they are rehearsed they are relived, and relived with all the potency they once had for their original audiences and participants. There is surely a paradoxical element in this dynamic sense of "recall," but it is not without a parallel, admittedly not complete. One of Harold Pinter's characters (in his play *Old Times*) remarks: "There are things I remember

7. The meaning of *anamnesis*, "remembrance," is still keenly debated, with the specific issue centering on the question whether the action has a Godward or manward reference. D. R. Jones, *"Anamnesis in the LXX and the interpretation of 1 Cor. xi. 25," Journal of Theological Studies* n.s. 6 (1955), pp. 183-191 wants to include both ideas. For a discussion that takes in wider interests, see G. Wainwright, *Eucharist and Eschatology,* 2nd ed. (London: Epworth Press, 1978), pp. 60-68, and D. Gregg, *Anamnesis in the Eucharist* (Bramcote: Grove Books, 1976).

which may never have happened, but as I recall them so they take place."

We have seen the evidence for this "realism of remembrance" in Israel's history—at Passover, at the nation's credal recitations (notably at the festival of Booths), and in such episodes as the widow's complaint in 1 Kings 17:18. The new Israel's "remembering" has the same quality about it—whether at the Last Supper or such practical considerations as Paul's "remembering the poor" (Gal. 2:10). The legacy is handed on to the church, as in worship we dramatize and enact God's saving mercies to his people long ago. The past events are reenacted so that their present influence may be felt and their appeal registered to each succeeding generation of believing people. Here is one of the great arguments for the conserving of traditional usages in our common worship, since we today have a duty to receive and experience what has been committed to us, and to pass it on to those who come after us—that they too may learn from our rehearsal what God has done and is doing with his people.

If Christian worship celebrates the past goodness of God and focuses on his redeeming acts in Christ, it will remind us that this is a contemporaneous event. We are not looking back as the historian or archaeologist does. We are recovering the past in order to let it speak to the present. Worship has its foundation in the presence of God with his people. But such evocation is not produced simply by the exercise of human imagination, nor is it under the control of the unaided human spirit. It needs the interplay of the Holy Spirit whose work in worship is to lift the past from its time frame and make God's redeeming grace and love contemporary to the present generation of the church. Exactly this role is ascribed to the Johannine Paraclete (John 14:26; 16:21-25); and it remains the church's one hope of rendering worship both acceptable to God and satisfying to present-day worshipers.

The other side to this understanding of worship deserves a separate treatment: it is *worship as dialogue,* involving the interchange of the divine initiative and the human response. Worship pulsates with a two-beat rhythm expressed simply as "we come to God" and "God comes to us." Provided we remember that in worship—as in all things—God's grace is prior to our endeavors and the initiative is always with him, we may use this model to construct a structure of worship and gather together the results of our preceding chapters as components to make this model. The biblical image is drawn from the story in Genesis 28:10-22.

Worship as Dialogue: Jacob's Ladder

The episode of the patriarch at Bethel is rich in symbolism; but it must be read through Christian eyes. Fortunately this exercise has already been done by the fourth Evangelist. In a parallel story involving another Israelite, whose name and character (Nathanael, "a man without deceit," John 1:47) set him over against Jacob ("the deceiver"), the promise is given: "I am telling you the truth: you will see heaven open and God's angels going up and coming down on the Son of Man" (John 1:51). Some of the details are obscure, but the contrast is plainly drawn for the Christian reader of the Genesis account. The "ladder" reaching from earth to heaven is Jesus the Messiah who as "Son of man" mediates the true worship of God and conducts the traffic between God and man. We are in touch with a fundamental postulate of Christian worship: it is centered in Christ "the essence of worship," as William Nicholls calls him.

> In Him is embodied the downward movement of God's love and grace, as He reveals Himself to man, and reconciles man to Himself; and also the upward movement of man's response, perfectly dependent upon that love, and drawing from it all the resources of strength which are needed to make that response in all the circumstances of life, and even in death itself.[8]

We are faced in this christological midrashic interpretation of the experience of Jacob with the twofold response that Christ embodies: he offers to the human race the perfect service (Greek *latreia*) that climaxes in his obedience unto death. Mark 10:45 epitomizes his role as the "Son of man" who, like the *ebed Yahweh* of Isaiah 53, did not come to receive service but to give it, and ultimately to lay down his dearest possession vicariously for the sake of the nations. But *latreia* as Christ's downward movement tells only half the story. As the risen one he offers an oblation of praise (Greek *eucha-*

8. W. Nicholls, *Jacob's Ladder*, pp. 26, 27; cf. T. F. Torrance, *Theology in Reconciliation* (Grand Rapids: Wm. B. Eerdmans, 1976), ch. 3.

ristia) to God in which he represents in his glorified humanity
the perfect response of thanksgiving—which we may claim to
be the genius of Christian worship.

These two terms, *latreia* and *eucharistia,* combine the
double role of worship in its kinetic aspect. There is the
movement of "coming to," as God in his son has come in
revelatory and reconciling power to humankind; and there is
the movement of "offering to," as Christ's perfect sacrifice is
presented to the Father in an act of vicarious and victorious
thanksgiving. In a remarkable way these twin ideas come over
—or are read back—into the structure of Christian worship as
seen in Jacob's vision at Bethel, but it is in reversed sequence.
The downward action of God becomes the upward act of our
addressing the God and Father of our Lord Jesus Christ. The
"descending angels" stand in a figure for God's coming to us
with his gifts of grace. The hinge on which the twofold movement turns and from which it, so to speak, changes course is
the *eucharistia* of Christ, which is both a sign of what Christ
has done for us and a vehicle of our offering to God in him.

The diagram of liturgical movements may be set out like
this:

We come to God   *God comes to us*

But such a schema needs to be understood as completed in
another chart:

God in Christ   *Christ offers to*
comes to us   *God our worship*
(latreia)   (eucharistia)

The composite picture looks like the following, with the
hinge shown in prominence at point X:

The incarnation /   *The resurrection / high-*
cross of the lowly   *priestly intercession*
Christ   *of the exalted Christ*

Our approach   *God's approach*
to God   *to us*

Although diagrams and schematics tend to be misleading, at

least one item stands out in the above version. All turns on the point of intersection and it is at that pivotal point that worship takes on its basic christological and soteriological character. For all worship, identified as Christian, stems from and is expressed by the coming of God's presence in Christ incarnate, crucified, and triumphant, who by virtue of his obedience and risen life offers the perfect oblation to the Father. The church lives by that drama, with its downward and upward sweep; and it worships by identifying its liturgy with the ongoing liturgy performed by the exalted son of God, an act which in turn "remembers" and rehearses the "one offering of himself once offered."

If the "divine-human model" of what we have tried to depict is borne in mind, we can now go on to explore more fully the nature of the dialogue structure of the "human-divine model," based on our approach to God which is answered by God's coming to us. Once again a diagram may assist:

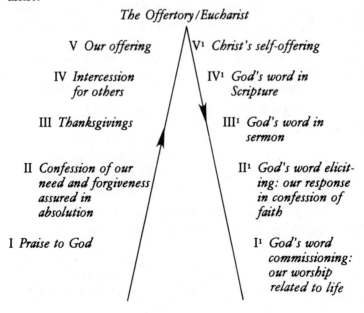

The Offertory/Eucharist

V *Our offering*   V¹ *Christ's self-offering*

IV *Intercession for others*   IV¹ *God's word in Scripture*

III *Thanksgivings*   III¹ *God's word in sermon*

II *Confession of our need and forgiveness assured in absolution*   II¹ *God's word eliciting: our response in confession of faith*

I *Praise to God*   I¹ *God's word commissioning: our worship related to life*

The ascending steps on the left-hand side of the chart denote the progress of worship in its upward spiral of approach to God. Let us look at these steps more closely.

I. *Praise*. All true worship arises out of a recollection of the divine presence, which in turn evokes our adoring praise. As Isaac Watts's memorable line puts it, ''God is a name my soul adores.''

In line with the church's inheritance in Temple and synagogue, the opening note of worship is struck in the ''praises of Israel,'' both old and new. We have already seen the propriety of this act to set worship on its ''proper'' basis as an acknowledgment of God in his work and a reaching out to him in adoring love, gratitude, and praise. All such outgoing is responsive to God's prior gift to us in Jesus Christ.

II. *Confession and Absolution*. It is a natural and needful transition to see ourselves in the white light of divine holiness and glory. The *Sanctus*, celebrating such awesomeness of God who is altogether ''holy,'' impresses upon us the frailty and finitude of our own nature; and our unworthiness answers to the divine worthiness. So we proceed to an admission of our tainted lives and flawed character, and we cry out for his forgiveness. This plea is met by the assurance of God's pardon, which comes to us in a language that is both assuring and performative; that is, in the announcement that ''we are forgiven'' the present availability of grace is grasped, renewed, and experienced.

The place of penitence and pardon in both western and Orthodox liturgies is well established, but the introspective conscience with its complaint of *mea culpa* must be kept firmly in place and not allowed to dominate the scene. Also, sin once confessed and forgiven should not be raised again in the flow of the liturgy. This is one practical and pastoral value of a sequential order.

III. *Thanksgivings*. The promises of the gospel, as pledges of divine succour and strength, lay the foundation of our approach as penitent believers; they also are the occasion of the truly thankful spirit. So worship is led on to offer spoken gratitude for God's goodness and grace, traditionally sung in the noble language of the *Gloria in excelsis Deo:*

> Glory be to God on high
> And on earth peace, good will towards men

> We praise thee, we bless thee,
> We worship thee, we glorify thee
> We give thanks to thee for thy great glory.

The *Agnus Dei* follows on:

> O Lord God, Lamb of God, Son of the Father,
> that takest away the sins of the world,
> have mercy upon us . . . receive our prayer

The final section responds to the call of the *Sanctus:*

> For thou only art holy;
> thou only art the Lord;
> thou only, O Christ, with the Holy Ghost,
> art the most high, in the glory of God the Father. Amen.

IV. *Intercession.* The ground is now cleared and the "atmosphere" right and conducive for a widening of the horizons to take in the angle of intercessory prayer. The tradition of the "collect"[9] appointed for the church calendar fits in here; the name derives from the prayer thought of as representing the mind of the "assembly" *(collectio)* who are greeted by the president or leader, the people responding to his bidding or suggestion to emphasize that it is the prayer of the corporate assembly who share a common mind. Cranmer's "collects" in the Book of Common Prayer are classic (of the eighty-four prayers in that liturgy he is credited with twenty-five of them) and adopt a set pattern that has never been excelled: (i) an address to God; (ii) a description of some attribute of the divine character as the basis for prayer; (iii) the prayer itself—short, simple, direct; (iv) a concluding doxology:

> (i) O God (ii) who art the author of peace and lover of concord, in knowledge of whom standeth our eternal life, whose service is perfect freedom: (iii) Defend us thy humble servants in all assaults of our enemies; that we, surely trusting in thy defence, may not fear the power of any adversaries; (iv) through the might of Jesus Christ our Lord. Amen.

The alternative to this type of united praying is the *ad hoc* intercession that reaches out to embrace a wide range of persons, topics, and needs. In the history of Christian worship

9. L. E. H. Stephens-Hodge, *The Collects* (London: Hodder and Stoughton, 1964).

several items have a time-honored place: the church throughout the world, as Polycarp nobly remembered his share in the
larger family, even when arrested and later called to be a martyr *(Martyrdom of Polycarp,* 8:1); the peace of the world and
its nations; the sick, sorrowing, and bereaved, along with
prisoners (see 1 Clement's prayer, 59:4). Christ's own teaching requires the church to remember its enemies and persecutors. Within this framework personal and relevant supplica-
tions for specific needs are added to give the worshipers a
broad outlook and a reminder that by their intercession "the
world stands" (Tertullian).[10] There should be some time for
silence, prefaced by a "bidding" prayer that suggests specific
guidelines.

   V. Intercession takes on a practical shape with *the Offering,* by which our commitment to Christ's church and his
cause in the world with its needs—spiritual, social, and
material—is measured. The people's offerings are, however,
impossible to dissociate from the "one offering" of the
Savior. Therefore the more comprehensive term is *Offertory,*
which links both the oblation of Christ and the species of the
eucharistic offering that the people of God furnish first to the
presiding minister (or priest, in the Catholic tradition) to be
received and "consecrated" by being "set apart" for holy
use; but the people's gifts of bread and wine equally represent an offering to God of that which they give as the fruits of
their daily labor and service. The *Offertory* thus combines in
one act the essential and unique sacrifice of Christ in his body
given and his blood outpoured, and the people's share in
that sacrifice by the token presentation of bread and wine.
The *Offertory* functions as a hinge in our diagram, as we saw,
and stands at the apex of the liturgical pyramid, gathering up
all that precedes and determining the course of what is to follow. This pivotal locating of the eucharistic offertory involving the celebration of the rite breaks with the early tradition
of a separation between "the liturgy of the word" and "the
liturgy of the upper room." But its place here in our scheme
is justified, we maintain, by its function of representing the

   10. Hence Tertullian's wish for a "secure reign [of the imperial house],
a safe home, a strong army, a faithful senate, a good people, a quiet world,
and in fact all that both man and emperor could desire" *(Apology* 30.4).
Tertullian's basis for these sentiments is 1 Tim. 2:2 *(Apology* 31.2,3).

transition from "we give" to "we receive." The central position in the flow of the liturgy also emphasizes its central importance, and gets us decisively away from the popular idea of the communion service as an addendum, awkwardly tacked on the (main) preaching service in the Free church tradition. Certain parts of the Protestant church, for example the Disciples or Church of Christ (at least in their pristine "liturgy"), have seen the value of a central eucharistic service as an invariable part of the regular Sunday morning worship.[11] Its rationale may be especially valid in our day when "family worship" often welcomes children to attend, if not to participate in, the Lord's Supper, and when there is not a clear demarcation, formerly rigorously insisted upon, between the "first" service open to all and sundry and a "closed" communion service restricted to baptized or committed Christians, mainly church members.

IV[1]. *Scripture lections.* The congregation is now ready to receive the good news through the medium of the spoken word, which acts as an interpretation of the drama just enacted. The biblical reasoning lies in the Passover exposition or *haggadah*, which is to accompany every family celebration. The story of the exodus is told and "explained" (Exod. 13:8) to every succeeding generation. The *drōmenon* or enactment of worship is both rehearsed and explicated in the most obvious and accessible mode of communication: the spoken word. Paul's carry-over of the same linkage of act and word is seen in 1 Corinthians 11:26: "every time you eat this bread and drink from this cup *you proclaim* the Lord's death"; the verb (Greek *katangellein*) signifies the preaching of the cross both in the dramatized rituals of eating and drinking and the accompanying commentary, possibly in the recital of the Passion narrative, as C.H. Dodd suggested.[12]

11. Keith Watkins, "Liturgies. Christian Church (Disciples of Christ)," *The Westminster Dictionary of Worship*, ed. J. G. Davies (Philadelphia: Westminster Press, 1972), pp. 233, 234. See also, for Brethren practice, F. F. Bruce, p. 242.

12. C. H. Dodd, *History and the Gospel* (London: Hodder and Stoughton, 1938), p. 83: "Some form of Passion-narrative accompanied the preaching of the Gospel and the celebration of the Sacrament."

The reading of Scripture is, of course, of wider appeal and significance than explicating the Lord's Supper rite, though that focus certainly confirms Scripture's underlying message or "point." Holy Scripture in its canonical shape is seen as a unity, composed of authoritative books, in so many ways diverse and assorted, and linked by the single token that each part contributes to a declaration of God's saving intention, redeeming power, holy design, and undefeatable purpose—which is "to bring many sons [and daughters] to share his glory . . . [in] Jesus [who] is the one who leads them to salvation" (Heb. 2:10).

The word-of-God character of Scripture ensures its indispensable and vital place in the curriculum of Christian worship. For that reason—since through this medium God has spoken of old and still speaks in his son (Heb. 1:1, 2)—the lessons of the Old Testament, the Gospels, and the Epistles are to be read out in the hearing of the people, following and enriching the synagogue practice and guided by the precedent of our Lord in Luke 4:16-21 (cf. John 5:39-40; 2 Tim. 3:15-17; Heb. 4:12, 13). These verses agree on one important feature: Scripture is a living message of God to men and women and finds its chief "thrust" in its witness to Christ the living word who issues a call to the hearer to respond in living faith and obedience to his gracious summons.

The congregation's responses to the lessons is important, as enforcing the dialogue pattern. Sometimes the most suitable way to respond is the singing of a hymn. Or before the Gospels are read, the people may say:

Glory be to you, O Lord.

And after the reading:

Praise be to you, O Christ.

III[1]. *The sermon* attains its true dignity when its preacher takes on the privileged task of clarifying and enforcing the will of God as Scripture reveals it and human experience illustrates it. The sermon stands in a mid-way position between the age-old purpose of God in salvation-history and the present-day needs, aspirations, and ambitions of the people of God. The several ways the divine will may be seen to impinge on human activity—personal, social, national, and worldwide—are the agenda items of the Christian preacher as he or she comes before the congregation with that unique utterance called "the sermon." No other means of communication is quite the same, nor is fraught with such solemn significance, as is the preacher's "message." The words spoken are both idiosyncratic (i.e., they are the preacher's own possession, since he or she has prayed, meditated, studied, and listened in the study prior to the utterance, however ex tempore the sermon may seem to be at its delivery) and authoritative (i.e., the words of the sermon share a sacramental quality by reason of their relating "the word of God" in the words of men).[13]

There is thus a local and a transcendent significance about preaching. The preacher confronts a people who are well known to him and he looks into the faces of men and women, young and old, who embody a wide variety of the human condition in all its joy and despair, its optimism and defeat, its self-satisfaction and yearning, its indifference and attentiveness. If it were simply the "word of man" he or she speaks, the task would be hopeless before it began, or else too demanding if only native powers of rhetorical skill, homiletical expertise, personal charisma, or inventive gimmickery were called into play. The preacher, however, knows ,his limitations—and his resources; not least he awaits the congregation's evaluation of the words he speaks as "the word from God" for their situation. So the sermon is yet one more vehicle by which God comes to his people.

II[1]. *The response* they make to all that has gone before is an integral part of worship. Whether that assent which leads to action is expressed in "Amen," or silent prayer, or firm resolve, or public commitment is not important, and local customs and past heritage will shape that way this part of the service is understood and handled.

The traditional form is the *confession of faith* as expressed in the creed or some other suitable form of words. The value

13. J. F. White, *Introduction to Christian Worship* (Nashville: Abingdon Press, 1980), p. 138 has remarked on "four items [that] are vital in conceiving of preaching: power of God, source in scripture, authority from the church, and relationship to people."

of placing the creed, whether historical or ecumenical (the Apostles' or the Nicene Creed), here is considerable, since it gives the opportunity for the gathered company to feel its kinship with the church of all ages, to gain a sense of the dignity and yet personal privilege of responding to Christ's present call, and to share faith with one's neighbor in a way that is both objective (avoiding embarrassment for those whose faith is as yet incipient) and also existential (making clear that each one is invited to register his or her own committal). The nature of a person's affirmation will be as wide as the sermon's content and the current demands and promises of the good news extend. Yet in a basic way all human responses are enfolded and expressed in one single response: to enthrone the will of God in our lives, and to yield those lives in all their facets and features to a practicing of that "grand design" all our days.

I¹. *Worship related to life* is therefore the "end" of the service in its customary sense: there is no more, apart from the dismissal and final "peace." In its technical meaning "end" takes on another sense: it is the goal of all that has been said, sung, and rehearsed in act and gesture. The congregation is bidden to "live out" in the practicalities of everyday experience and responsibility the meaning of its cult. So some "commissioning" is needed to round off the service, whether by hymn or prayer of discharge into the business of life—the Lord's Prayer is exactly in place here—or exhortation to take up the challenge in some definite "service." Romans 12:1-2 is immediately followed by a recital of such "services" related to "everyday life" (so E. Käsemann who adds this far-reaching comment: "Salvation activates a person and thus manifests itself as a power over our lives and the community").[14] The "sacred" is no longer confined

---

14. E. Käsemann, *Commentary on Romans* (Grand Rapids: Wm. B. Eerdmans, 1980), p. 327. See also his chapter, "Worship and Everyday Life," in *New Testament Questions for Today* (Philadelphia: Fortress Press, 1969), pp. 188-195:
   Just as love in 1 Corinthians 13 is the determining and unifying force of all *charismata,* the point here [in Rom. 12] . . . is that every activity of the Christian community is to be characterized as charismatic, because in this total activity the "spiritual worship" becomes real in the world. (p. 195)

within the territory of the sanctuary and its cultus; it invades and transforms the world of the secular, and it does not work in any mechanical or *ex opere operato* fashion as a magic power mysteriously released. The "sacred" in worship touches human life in this world as a moral force requiring personal obedience, social concern, and down-to-earth service. All of this Paul works out in a way that grounds the spiritual or charismatic gifts in the rough and tumble of activity in the Greco-Roman world; he never allows his reader to escape into a shell of isolation on the pretext of becoming absorbed with "pure worship." Instead, the "spiritual worship" (Rom. 12:1) takes on valid meaning as it leads out into the world of human relationships with all their strain, conflict, needs, and opportunities of serving the Lord (12:11) by serving the lowly members (12:13, 16).

The concluding benediction, fashioned after 2 Corinthians 13:13(14), informs us that we are not left alone in this task. We are not summoned to a display of heroics or an advertised profession of altruism, but to a sensitive awareness of our Christian duty and privilege in God's world where we may discharge the obligation only as we are reinforced by:

The grace of the Lord Jesus Christ,
the love of God,
and the fellowship of the Holy Spirit.

Concluding Remarks

The plan of a "service of worship" now offered should not leave the impression that such is "fixed" in the sense of unalterable rigidity requiring punctilious following. Obviously that is the way of formalism and death; and such an impression tends to give a liturgical service a bad name. The skeletal frame leaves room for adaptation and innovation, permitting the "freedom of the Spirit" to be recognized.[15] But what such a structure does stress—and herein is its importance—is that corporate worship is not an accidental assortment of items that "happen" to come together. There is a reason for each part in its "right" place, and there is a logical

15. See the example mentioned in G. Wainwright, *Doxology. The Praise of God in Worship, Doctrine and Life* (London: Epworth Press; New York: Oxford Univ. Press, 1980), p. 349.

sequence and progression, which means that the pace of the service flows in sequential and meaningful order, with clearly marked transition points and advancement from one part to the next.

The role of the worshiping congregation is all-important, so that worship is not a ministerial preserve nor under the control of the organist or choir director. Music offers a significant contribution, as do the hymns sung by the congregation. But the people of God are deserving of a richer share in the service than simply hymn-singers and offering-givers, while for the rest of the service they remain a body of inert auditors and passive spectators.

One supreme way in which the people can gain enrichment from the worship is to give them an understanding that each facet of the public worship of God has meaning in which they are invited to contribute a significant activity—in praising, praying, giving, as in remembering, listening, confessing, believing, and acting out. These are all verbs of involvement and choice.

Worship offers the best and demands it. Its agenda needs a serious overhaul in our churches. But even more it is a practice seeking a rationale, and that rationale is at heart theological.

If the preceding pages have stimulated some theological thinking that will lead on to a reshaping of our services of divine worship, the result will be that some areas of ignorance and prejudice may be banished,[16] and modern-day Christians will come to appreciate more keenly and thankfully that the worship of the triune God is both our high responsibility and our joyful privilege.

---

16. W. R. Inge, former Dean of St. Paul's Cathedral, was once asked if he were interested in the study of liturgy. His reply was No; nor (he went on) did he collect postage stamps (an anecdote cited by Prof. Hugh Lloyd-Jones in his Viewpoint article in the *Times Literary Supplement*, Feb. 29, 1980, p. 232).

Index of Subjects

Shema 87, 89
Shemoneh Esreh 34
Sunday (Lord's Day) 74, 113, 168
Synagogue worship 32, 33, 102,
  224
Synaxis 14, 113

Te Deum 55, 81
Tertullian 134, 138, 139, 190,
  193, 222

Upbuilding 199, 201

Watts, Isaac 8, 39, 40, 46, 49, 56,
  59, 220
Wesley, John, Charles 8, 43, 44,
  46, 57, 116, 178
Worship
  and celebration 215

in Christ 209, 217
definition of 3, 4, 17, 26, 29,
  171
dialogue pattern of 6, 216,
  217, 224
and everyday life 15, 226, 227
freedom in 7, 8, 11, 227
importance ix, 227, 228
meaning 1
renewal of 1, 227, 228
and salvation-history 211-212
sequence of 37, 217-227
theocentric character 17, 171
theology of 2, 228
trinitarian 27, 92, 180, 210,
  211, 228
unity and diversity 187-208

Zwingli 136, 147, 165

Index of Principal Scriptural Passages and Other Writings

JEWISH, PAGAN, AND
CHRISTIAN TEXTS

Index of Modern Authors